What Do You Think?

Are Girls Smarter Than Boys?

Andrew Langley

Heinemann Library
Chicago, Illinois

Editorial: Andrew Farrow and Rebecca Vickers
Design: Philippa Jenkins
Picture research: Melissa Allison and Ruth Blair
Production: Alison Parsons

Printed and bound in China

13 12 11 10 09
10 9 8 7 6 5 4 3 2 1

Library of Congress Cataloging-in-Publication Data
Langley, Andrew.
 Are girls smarter than boys? / Andrew Langley.
   p. cm. -- (What do you think?)
 Includes bibliographical references and index.
 ISBN 978-1-4329-1671-8 (hc)
 1. Intellect--Sex differences. I. Title.
 BF433.S48L36 2008
 155.3'3--dc22
                                            2008014752

Acknowledgments
We would like to thank the following for permission to reproduce photographs:
© cartoonstock.com p. **28**; © Corbis/Randy Faris pp. **18**, /Gideon Mendel **48**; © Getty Images pp. **12**, /Iconica **16**, /David Nevala Photography **44**, /News **22**, **40**, /Photographer's Choice **10**, **31**, /Photonica **36**, /Riser **32**, /Stockbyte **42**, /Stone **38**, /WireImage **34**; © Library of Congress p. **14**; © Masterfile pp. **4**, /David Schmidt **26**; © Rex Features pp. **15**, **17**, **24**, **46**, /Marion Curtis **7**; © Science Photo Library/American Institute of Physics pp.**12**, /Mehau Kulyk **20**, /Wellcome Dept of Cognitive Neurology **8**.

Cover photograph: Cover photograph reproduced with permission of © Getty Images/PhotoAlto/ Laurence Moulton and © Getty Images/Photodisc.

Every effort has been made to contact copyright holders of any material reproduced in this book. Any omissions will be rectified in subsequent printing if notice is given to the publishers.

The publishers would like to thank Dr. Jenny Parkes for her assistance with the preparation of this book.

Disclaimer
All the Internet addresses (URLs) given in this book were valid at the time of going to press. However, due to the dynamic nature of the Internet, some addresses may have changed, or sites may have changed or ceased to exist since publication. While the author and publishers regret any inconvenience this may cause readers, no responsibility for any such changes can be accepted by either the author or the publishers.

Table Of Contents

Some words are printed in bold, **like this**. You can find out what they mean in the glossary on pages 54–55.

> *Something to cheer about*

Men have dominated society throughout most of history. However, women have taken giant steps lately toward a more equal role in world affairs.

Are Girls Smarter Than Boys?

There are more than six billion humans in the world. Roughly three billion of these are male, while the other three billion are female. In almost all ways, men and women are much the same. The most obvious physical difference between the sexes is that women can have babies and men cannot.

But is there another big difference? Are women more intelligent than men? Or is it the other way around? Perhaps there is nothing to choose between them and no reliable method of measuring intelligence anyway. Nevertheless, men and women have been arguing about it for hundreds of years.

It is safe to say that readers of this book will be either male or female. This gives everyone a stake in the subject. Are girls smarter than boys? Is it an important question? Is it worth arguing about? The answer must be yes. Throughout history, men have made most of the rules. They have believed themselves to be stronger, more capable, wiser, and smarter than women.

It is only in the last hundred years that this situation has started to change. Women have begun to assert themselves as equal and to claim the right to equal treatment. This includes the right to be treated as intellectually equal to men—at the very least.

Your opinion really counts

This series of books is called "What Do You Think?" This is a question aimed at you—the person reading the book. You are involved, and your answer to the question really matters. You have the chance to tell other people your views.

At this point you may not have an answer ready. You may not even agree that there is much use in discussing the topic. But you are being asked to think about it. That means accepting the subject is serious and concerns you. Then it means figuring out your own opinion, and not just copying someone else's. The purpose of this book is to help you along the way, without trying to push you one way or the other.

Is there a "right" answer?
Suppose someone asks you, "What is two plus two?" It is a simple question, and it has one correct answer: four. If you said "three" or "five," you would be wrong. This is not something you can argue about. It is a matter of fact, not opinion.

The title of this book asks a different kind of question: "Are girls smarter than boys?" This may sound like a simple question, but there is no correct answer to it. Nobody can definitely say that girls are smarter or less smart than boys. But everyone can argue about it. It is a matter of opinion, not fact.

Why have an opinion?

Do you like to argue? Or are you someone who keeps out of discussions? You may feel you do not have anything to say. You may even feel you cannot be bothered. Now is the time to change that. A person without any opinions is no fun at all. Besides, some arguments are good for you. They can:

- get you involved with an issue
- give you a broader view of the world
- encourage you to think logically
- give you the chance to interact with other people
- help you learn to stand up for yourself in a lively debate.

✔ Support your opinion

A supported opinion is called an argument. You can remember how to support your argument using these three **A–R–E** steps:

✔ **A**ssertion: This is a statement of your opinion.

✔ **R**easoning: These are your views on why you think your opinion is correct.

✔ **E**vidence: These are the facts you use to back up your opinion and show that your argument is valid.

How do you form an opinion?

Everybody has opinions about all kinds of topics. Some people feel very strongly about the mental differences between the sexes. But you need a lot more than strong feelings to reach an opinion that will stand up to argument. It is much better to look at the subject calmly and with an open mind.

The aim of this book is to help you think for yourself about whether girls really are smarter than boys. It shows you how to form your own opinion on the subject. To do this successfully, you need a clear set of steps, which will lead you to a balanced and well-informed point of view. You will be surprised at what you may discover on the way.

> *What do you think?*

Everyone can have his or her own opinion about a subject. However, opinions are only effective and persuasive if backed up with good evidence. With complex and challenging subjects, there is usually a wide variety of contradictory information. You will need to weigh the evidence and reach your own conclusions.

Make use of research

You need to research your evidence. This is the raw material that gives you a firm base on which to build your opinion. Without facts you will not be able to back up an argument, no matter how passionately you believe in it. This material comes in many forms, including columns of statistics, eyewitness accounts, public statements, and scientific reports.

Where do you find evidence?
Library books and Internet websites will give you facts and figures. Look out for news stories about **gender** difference and intelligence in the media. Cut out newspaper stories that give you some fresh facts. Talk to people who know something about the topic. Don't forget that your own experiences can also be useful. Has something happened in your life to make you think one sex is smarter than the other?

Listen to other people
There are two sides to any argument. Don't begin with a fixed opinion in your head and then try to justify it. And don't fail to listen to others with opposing views. Keep an open mind and listen carefully to the ideas and evidence for both sides—even when you disagree with them strongly.

Above all, do not get frustrated and lose your concentration. Always remember that an argument is not always won by the person who is right, but rather by the person who is best at arguing and has the strongest evidence. (Read more about debating skills on pages 48–51.)

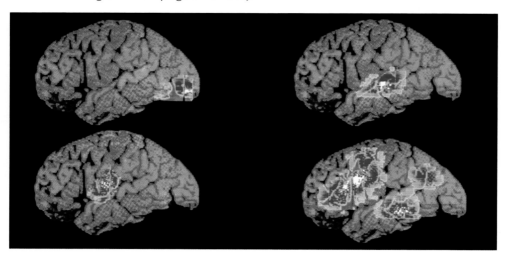

> *Brain power*

Everybody's brain is different. Some brains are physically bigger than others, while some individuals have a stronger ability to use certain brain areas. Does bigger and stronger automatically mean smarter?

Think critically

Be critical of what you read and hear, and do not accept things at face value.

Checklist for critical thinking

Critical thinkers . . .

✔ understand the difference between fact and opinion, and can distinguish facts from opinions in spoken and written text.

✔ assess the available evidence, evaluating it fairly and completely.

✔ acknowledge the multiple perspectives on an issue and identify the points of disagreement.

✔ identify the assumptions being made by authors or advocates on an issue, evaluating those assumptions for validity and bias.

✔ evaluate different points of view to inform their own opinions.

✔ support their own ideas with sound reasoning and evidence, taking into account opposing ideas and facts.

Analyzing evidence: Differences in height

What can you find out from this evidence about the average height of boys and girls? Do you need to know more about it to assess its validity?

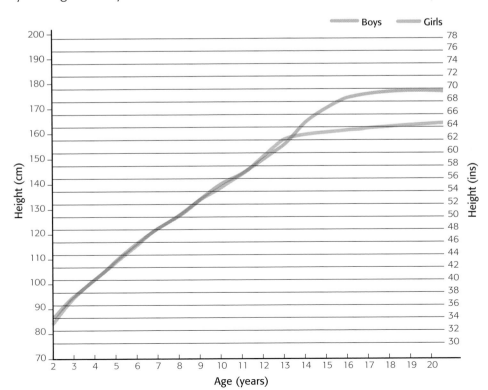

> *Does science have the answer?*

Scientists have developed many ways to test for and measure intelligence. **Neurologists** examine the brain and brain chemistry, while **psychologists** have developed tests for individuals to take. However, not everyone agrees that these tests are fair or accurate.

What Is Intelligence?

The first step in forming an opinion is to decide exactly what you are talking about. You have to know the meaning of the question you are debating. The question here is, "Are girls smarter than boys?" So, how do you define the word "smart"? Does it simply mean "clever"? Is it the same thing as "intelligent"? If not, what makes them different?

Think of some famous people whom you would describe as smart. You will probably include successful businessmen and women, as well as crafty politicians and sharp-witted TV show hosts. Now think of famous people who are highly intelligent. This list may well be different and feature scientists, inventors, and artists. Being smart or intelligent can bring a person success, power, and wealth. But does everyone get an equal chance? In many parts of the world, women traditionally have been regarded as less intelligent than men. This is partly because they have been given fewer opportunities to prove themselves. Today, these old attitudes are changing— but is change coming fast enough?

How can we decide one person is more intelligent than another? Scientists have devised various ways of measuring intelligence, the best-known of these being the IQ (Intelligence **Quotient**) test. But many people believe tests can be inaccurate and misleading. Others argue that we should not judge others by the results of just one type of test.

Intelligence: The basics

Can we say exactly what we mean by "intelligence"? Many people have tried to define the word, but there is still a lot of disagreement. Nevertheless, most of us agree on some of the basic ingredients. An intelligent person can use his or her mind to:

* reason things out
* plan ahead
* solve problems
* understand complex ideas
* learn from experience
* use language well.

Humans are not all the same. Some people are bigger and stronger than others or are better at sports. Some are gifted musicians, while others are tone deaf. In the same way, some are brighter than others. This means that they are better equipped to do the things listed above.

Being smart and being intelligent: Is there a difference?

"Intelligent" is not the word used in the title of this book. The question asks whether girls are "smarter" than boys. Is "smarter" the same thing as being "more intelligent"? This is how it is generally understood in many cultures. But does it mean something different?

> Wife and husband

Marie Curie and her husband, Pierre, made breakthrough discoveries about radiation in the early 1900s, leading to the development of nuclear physics. Both of them were exceptionally intelligent and both became successful in the same field of science.

"Smart" generally means quick-witted and sharp. People who are very good at selling things, or striking deals, or building up business empires are often described as smart. This does not necessarily mean they are brainy with high IQ results. Many successful business **tycoons** have failed in school, just as many brilliant school students have ended up as unsuccessful adults, never fulfilling their early potential.

Case Study 1

International businesswoman Anita Roddick (1942–2007) was not a big success in school in England. She flunked her exam to get into a high-level secondary school and later failed to get accepted into drama college. In order to make a living, in 1976 she opened her first Body Shop, selling natural cosmetics. By 2006 her products had 77 million customers worldwide, and she was able to sell the Body Shop chain for over $1.14 billion.

Case Study 2

When Stephen Hawking (born 1942) was a physics student at the University of Oxford, in England, his teachers soon saw he was exceptionally intelligent. He learned with amazing speed, without reading many books or even taking notes. "Examiners realized they were talking to someone far more clever than most of themselves," said his teacher. Hawking went on to gain a **doctorate** from the University of Cambridge and is recognized as one of the most brilliant and famous scientists of his time, despite suffering from an illness that has left him nearly completely paralyzed.

What do these case studies tell you about the different kinds of intelligence? Find out about other very successful people, and decide in which ways they are intelligent.

What do they think?

"I know that I am intelligent because I know that I know nothing."
Socrates, Greek philosopher (c. 470–399 BCE)

"An intellectual is a person whose mind watches itself."
Albert Camus, French writer (1913–1960)

"It's not that I'm so smart, it's just that I stay with problems longer."
Albert Einstein, scientist (1879–1955)

"It is not enough to have a good mind; the main thing is to use it well."
René Descartes, French philosopher and mathematician (1596–1650)

"Intelligence is quickness in seeing things as they are."
George Santayana, Spanish-born U.S. philosopher and writer (1863–1952)

The weaker sex?

Throughout much of history, most societies have classed women as **inferior** to men. This was usually because women seemed to be weaker. They were smaller than men and were seen as less decisive and more emotional. On top of this, of course, they had babies, which placed them in a more vulnerable position. People believed women were less intelligent than men because of their inferior status.

Men were in charge of most areas of life, including government, the law, the armed forces, and making money. They also had most of the important rights in life. Even in the early 1800s, women in the United States and Europe had few rights. They were not allowed to vote in elections or take responsible jobs in law, medicine, or the church. Husbands had legal power over their wives, and married women could not own property.

The battle to be equal

From the 1850s onward, women in many countries began to demand equal rights with men. The most important of these was **suffrage** (the right to vote). Women formed organizations to state their case. They often took direct action to get their message across, from breaking windows and burning mailboxes to holding **mass demonstrations**. Many women were put in prison for their actions. But the "Women's Movement" was winning its first victories. New Zealand was the first nation to give women voting rights in 1893. It was followed by Australia (1902), the United States (1920), Sweden (1921), and the United Kingdom (1928).

> Fighting for the vote

Women have had a long struggle to gain equal rights. One of the biggest battles was the fight to win the right to vote in elections. This demonstration was in the United States in 1908.

In what ways are women better off today?

Women's lives have changed hugely in the past hundred years. Probably the biggest change of all has been in employment. Today, in most of the developed

> *At the center of things*

German Chancellor Angela Merkel is one of several women
who have become powerful world leaders in recent years.

world, over 60 percent of women are now part of the paid **workforce**. There
are female presidents, female astronauts, female business leaders, and female
judges. According to the law, women and men are equal.

But are women treated as equals? Do they get the same chances and
the same treatment in life? Certainly, women are not given the same job
opportunities as men. There are still very few women in senior positions. And
there is still a large gap between the pay levels of male and female workers. Is
this because people still think of women as the "weaker sex," or does it have to
do with intellectual ability?

 Some female firsts

1872	Victoria Woodhull: First female U.S. presidential candidate
1910	Blanche Scott: First woman to fly an aircraft
1917	Jeannette Rankin: First woman in U.S. Congress
1960	Sirimavo Bandaranaike: First woman prime minister (Sri Lanka)
1974	Isabel Perón: First woman president (Argentina)
1979	Margaret Thatcher: First woman British prime minister
1997	Madeleine Albright: First woman U.S. secretary of state
2007	Nancy Pelosi: First woman speaker of the house in U.S. Congress

Can you measure intelligence?

Nobody can agree about what exactly the word "intelligence" means. So, it is no surprise that there is even less agreement about whether we can measure a person's level of intelligence. The subject has caused a lot of controversy in the last 50 years, yet intelligence tests are widely used to assess students in schools and colleges.

Several psychologists have figured out different ways to test people. Most of these tests feature questions or tasks that involve reasoning, counting, remembering, and using definitions. The scores are used to show the level of intelligence. The most famous system is the IQ (Intelligence Quotient) test.

How does an IQ test work?

There are many types of IQ test. Most of them ask people to solve a series of problems within a set time. These problems include completing sequences of letters or numbers, arranging shapes or pictures, correctly defining words, and spotting similarities. Skill in math and speed in understanding are also tested.

The average for an IQ is fixed at 100. Most people score somewhere in the middle of the range, roughly between 85 and 115, 15 points on either side of 100. Testers believe that anyone scoring below this range may have learning difficulties. Those with higher scores (and some have even passed the 200 mark) are likely to be highly intelligent.

What do the tests tell us?

Many schools use IQ test results to monitor the progress of their students. For example, a student may do poorly in class, but score high on the test. This suggests that he or she has plenty of ability, but difficulty with learning. A child with poor performance in class and a low IQ score can be given special attention.

> *Testing time*
Students in some states take regular intelligence and achievement tests. The results can have an impact on their education and the career advice they receive.

But what causes IQ ratings to vary so widely? Again, nobody knows exactly. Most scientists agree that our intelligence levels are often inherited from our parents. Others say that intelligence is affected by the environment in which we are raised. Children from more stimulating and interesting home backgrounds are likely to have higher IQs.

Can we trust intelligence tests?

Have you ever taken an IQ test? Did you think your score was a fair reflection of your intelligence? Or was it a bit of a shock—one way or the other? Some people think these tests are often unfair, and that the results can be misleading.

Some children are simply good at written tests, but this does not necessarily reflect their intelligence. Besides, the questions can be easier for those of certain cultures. For instance, a child born to English-speaking parents will probably perform better in an English-language IQ test than a child who was raised in another country and who has learned English as a second language.

> IQ queen

Intelligence tests can never be exact. Marilyn vos Savant is usually cited as the holder of the world-record high IQ, but her test results have varied between a low of 167 and a high of 230.

Famous high IQs

Here are some famous people with IQ ratings above the average. Obviously, celebrities with below-average IQs keep quiet about it!

George W. Bush	125
Bill Clinton	137
Hillary Clinton	140
Jodie Foster	132
Bill Gates	160
Stephen Hawking	160
Madonna	140
Arnold Schwarzenegger	135
Shakira	140
Sharon Stone	154

> *All shapes and sizes*

Human beings of both sexes vary hugely in almost every way. Big, small, weak, strong, sporty, clumsy, brilliant, intelligent—they come in all varieties.

Are The Sexes Different?

In many ways, men and women are much the same. Both sexes are human animals, with the same basic body shape, the same physical needs, and the same abilities. More than that, the two sexes depend on each other. Without both males and females, there would be no babies. This makes them equal in their ability to keep the human race going.

So, what are the differences between men and women? Obviously, there are physical differences. Men tend to be taller than women, with greater upper body strength. They have more body hair and thicker skin. Scientists have found that men on average have slightly larger brains than women. But, of course, men cannot bear children. There are plenty of unseen differences as well. Research shows many of the ways in which people behave are probably linked to their gender. Men are seen as more aggressive than women. Women are believed to like to agree and give support, while men like to argue.

Both sexes have their areas of strength and weakness, and these differences can show up on intelligence tests. However, the line dividing men and women is not clear. Each sex shares some of the psychological features of the other.

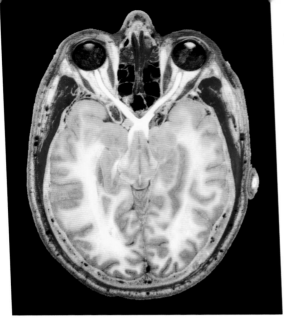

Who has the brains?

Men have bigger bodies than women. So, do they also have bigger brains? Here are some of the findings of a long-term Canadian study of male and female brains:

Sandra Witelson Had Studied Scores of Brains Looking for Gender Differences

Inside Witelson's walk-in refrigerator at McMaster University in Ontario, her collection of brains filled three walls of metal shelves. Every one posed a riddle: How does the structure of the brain influence intelligence?

In 1987, 120 men and women had agreed to donate their brains after death. They all submitted to thorough psychological and intelligence tests so that each brain would be accompanied by a detailed profile of the mind that had animated it. With so many well-documented donors, Witelson could conduct comparative brain studies on an **unprecedented** scale.

She measured her brains. She weighed them. She cut them up and counted the cells. Her findings buttress [support] the proposition that basic mental differences between men and women stem in part from physical differences in the brain. Witelson is convinced that gender shapes the anatomy of male and female brains in separate but equal ways beginning at birth.

```
On average, she said, the brains of women and men are
neither better nor worse, but they are measurably
different. Men's brains, for instance, are typically
bigger—but on the whole, no smarter. Women's brains
seem to be faster and more efficient than men's.

"All in all, men appear to have more gray matter, made
up of active neurons, and women more of the white
matter responsible for communication between different
areas of the brain."

[By Robert Lee Hotz, LA Times, June 16, 2005.]
```

This story tells us several important things. It has to be read carefully and critically. First of all, does the research sound thorough? What gave Sandra Witelson the basis for making her comparative study? Second, what kind of differences did her work show up? Make a list of the differences explained in this article. Do the findings tell us anything about whether men or women are the more intelligent? Or are they just different? How does this research affect your opinion?

Does bigger equal better?

So, men on average have larger and heavier brains than women. Their brains also contain more neurons (the cells that send and receive messages between the brain and the nervous system). But does this mean that men are smarter? Do bigger brains make you more intelligent?

The answer is, not necessarily. Elephants and whales have much bigger brains than humans do. If brain size were all that mattered, they would be the smartest animals on the planet. Size isn't everything. The important factor is the relationship of brain size to body size. Women in general have slightly smaller bodies than men, and this is reflected in their brain size.

Brain facts and figures

	Male	Female
Average brain weight	1,375 grams	1,275 grams
Average neocortical neurons	22.8 billion	19.3 billion

[Source: http://faculty.washington.edu/chudler/facts.html]

Survival of the fittest

Men may have more muscles, but does this give them better chances of survival? Figures show that it does not. On average, women throughout the world live longer lives (see page 24). However, some scientists now believe that men are closing the **life expectancy** gap. This is partly due to the development of better ways of treating the congenital and inherited conditions and deadly illnesses that affect men more. These include heart disease, cerebral palsy, muscular dystrophy, and **hemophilia**. But that's not all. Women seem to be tougher than men in other ways. Here is another piece of evidence showing that women have a better chance of survival—even before they are born:

> "Despite their size, speed, and strength, men just seem to die more easily and frequently than women—even in the womb. Boys are conceived far more frequently than girls—about 115 male for every 100 females. From that point on, however, women quickly make up ground, and they soon surpass men handily. For some reason, male fetuses are miscarried, stillborn, or spontaneously aborted more often than female fetuses. Consequently, by the time of birth, the ratio of boys to girls has dropped to 104 boys for every 100 girls... It doesn't stop there, though. Boys die more frequently than girls in infancy, during childhood, and during each subsequent year of life."
>
> [By Dr. Robert W. Griffith, *Health and Age*, July 16, 2004. www.healthandage.com/public/health-center/4/article-home/2872/The-Longest-Living-Sex-and-Why.html]

What does this story tell us? Why are more male babies conceived than female ones? And why are there still more women in the world than men?

Moms and dads

Both men and women can become parents. But only women can actually have babies. Female bodies are specially equipped to bear children. For instance, the bones of the female pelvis are set wider apart than the same bones on a male, so that babies can pass through when they are born. Women also have breasts in order to produce milk to feed their newborn children.

These biological differences between the sexes have also encouraged social differences. Throughout human history, a woman's main role has been to raise and look after her babies. This can obviously put mothers in a more vulnerable and dependent position than men. Men, on the other hand, have been seen as protectors and providers for their families. This means fathers are generally able to behave in a more independent way.

Some differences are harder to spot

On the face of it, both sexes look pretty much the same. But there are many physical differences that do not seem obvious to the naked eye. For example:

- Men are taller than women.
- Men grow more body hair.
- Men have thicker and oilier skin.
- Men have a greater mass of muscle tissue.
- A man's blood has more red corpuscles (cells).
- Women have lower blood pressure than men.
- As they get older, women lose less brain tissue.
- Women have a smaller waist in comparison to their hips.
- Women have a lower center of gravity, with longer upper bodies and shorter legs (relative to their height).

What influences do you think these differences have on people's lives? Do they tend to give the sexes different abilities? Do they affect our health differently?

> *Buddies in arms*

The armed forces in many countries have merged what used to be separate sections for men and women. Does this recognize the fact that men and women can perform most of the same military jobs at the same level, or is it just political correctness?

Who lives the longest?

Average life expectancy (in years)	Women	Men
World	67.84	64
Andorra (highest)	86.23	80.62
Japan	85.56	78.67
Australia	83.63	77.75
United Kingdom	81.3	76.23
United States	80.97	75.15
China	74.8	71.3
Russia	72.6	59
India	71.7	66.28
South Africa	49.7	48.8
Swaziland (lowest)	32.62	31.84

The skills divide

Do the sexes have different mental skills? Are males necessarily better at some things, and females better at others? Researchers have conducted hundreds of studies aimed at finding this out, based on different ability and reasoning tests. The best known of these are IQ tests and the SAT (Scholastic **Aptitude** Test), taken by college applicants.

Many people criticize these ways of measuring ability as being unfair. They point out that the tests are usually set by men, and that the questions tend to refer more to men than women. They also use situations and contexts that are more familiar to men. Even so, most studies show clearly that males and females have abilities that are different. Men are better in some areas, while women are better in others.

What are females best at?

In general, women can use words better than men. In order to perform the verbal tasks in the tests, they show greater skill. This is backed up by other evidence. Males are more likely to stutter and to suffer from dyslexia (word blindness) and other reading difficulties in their early years. Because of their role as mothers, women are naturally seen as the more caring and sympathetic sex. For the same reason, they tend to spend more time in the home and take the bigger share of housework and bringing up children. Studies also show that in conversation, women are more likely to support and agree with others. Men are more likely to disagree and argue.

Mothers usually play the biggest part in bringing up children. Is this because of their instinctive natures, or because they are the ones who bear children and tend to spend more time in the home?

What are males best at?

Studies suggest that men also have much stronger "spatial" ability. This means that they are better at judging the distances between objects—especially moving objects. They are better able to "track" these objects as they move and anticipate where they will go. This could give them a mental advantage, because they may be more able to think through practical problems. The advantage can also be physical—most obviously, when kicking or hitting a moving ball in sports, such as when playing soccer and tennis. Men tend to be able to use numbers better than women. They are also likely to have a broader range of general knowledge. Given all this evidence, it is no surprise that male students outnumber females in science, mathematics, and technology classes in U.S. colleges. On the other hand, there are more female students than males in most other areas of study.

What do they think?

"If women are expected to do the same work as men, we must teach them the same things"
Plato, Greek philosopher (c. 427–347 BCE)

"Women are not men's equals in anything except responsibility. We are not their inferiors either, or even their superiors. We are quite simply different races."
Phyllis McGinley, U.S. writer (1905–1978)

Thinking and feeling

According to some surveys, up to 75 percent of women prefer acting on feelings, while up to 80 percent of men prefer acting on thinking. What can we learn from these tests about men and women? Psychologists and **sociologists** are always designing new ways to study intelligence and gender differences. The results of their research often become big stories in newspapers and on TV. We are all endlessly fascinated by the subject. But what do all these studies add up to? Do they agree with each other? And do they give us any clearer idea of the different abilities and thought processes of men and women?

Many academics point out that, overall, many research and test results find little or no difference at all between the abilities of men and women. However, we rarely hear anything about these results. Why not? Because they do not make interesting news stories!

> *The greatest*

Roger Federer is probably the finest tennis player of the 21st century. The men's game is faster, longer, and more powerful than the women's game, but does that make it better or more fun to watch?

Here is some evidence from a psychologist. Read it and judge for yourself whether the gender gap in intelligence is huge or tiny:

Think Again: Men and Women Share Cognitive Skills. Research debunks myths about cognitive difference. What the research shows

Are boys better at math? Are girls better at language? If fewer women than men work as scientists and engineers, is that aptitude or culture? Psychologists have gathered solid evidence that boys and girls or men and women differ in very few significant ways—differences that would matter in school or at work—in how, and how well, they think.

At the University of Wisconsin, Janet Shibley Hyde has compiled meta-analytical studies on this topic for more than 10 years. By using this approach, which aggregates [gathers] research findings from many studies, Hyde has boiled down hundreds of inquiries into one simple conclusion: The sexes are more the same than they are different.

If males and females are truly understood to be very much the same, things might change in schools, colleges and universities, industry and the workplace in general.

In half the studies, sex differences were small; in another third they were almost non-existent. Thus, 78 percent of gender differences are small or close to zero.

[From *Psychology Matters*, American Psychological Association, January 2006.]

Are there other reasons for test differences?

Of course there is going to be some truth in these research findings. After all, they are based on strict scientific methods and organized by genuine college academics. But is there enough evidence in them to draw major conclusions about male and female behavior?

Some experts think you should not read too much into the studies. Aren't the answers of both men and women likely to be influenced by the way they were raised? In most cultures, males are often encouraged to be aggressive and practical. Females are encouraged to be more passive. These different attitudes may be reflected in survey results.

"HANG IN THERE, SANDRA. IN A FEW YEARS WE'LL BE TORMENTING THEM"

> *Who is a kid longer?*

Psychologists and educators recognize that girls usually reach social and physical maturity earlier than boys. This can have effects on how they interact and learn.

Children And Adults

Everybody is born with a certain amount of intelligence. And, however hard you try, you will not be able to make yourself more intelligent. On the other hand, you can learn to use your intelligence in the best way possible.

But do things stay exactly the same throughout your life? Does your brainpower develop at the same speed as your body, or does it vary? Research in the West shows that your level of intelligence can certainly change as you get older. It also shows that the intelligence of males and females often develops at different rates as they grow up. As young children, many boys are slower at learning to read than girls. As teenagers, boys tend to do better in math and science than girls, while girls do better in English. By the age of 16, girls have overtaken boys in all three subjects. When they go on to higher education, female students on average achieve better results than male students.

Do these differences continue into adult life? Do they give women career advantages? This is much harder to figure out, because worldwide males still dominate most areas of the workforce. Although there are large numbers of highly successful women workers, they are greatly outnumbered by men. Is this because women are less intelligent, or simply that they are denied equal opportunities?

In school

What do you remember about your early years in school? You must have met all kinds of people, with different abilities and different talents. Did you notice how much they changed as they grew older? Did some children seem much brighter than others right from the start? Did they stay that way all through school, or did others catch up with them? Children are developing all the time, but not at the same speeds. Some grow tall early, while others have a growth spurt in their teens. Some start out funny-looking and turn into beautiful or handsome teenagers. Some can read before they get to school, while others do not learn until they have been in school a few years. Does this prove anything about their intelligence or not?

The reading debate

Many people see reading as one of the big tests of a child's intelligence. Learning to read is one of the first big hurdles you have to jump in school. So, what does it tell us about the differences between boys and girls? Figures show that for many years school teachers have been picking out boys as slow readers. A study in the United States in 1990 found that teachers were referring up to four times more boys as girls for special teaching in this subject. Why should this be? Was it true, as some have suggested, that teachers were biased against boys and were treating them unfairly?

> *Student life*

Girls and boys develop intellectually and physically at different rates during their school years.

Are boys slower readers? Another study in 2004 examined the question in even more depth. This involved more than 10,000 young people in the United Kingdom and New Zealand. Researchers discovered that boys are twice as likely to have reading difficulties as girls. At the same time, another study was comparing the achievements of 15-year-olds in 32 countries throughout the world. This confirmed that girls are more literate than boys at this age. So, had the teachers been acting unfairly? Professor Robert Goodman of the Institute of Psychiatry and co-author of the research, said: "Our study has found teachers have been right all along and that there are more boys with difficulties."

What other differences are there in school?

In many parts of the world, there is a clear gap between girls and boys in the early years of learning (though not in all countries—see page 40). Moreover, as children get older, the gap seems to close and then widen even further than before. Some research shows that, by the age of 14, boys tend to perform better than girls in math and science. Girls do better in English and other subjects needing verbal skills. But by 16, girls get better results than boys in tests for math, science, and English.

What do they think?

"It's easy—females have always been smarter than males."
Sarah, United States

"Boys don't like to learn or work hard at school—it's seen as uncool."
Hazel, United Kingdom

"Girls are more eager to please teachers and more disappointed than boys if they don't do well."
Mae, Norway

"You can only get away with being a male science nerd if you are cool in other ways."
Tom, United States

"Girls can do their work and stay clean and tidy all day, but the boys are always scruffy and dirty by the time they go home."
Bola, Nigeria

"From an early age girls are encouraged to take part in 'quiet' activities which help equip them for studying later while boys are not."
Mark, United Kingdom

[From various sources]

In higher education

There may be big differences in the progress of males and females in school. But do these carry on into college? After all, students who continue on to get degrees in higher education are likely to be among the most intelligent part of the population. So, do female students do better than male students?

Has the picture changed over the years? Since the 1900s, women have gone to college in increasing numbers. Now that there are just as many females as males studying for college degrees, how have the females performed? National and international statistics tell us the big story. Here is how it looks at one college, Bradley University in Peoria, Illinois:

The New Gender Divide

As my husband perused the *Journal Star*'s high school graduation supplement in May, he picked up a pen and started calculating. Here's what he found:

- Girls comprised 71 percent of the Top Ten graduates reported by 29 area high schools; the hapless boys held just 85 of 282 spots.
- Among May graduates the last four years, just 35 men completed the university's rigorous honors program. Eighty-five women did. Where men once dominated, women now do, and the gap is widening:
- Men made up 59 percent of Academic Hall of Fame honorees in the first 10 years of its existence at Bradley (1982-1991). In the last 15 years, they've made up just 22 percent.
- In 1967, the year I graduated from Bradley, half of all summa cum laude [the highest graduation level] awards went to men. Today fewer than one in four top students are male.
- In high schools the gap is apparent as well. Peoria [Illinois] District 150 says 85.4 percent of the entering girls in the 2006 graduation class stuck around to finish. Among the boys, just 80.6 percent did.

Similar gaps between male and female achievement are being observed virtually everywhere in the industrial world. In Australia, taxpayers are underwriting a multimillion-dollar educational initiative called *Success for Boys*. For one thing, in the knowledge-based economy, jobs available to men and women without college degrees are shrinking. Girls have responded by enrolling in college in unprecedented numbers while the boys have flat-lined. Last year 270,000 more women than men got bachelor's degrees in America.

[By Barbara Mantz Drake, *Peoria Journal Star*, July 22, 2007.]

Do these figures surprise you? What do they tell you about the changing status of women in education? Do you think these findings would reflect the general picture across the United States—and in other parts of the world? And how do they affect the way you think about gender differences in intelligence?

Who has degrees?

These statistics show how student achievements have changed in the United States. These figures show the number of students gaining bachelor's degrees in two four-year periods, forty years apart:

	Male	Female
1962–1966	1,040,000	905,000
2002–2006	862,000	1,310,000

What's the big difference in these figures?

[Source: NCES Digest of Education Statistics, 2006]

> *Degree day*

In the western world, more females now graduate from higher education than do males. Is this the sign of a new gender divide in learning?

> *Woman at the top*
> Oprah Winfrey has carved out a sensational career in television. She is now one of the most influential and well-known people in broadcasting worldwide.

At work

Female students are now achieving better overall results than male students in higher education. So, it seems that women leaving college with a degree are likely to be at least as bright as men. They should, surely, have the same opportunities as men. But does this mean they go on to do equally well—or even better—in their careers?

Sadly, the answer is no. At work, the signs of gender inequality become glaringly obvious for the first time in a person's life. Let's assume that most graduates will get jobs in the upper levels of the worldwide workforce. Employment figures show that men still hold most of the important and powerful jobs and earn much more money.

How wide is the salary gap?

A study by the American Association of University Women (AAUW), published in 2007, examines the salary gap between males and females in the United States. It first appears early in a person's career—and gets worse. One year after leaving college, women working full time earn 20 percent less than their male colleagues. After 10 years, women have fallen even farther behind, earning 31 percent less than men.

Earlier research findings back up these figures. A 2005 study found that average salaries for female attorneys lagged behind those of male attorneys by $14,000. The gap was much the same in finance and accounting jobs throughout the country. Also, in a 2007 survey, the majority of business leaders were aware that men and women were not paid equally for similar jobs.

```
One Woman's Story

Takako Ariishi, 36, grew up [in Japan] as the only
child of the president of a small business owned by
her family that supplies gauges to Nissan. At first,
her disappointed father cut her hair like a boy's
and forbade her to play with dolls. When she had her
first son 10 years ago, he fired her from the company
and anointed the infant grandson as his successor.

Still, Ms. Ariishi took over as president three years
ago after her father died. She is the only woman
in a group of some 160 heads of Nissan suppliers.
The first time she attended the group's meetings,
she says she was asked to wait in a room with
secretaries. "I still have to prove all the time that
a woman can be president."

[Source: New York Times, August 6, 2007.]
```

 Female high flyers

Here are a few of today's outstanding women—political leaders, athletes, businesspeople, and writers:

Venus Williams, tennis player   **Hillary Clinton**, politician

Ellen McArthur, around-the-world sailor   **Condoleezza Rice**, politician

Aung Sun Suu Kyi, politician   **Meryl Streep**, actor

J. K. Rowling, writer   **Maya Angelou**, writer

Oprah Winfrey, broadcaster and businesswoman

Find out more about them. Ask yourself: How have they achieved so much? How much was due to intelligence, how much to natural gifts, and how much to sheer determination? And did they have to work much harder than their male rivals in order to succeed? If so, why?

> *Unequal opportunities*

In many areas of the world, the gender gap is closing. But women in the developing world are still likely to suffer from sexual **discrimination** in school and work, and will find fewer chances to prove their intelligence.

Are There Equal Chances To Be Smart?

Here is a reminder of the question that is the title of this book: Are girls smarter than boys? We have already looked at some types of evidence that can be used to answer the question, such as statistics and survey results. But do you think this is enough to reach a full answer? Are there other ways to find evidence?

The facts we have seen so far suggest that men and women should be equally intelligent. Girls do slightly better, on balance, than boys at school. Female students outnumber males in colleges in many parts of the world. They also gain more degrees. On the face of it, they should be just as successful as men in their later careers.

So, there may be other reasons why females still lag behind in both pay and job opportunities. Are women bound to have different lives than men simply because of their sex? Are they treated differently and given fewer chances? Does this kind of treatment have an effect on what they expect from life? And does it alter the way they use their intelligence?

The future for female equality is looking brighter in many parts of the world, as attitudes change. But in other areas, notably some developing countries, girls are seen as inferior to boys. They are discouraged from gaining an education or a career. They do not get an equal chance to show whether or not they really are smarter.

Why do women lose out at work?

Do female workers—especially mothers—get the same chances as male workers? The evidence shows that they do not, in spite of a small improvement in some areas in recent times. So, do fathers and childless people have an advantage? Is it an unfair one?

There has been a lot of research into the possible reasons for the "gender gap" at work. The reports usually agree that there is not just one likely cause, but a whole list. Here are some of them:

The glass ceiling

Most employers have **conventional** attitudes toward gender difference. They are likely to treat women as inferior, simply because this is a common **prejudice** in many societies. The result is that they rarely promote female employees to top positions. Many women only rise to a lower level before they hit what is called "the **glass ceiling**."

> *Family life*

Many fathers do an equal share of work in the home. But on average throughout the world, within families most of the housework and caring burden still falls to women.

Family responsibilities

Women have babies. This means, of course, that many women give up their jobs to look after their children—even if only for a few months. This period—the "career break"—can have a big impact on a woman's working life. Many employers say that women who take a break are bound to have less working experience than men who do not. Therefore, they should be paid less.

Men are more pushy

Are women less competitive than men by nature? Many people think so and believe that a man's aggression is more likely to bring him success and promotion at work. Women, they say, are more anxious than men to find peaceful solutions to problems and give support. Other people believe this view is old-fashioned and inaccurate.

Women tend to choose less well-paid jobs

There are far more women than men working as secretaries and cleaners, or in catering or the "caring" professions, such as nursing and teaching. These are jobs with lower pay levels and generally lower expectations than most others.

Can you think of any more reasons? What about adults you know—do you recognize any of these issues affecting their working lives? Talk to them and find out if they have noticed any changes in attitudes in recent years. You should also ask yourself: What does this have to do with being smart? Do discrimination and social attitudes have an effect on how a person uses his or her intelligence?

Paternity leave

How much paid **paternity leave** is a man legally entitled to get when he becomes a father? This varies widely across the world.

- ✔ Argentina — 2 days
- ✔ Australia — 0 days
- ✔ Chile — 7 days
- ✔ France — 2 weeks
- ✔ Italy — 13 weeks
- ✔ New Zealand — 0 days
- ✔ Saudi Arabia — 1 day
- ✔ South Africa — 3 days
- ✔ Switzerland — 0 days
- ✔ United Kingdom — 2 weeks
- ✔ United States — 0 days

[Source: Emplaw website, 2007 figures]

Women's fight to be educated

Women may have an uphill struggle for equal education and work opportunities in the United States and Europe. But things are much more difficult for them in some other parts of the world. Here is a report from Malawi, in southeast Africa:

Girls Lag Behind Boys in Education
China Limau is the only girl out of the 35 students in Standard 8 at Muona Primary School in Nsanje, south Malawi. She wants to be an engineer after completing school. She does not want to be like other girls who opt for more female related careers. She wants something **distinctive**. However, the possibility of achieving her goal looks grim. In Malawi, girls still drop out of school more frequently than boys. It is estimated that only 28% of the Standard 8 pupils in the country are girls and of that percentage only 36% pass their examinations. China Limau, however, is not deterred by these statistics. "I want to be educated like you," she told a group of journalists who recently visited her town during a countrywide tour.

[Source: University of Pennsylvania, *Malawi News Online*]

How does the situation in Malawi compare with girls' chances in the West? How hard is it for a Malawian schoolgirl to use her intelligence to its full potential?

Women in the developing world
Girls in many poor and developing countries can face discrimination at the very start of their lives. The practice of female infanticide means there are girls who never survive to reach school age. Then, many are not allowed to go to school at all, because their parents want to keep them at home. Some are fortunate enough to start school at the same age as boys, but a large number drop out of education early, simply because of their gender. Why is there this difference? Both the sexes are equally intelligent and capable. But traditional attitudes are still strong. The teachers in many of these countries, who are mostly male, see girls as less bright than boys. They tend to give the boys more attention and expect girls to be quiet and passive.

Poverty and puberty
But the main thing that prevents girls from getting an education is simple: poverty. Many parents take their girls out of school because they need them to work and earn money or to help in the home. It is much more important to them financially that boys should be given a proper education.

> *Country classroom*

These schoolgirls listen to their teacher in rural Malawi. Drop-out rates for girls are especially high in parts of Africa, due to intimidation, early marriage, and social pressure to work in the home or fields.

Other parents stop their daughters' schooling as soon as they reach **puberty**. They fear the girls may become pregnant and want to keep them away from male students. Many girls are married while very young to husbands they do not necessarily want. After this, they are very unlikely to obtain any more education. For some, school can be a dangerous place:

"South African girls often encounter violence...
they are confronted with levels of sexual violence
and sexual **harassment** in schools that impede their
access to education on equal terms with male
students."

[Source: Human Rights Watch Website]

 No school today—or ever

"Over 100 million children have no opportunity to attend school. Of this number, girls account for 60 percent."
[Source: UNESCO]

> ## Being the boss

This male doctor is the one in charge here—the conventional position of the man. How unusual would it look in some societies if the roles were reversed, with a female doctor and male nurse? Are times changing in most places?

How Can We Make Things Fairer?

Why should girls be smarter than boys—or the other way around? The two sexes may be different in many ways, but they are also amazingly similar. So, why shouldn't they be equally smart? Some studies still suggest that there are differences in intelligence between men and women. Are these differences real and permanent, or are they artificially created by the society we live in?

One thing is certain. If we want to judge male and female intelligence properly, we need to be able to treat both in a fair way and give them equal opportunities to reach their full potential. And to do that, we have to make changes in our attitudes and—maybe—our laws.

In most parts of the world, including supposedly enlightened developed countries, such as the United States, women are still seen by many as "the weaker sex." Are people with these views right, or do they need to be better educated, to encourage them to treat everyone equally?

There may also be better ways of measuring people's intelligence. Many psychologists and sociologists have criticized older systems, such as IQ testing, because they are not completely fair. Researchers are constantly looking for new methods that will give them more reliable results.

Should we change our attitudes?

You have seen plenty of evidence in this book about the intelligence of men and women. Maybe you have found more information on your own. All this may have changed your opinion about the subject. Do the facts really show that one sex is smarter than the other? Or are you choosing the evidence that suits your opinion? Everyone has a view about the differences between the sexes. Often this view can be based on no real evidence at all. It may have been influenced by what you have been told, how your parents behave, or what you see on TV and in movies. Even today, many people believe that females are inferior to males. Do you think more action should be taken to change attitudes like this? Or is the present situation acceptable? What can be done to change the conventional view of men and women, at every stage of life?

> *Successful or held back?*
>
> **Is sex discrimination still a barrier to women's advancement? The evidence seems to support both sides of the debate.**

At birth

Parents are the biggest influence on our character. Their behavior and beliefs can affect us for life. How can mothers and fathers learn to treat their babies in exactly the same way, whether they are boys or girls?

In school

School can be a scary place for girls, with widespread bullying and strong peer pressure to conform to a sexual **stereotype** (which often means girls have to be girly and unassertive). Counseling and complaints procedures are already in place. But what can be done to strengthen the non-sexist message among boys?

In college

Sex discrimination (as well as harassment) are banned in most colleges. But do female students get treated in the same way as the males? Are they encouraged to study subjects usually thought of as "male," such as engineering or construction?

At work

Employers need to find ways of closing the "gender gap" over pay and career prospects. They should make sure they use the same standards for hiring men and women and should give them equal starting salaries. They could also offer flexible work arrangements for parents with children.

 What do they think? Famous sexist quotes

"Women should remain at home, sit still, keep house, and bear children."
Martin Luther, German religious leader (1483–1546)

"[Feminism is] a socialist, anti-family, political movement that encourages women to leave their husbands, kill their children, practice witchcraft, destroy capitalism, and become lesbians."
Pat Robertson, TV evangelist (born 1930)

"Nature intended women to be our slaves. They are our property."
Napoleon Bonaparte, French leader (1769–1821)

"Women have a right to work wherever they want—as long as they have dinner on the table ready when you get home."
John Wayne, movie actor (1907–1979)

Equal opportunities worldwide

Are things getting better? Certainly, most governments are now trying to promote equal rights for women. Many have passed laws that aim to stop sex discrimination in education, work, and other areas. The United States set up an Equal Employment Opportunity Commission over 40 years ago. This good example has been followed by other countries. Yet, surprisingly, it seems that the best news now may be coming from the developing world:

Developing World Cracks Glass Ceiling

Women in developing countries find it easier to break through the so-called glass ceiling than their colleagues in the west, according to a global study.

More than a hundred business people were interviewed across eight countries, including China, India, and Germany, for the report on women's economic participation for the Women's Forum held in Deauville, France. There was "considerable **optimism**" in developing countries regarding the growth of women's participation in the workplace—not just in the numbers entering the workforce but also their entry into middle and senior management.

In some countries, such as Germany and Switzerland, there are cultural and social perceptions of women that make advancement much more challenging. Whereas in the developing world, where there is a huge cry for talent, where there is enormous growth, you must be able to adjust to these norms faster.

The report highlighted some business responses that had helped the inclusion of women in the workplace. Some interviewees in Brazil, France, India, and the U.S. pointed to the establishment of a diversity committee in a company as a great help to eliminate bias.

Others mentioned women-only networks as a good measure. One interviewee in India said that in some of the hi-tech industries where networks were newly developing, women were doing very well.

[By Marianne Barriaux, *The Guardian*, October 15, 2007. Copyright Guardian News and Media 2007.]

How different is this from other stories about women in the developing world? Why do you think there is now a divide between more developed and less developed countries? Will this trend help all women to make better use of their intelligence?

New ways of testing intelligence

How many times have you seen headlines like these?

MEN CLEVERER THAN WOMEN CLAIM (BBC)

MEN MORE INTELLIGENT AND MORE STUPID THAN WOMEN (Express India)

WOMEN BELIEVE WOMEN MORE INTELLIGENT THAN MEN (CNN)

They seem to appear every few months, when a new opinion poll or survey is published. But how seriously should we take these stories?

Many academics have expressed doubts about IQ testing and other ways of measuring intelligence. They say that these methods only test a narrow range of a person's abilities. New kinds of measurements are being developed that may be fairer and more effective. They include psychological tests, interviews, and observation of people's behavior.

> *Girl power*

These women in Pakistan march in support of equal rights for minority groups—one of the many worldwide activities on International Women's Day.

> *Working together*

Armed police patrol a railroad station during a
terrorist alert. Throughout the world, men and
women now operate together as equals in many
areas of the workforce.

Debate
The Facts

Are girls smarter than boys? Have you made up your mind yet? This book has not tried to persuade you to take a view one way or the other. Its purpose is to show you some of the evidence from both sides. It also helps you learn to think critically, to find and look at evidence, and to make your argument effectively to others. Now you should be ready to explain your opinion to other people and persuade them that it is the right one. The best way to do this is to organize a debate with your classmates.

What kind of debate should you have? The simplest kind of debate may not be the best. You could just start a discussion with other students. But this can easily turn into a shouting match, and nobody will learn anything from it. An organized and structured debate is a better option, even though it can be more difficult to set up.

This kind of formal debate has two equal sides. You start with a **motion**. This is an agreed statement or question to argue about. In this case, of course, it is "Are girls smarter than boys?"

Who takes part?

The two teams of speakers
It is essential to find teams of people who can present both points of view. They must also be able to speak clearly and confidently on the topic. The audience will benefit from hearing something that both challenges and informs them.

The moderator
Choose someone to be the "**moderator**," or referee. This person does not take part in the arguing, but rather directs the debate. He or she introduces the motion and keeps control of the speakers and the audience.

The audience
The more, the merrier—but all audience members must keep to the debate rules. Nobody may speak unless the moderator gives them permission.

How to be a good debater

- ✔ Research your subject and prepare your speech thoroughly in advance—this will give you confidence.
- ✔ Have plenty of facts and other evidence ready.
- ✔ When speaking, stand up straight and don't move around too much.
- ✔ Look up and make eye contact with your audience.
- ✔ Read your speech clearly and loudly enough for everyone to hear, using your natural voice.
- ✔ Vary the pitch of your voice—this helps to keep the attention of the audience.
- ✔ Emphasize the key points in your speech.
- ✔ Speak only when the moderator allows you to.
- ✔ Listen carefully to what other speakers have to say.
- ✔ Allow others to express their opinions and do not interrupt.
- ✔ Make notes of the weak points in your opponents' speeches.

What happens during a debate?
The moderator explains the rules of the debate and introduces the motion. Then, the first speaker puts forth an argument in support of the motion. He or she is followed by a speaker from the other team, who puts forth an opposing argument. The third speaker argues for the motion, and the fourth speaker against. Each speech should last no longer than five minutes.

After this the moderator can invite the audience to pose questions to the speakers. The debate winds up with short closing statements from both sides, restating their opinions. Finally, the audience votes either for or against the motion. The moderator counts the votes and declares the winner.

What do you think now?

When you started this book, did you already think that girls were smarter than boys? Or did you think the opposite? Had you ever really thought about the subject before? Here is a quick reminder of the main points to think about regarding gender and intelligence:

- What do we mean by "intelligence"? Intelligence is the ability to use your mind to reason things out, plan ahead, solve problems, and understand complex ideas. There are many kinds of tests to measure intelligence—but can we trust the results?

- What is the real difference between women and men? Obviously, there are physical differences. Also, men are seen as more aggressive than women. Women are perceived as preferring to agree and give support, while men like to argue. Men are seen as good at organizing things, and women as good at identifying with the feelings of others. Are these non-physical differences valid, or are they just stereotyping?

- Does our intelligence develop as we get older? Research shows that the intelligence of males and females often develops at different rates. But do these differences continue into adult life?

- Do women get the same chances as men? Men and women should be equally intelligent. Yet women still lag behind in both pay and job opportunities. Women seem to get fewer chances than men simply because of their sex. Does this have an effect on what they expect from life? And does it alter the way they use their intelligence?

- Are things changing? The future for female equality is looking brighter in many parts of the world, as attitudes change. But in other areas, in both developing and developed countries, girls are still seen as inferior to boys. They are discouraged from gaining an education or a career. They do not get an equal chance to show whether or not they really are smarter.

So, are girls smarter than boys? What do you think?

Find Out More

Projects

◆ Are girls smarter than boys? Conduct your own personal survey among your classmates. Remember: Your class will not be an average sample, so do not read too much into the result.

◆ Talk to women and men from older generations—your parents, grandparents, and great-grandparents. Ask the women how they were treated in school and at work. Ask the men how they were encouraged to treat women. Compare attitudes of different generations.

◆ Check out your own IQ. You will find specimen tests on websites mentioned on the opposite page. But don't take them too seriously. Read the criticisms of the test system on page 17.

Books

Armstrong, Thomas. *You're Smarter Than You Think: A Kid's Guide to Multiple Intelligences*. Minneapolis: Free Spirit, 2003.

Macbain-Stephens, Jennifer. *Women's Suffrage: Giving the Right to Vote to All Americans.* New York: Rosen, 2006.

Macdonald, Fiona. *Equal Opportunities (Global Issues)*. North Vancouver, B.C.: Walrus, 2006.

Moore, Gareth. *Sudoku Makes You Smarter*. New York: Simon Scribbles, 2007.

Valenti, Jessica. *Full Frontal Feminism: A Young Woman's Guide to Why Feminism Matters*. Emeryvillle, Calif.: Seal, 2007.

Websites

- www.dana.org/resources/brainykids
  Online resources for brainy kids (and grownups)

- www.globalissues.org/HumanRights/WomensRights
  A survey of women's issues around the world

- www.archives.gov/research/alic/reference/womens-history.html
  Traces the history of the fight for women's rights

- www.iqtest.com
  One of dozens of sites offering free IQ tests

- www.kidshealth.org/kid/body/brain_noSW.html
  Learn more about your brain and how it works

Glossary

aptitude natural talent or ability to do something

conventional something that fits in with normal or accepted standards

discrimination act or make a choice or decision that is based on prejudice rather than reason

distinctive standing out or unmistakable

doctorate highest postgraduate college degree. It is also know as a PhD.

gender word used to identify a person's sex

glass ceiling invisible barrier that prevents many women from being promoted to top jobs

gray matter reddish-gray nerve tissue of the brain

harassment act of picking on, tormenting, or pestering someone repeatedly

hemophilia inherited disease that prevent's a person's blood from clotting, thus leading to internal bleeding

inferior naturally worse or of lower quality

life expectancy number of years a person is expected to live on average

mass demonstration meeting of a large crowd of people to protest against something or publicize a point of view

moderator person who controls a meeting or assembly

motion formal proposal or statement that forms the basis of a debate

neurologist person who studies the branch of medicine that deals with the nervous system, including the brain and its functions

optimism expecting the best possible outcome for something

paternity leave time off work a man is allowed when he becomes a father

prejudice judgment or opinion about something that is formed beforehand or without any knowledge of the subject

psychologist person who studies how we behave and think

puberty age at which a man or woman becomes physically capable of having a child

quotient number obtained when one quantity is divided by another. For example, 60 divided by 3 equals 20; the quotient in this case is 20.

sociologist person who studies how humans behave in society

stereotype person or object that conforms to an expected pattern

suffrage right to vote in elections

tycoon wealthy, powerful businessperson

unprecedented unheard of, something that has never happened before

workforce all the workers available in a project, or country, or even the world

Index

A Living Wage

AMERICAN WORKERS AND THE

MAKING OF CONSUMER SOCIETY

Lawrence B. Glickman

Cornell University Press

Ithaca & London

Library of Congress Cataloging-in-Publication Data

Glickman, Lawrence B., 1963–
    A living wage : American workers and the making of consumer
society / Lawrence B. Glickman.
      p. cm.
    Includes index.
    ISBN 0-8014-3357-6 (cloth : alk. paper)
    1. Wages — United States — History.   2. Cost and standard of living —
United States — History.   3. Working class — United States — History.
4. Consumption (Economics) — Social aspects — United States — History.
HD6983.G475   1997
331.2'973 — dc21   97-19264

First published 1997 by Cornell University Press.

Printed in the United States of America

Cornell University Press strives to utilize environmentally responsible suppliers and materials to the fullest extent possible in the publishing of its books. Such materials include vegetable-based, low-VOC inks and acid-free papers that are also either recycled, totally chlorine-free, or partly composed of nonwood fibers.

Cloth printing   10 9 8 7 6 5 4 3 2 1

For my parents, Sandra and Ronald Glickman

Contents

Illustrations

Preface

Living wage. The phrase is familiar, even totemic. Many commentators associate it with a world we have lost, a symbol of the wage level and social structure characteristic of the "good old days" when one breadwinner could support a family. The "notion of the 'living wage' has a quaint ring to it today, as more people labor longer hours for less pay and fewer benefits," observes Jacqueline Jones. In the midst of America's postindustrial economic woes, calls for a living wage have resurfaced in political rhetoric and on picket signs. President Bill Clinton, playing off the disparity between the legal minimum wage and the ability to live decently, asked Congress in his 1995 State of the Union address "to make the minimum wage a living wage." He is not the only politician to invoke the phrase. Colin Powell called for the restoration of a "decent living wage" in his address to the 1996 Republican National Convention; at the 1996 Democratic National Convention, Jesse Jackson called it a "moral imperative to provide a job with a living wage to every man and woman in America. That was Roosevelt's dream, and Dr. King's."[1]

Demands for a living wage have become a staple not only of national political speeches but of grass-roots movements as well. Several states and municipalities, prodded by the campaigns of organized labor and activist groups, have passed "living wage" laws, which usually set a wage floor half again that of the current minimum wage. North Dakota's pioneering "Living Wage Amendment," passed in 1992, requires businesses that accept government subsidies to pay their full-time workers enough money to keep a family of four out of poverty. In 1992 it was $6.71 per hour, far exceeding the national minimum wage of $4.25. Baltimore enacted a "living wage" ordinance requiring all city contractors to pay their employees at "a rate which exceeds the poverty level" — $6.10 per hour as of July 1, 1995, to increase to $7.70 over the next several years. Living wage bills have also been proposed in St. Paul, Milwaukee, Houston, and New York City, where in 1995 Councilman Sal Albanese sponsored legislation to set the minimum rate for city contractors at twelve dollars an hour. The platform of the New Mexico Green Party calls for a "national debate" on the living wage, and the recently formed Labor Party endorses a national "living wage" of ten dollars an hour. Living wage proponents argue that well-compensated workers are more likely to be active in political life and, conversely, that impoverished workers cannot constitute a vital citizenry. Linking economics to politics, these advocates stress the social benefits — for labor, capital, and the nation — that result from a well-remunerated working class.[2]

The call for living wages is frequently connected to movements for social justice. Demanded in recent years by Mexican garment makers, Canadian letter carriers, and South African Kentucky Fried Chicken employees, as well as by thousands of American workers, the living wage has become a universal in the language of labor rights. The United Nations has made the living wage a centerpiece of its worldwide antipoverty campaign.[3]

Contemporary living wage advocacy is not based solely on issues of politics and social justice but embraces family, gender, and moral obligation. Many proponents have echoed Congressman Richard Gephart's claim that "wages are the most important family value."[4] In 1992, for example, the mother of a minor league baseball player, Mike Gardella, complained about her son's inadequate income. For Gardella's mother, a living wage would enable a male breadwinner to support a family. "He's not making a living wage in the minor leagues," she declared. "He gets about $1,200 a month. And he has a wife and they have a baby on the way." In the wake of the 1992 urban uprising in his city, a resident of south-central Los Angeles explained the root of the problem: "McDonald's pays four dollars and fifty cents," he said. "That's not even a living wage for a teenager." The government "ought to raise the minimum wage to ten dollars an hour." He viewed lower wages as a threat to masculinity: "A man can't have any self-respect for less than that."[5]

With the globalization of the economy as well as revelations about some manufacturers' use of low-wage, prison, child, and even slave labor, living wage advocates have begun to emphasize consumers' moral responsibility to those who make the products that they purchase. "If the consumers only realized the horror and pain and suffering that goes into the strawberries they eat so pleasantly," maintains Arturo Rodriguez, president of the United Farm Workers union, they would support the unionization of exploited workers. A 1992 editorial in the *Los Angeles Times*, proposing a "minimum wage that is a living wage," acknowledged that higher wages "would raise the price on lettuce and frocks and many other things" but concluded that consumers had an obligation to pay workers well.[6]

However timely the contemporary living wage debate, the issues are not new. The meaning of democracy in a wage labor society, the theory of a symbiotic relationship between economic and political justice, the significance of good wages for the perpetuation of family life, and the importance of a politics of consumption were first debated when the idea of the living wage developed more than a century ago. Indeed, the continuities extend to the language of contemporary critics, whose indictment of the living wage as a dangerous, potentially socialistic violation of economic law recalls the arguments made by late nineteenth- and early twentieth-century American opponents of the living wage.[7]

In 1915 when the nation first debated minimum wage legislation, the journalist and pundit Walter Lippmann found it "hard to believe that America with all its riches could still be primitive enough to grunt and protest at a living wage."[8] At a time when an infinitely wealthier America is once again revisiting the issue, it is especially important to understand the complex history of this idea. In this book I examine the history of the "living wage," the term first voiced in the 1870s, whose seeming self-evidence obscures the history of debate about what exactly it means. Scrutiny of the long-term ruminations of labor leaders and reformers on the subject of wages uncovers three central and related transformations in modern American history: the acceptance of wage labor by workers, the concomitant consumerist reconstruction of working-class identity in the late nineteenth century, and the emergence of a new political-economic order in the early twentieth century which reflected these developments.

In Part I I describe how criticisms of wage labor gave way in the late nineteenth century to support for an economy based on high wages that would enable workers to reclaim citizenship, to consume more, and to preserve threatened gender roles. In Part II I examine the origins and development of the living wage and the related idea of the American standard of living, the central components of labor's late nineteenth-century "consumerist turn." In Part III I trace workers' attempts to define a consumerist class-consciousness through an analysis of the eight hour and union label movements. In Part IV I describe debates about the living wage from the Progressive Era through the New Deal and suggest that the living wage constituted a central tenet of the political economy of the "American Century."

Four interrelated arguments are central here.

Workers had long dismissed wage labor as a form of slavery, but with the notion of the living wage, they came to interpret it as consistent with and even constitutive of freedom. They did so by redefining wages in consumerist terms.

Workers played an active role in the construction of American consumer society, not just as participants in popular culture but as originators of a vision of a democratic political economy to which working-class consumption and consumer organizations were integral.

Workers attempted to shape the market for their own benefit, treating it not as a force of nature but as a human construction, an arena open to change through political and cultural struggle.

The living wage expresses the transformation of nineteenth-century republican into twentieth-century industrial America. As the labor radicalism of the post–Civil War years developed toward the New Deal, the debate shifted from the legitimacy of wages in any form to the possibility that the state should guarantee a minimum wage and promote an American standard of living. Endorsed by a variety of advocates from labor radicals such as Ira Steward to "pure and simple" trade unionists such as Samuel Gompers and later to religious leaders, politicians, and pundits, the living wage linked workers to reformers and to the state, and radicals to conservative trade unionists, thus setting the stage for the consumerist common ground of the New Deal order.

My 1987 datebook contains a fateful entry on September 27: "Look into the history of the family wage." Little did I know when I scribbled this reminder that I would spend nearly a decade doing exactly that. After all this time, it is a pleasure to thank some of the many friends, family members, teachers, and colleagues who have helped me along the way. I regret that there is not space to acknowledge all of them by name.

I have been blessed with excellent colleagues and a helpful staff in the History Department at the University of South Carolina. Two USC Research and Productive Scholarship Grants, encouragement from my colleagues, and generous departmental policies allowed me to complete this book. Three graduate students at USC, Tom Downey, Janet Hudson, and James Tidd, provided excellent research assistance.

This book was born in the vibrant intellectual community at the University of California, Berkeley. I am grateful to the amazing group of graduate students, hoops players, and faculty who provided inspiration and advice. Berkeley's Department of History, the Eugene Irving Mccormac Graduate Fellowship, and the Doreen B. Townsend Center for the Humanities provided financial support that amounted to a respectable living wage for a graduate student.

An earlier version of Chapter 4 appeared as "Inventing the 'American Standard of Living': Race, Gender, and Working-Class Identity, 1880–1925," in *Labor History* 34 (Spring–Summer 1993). It is reprinted with the permission of the Tamiment Institute.

The following people read portions of this book and dispensed especially valuable advice: Gregg Andrews, Amittai Aviram, Ed Davies, Elizabeth Faue, Ellen Furlough, Jon Gjerde, Jim Goodman, Victoria de Grazia, Alice Kessler-Harris, Steve Leikin, Ruth Milkman, and Kim Voss. For encouragement and interested response, I thank the audiences at the Bay Area Labor History Workshop, USC's "Scholars of Fortune," the Rutgers Center for Historical Analysis, and the Atlanta Seminar in the History of Labor, Industry, Technology, and Society. As readers for the Cornell University Press, Susan Porter Benson and Jean-Christophe Agnew gave the manuscript sympathetic and immensely helpful readings; they will detect their mark on this book. My friends Michael Berkowitz and Marc Schachter more than once took time from their own busy schedules to read and critique drafts of this book; I benefited enormously from their suggestions. Robin D. G. Kelley, Mary Jo Maynes, James M. McPherson, Peter Rachleff, John Risch, and Gerald Zahavi graciously answered specific queries from the author. My editor, Peter Agree, took an early interest in this project and encouraged me to produce the best book that I could write. Judith Bailey and Carol Betsch expertly handled the manuscript at Cornell University Press. I also thank the librarians and archivists at the Hagley Museum and Library, the State Historical Society of Wisconsin, the Tamiment Institute Library, the New York Public Library, and especially, the libraries at UC Berkeley and the University of South Carolina.

My biggest intellectual debt is to my mentor Larry Levine. His uncanny sense of what works and what misses the mark was invaluable to me as

I wrote this book, as was his constant support. His dissertation group (which I must thank collectively) provided fellowship, critical feedback, and some darned good dinners. I am proud to call Larry and Cornelia Levine my friends.

Other friends who helped me along the way deserve mention: Jesse Berrett, Pam Burdman, Marianne Constable, Peter Gordon, Leslie Kauffman, Cathy Kudlick, Jeff Lena, Mary Odem, Albert Park, Ann Powers, Stephen Shainbart, Marla Stone, Anita Tien, Eric Weisbard, Joel Westheimer, and Tim Weston.

My family was there for me time and time again. It was great luck to have my brothers, Cliff, a journalist, and Mark, an economist, to talk with about my work. Their love and friendship have been precious to me. Laura and Ellen Glickman, and their mother, Caroline, brought me joy. My parents, Ronald and Sandra Glickman, to whom this book is dedicated, have been consistently loving, encouraging, and generous.

Jill Frank read over my work with her usual, that is to say extraordinary, care. But more than this, I thank her for the joy of sharing a life together.

LAWRENCE B. GLICKMAN

Columbia, South Carolina

A Living Wage

Introduction:
Rethinking Wage Labor

Wage labor seems almost a natural aspect of the world, a system of remuneration so ingrained that it is difficult to imagine an alternative. Wage levels are hotly contested, to be sure; even in this era of weakened trade unionism, the struggle for decent wages continues. But that workers, however well or ill paid, earn wages seems only a matter of common sense. "This is a wage labor society," Susan Willis notes. "If you do not work for a wage, you are not felt to be a worker."[1]

This was not always the case. At the inception of the system in England during the first industrial revolution, workers "fought desperately to avoid the abyss of wage labor."[2] Nor did nineteenth-century American workers wish to live in a "wage labor society." Although most proudly accepted the label "worker," they did not want to work for wages. The "simple fact of employment," Daniel T. Rodgers points out, "deeply disturbed . . . many Americans."[3] Wage labor represented a dangerous, demeaning, and debilitating departure from traditional modes of financial reward. The ideal for these workers lay in a semimythical artisanal past or in an uncertain cooperative future.

Even after the independent craftsman had become more a symbol deeply etched in labor's collective memory than an accurate description of working-class reality, many workers continued to challenge the legitimacy of wage labor. For most of the nineteenth century, workers hoped to become independent producers, not permanent employees. They claimed that wage labor denied workers the "full fruits" of their labor and reduced the proud American citizen-worker to a "wage slave"— a derisive term popularized in the Jacksonian era as the incipient crisis of wage labor led to the rise of the organized labor movement. Free workers did not want to be identified with lifelong "hirelings," whom they saw as little different from slaves.

In the decades after the Civil War, however, a striking transformation began, as many workers for the first time considered the possibilities of wage labor. The unanimous aversion characteristic of the antebellum period splintered.[4] Some in the labor movement continued to condemn wage labor as a form of slavery, but a far greater number began to accept wages as permanent and to view them in a positive light.

This change in perspective was born of necessity; late nineteenth-century workers had little power to avoid wage labor. Fleeting political movements, successful unionization efforts, waves of strikes (of which there were approximately thirty-seven thousand between 1881 and 1905), and the formation of cooperatives indicated workers' strength, resolve, and fierce opposition to debilitating economic transformations. But these efforts did not stop the momentum toward proletarianization brought on by business consolidation and an adversarial state.[5] In the period between the Civil War and World War I, workers learned to accept wages and to identify themselves as wage earners because they had no alternative.

While acknowledging the encroaching reality of a "wage labor society," wage earners and their advocates refused to accept the meaning of wage earning as fixed and inevitable.[6] "The question of wages," noted Ira Steward, a labor theorist, was "one of the most disputed points in Political Economy."[7] He was only one of many workers to offer an alternative theory of wage labor. Rejecting the defeatist political economy of the "iron law of wages" as well as the "free labor" condemnation of wage workers as moral failures, living wage proponents struggled to make this new wage labor regime consistent with working-class notions of justice and democracy. A wage labor society, in their view, had no predetermined meaning; it could be inhabited by degraded "wage slaves," or in the version they preferred, it could be constituted by proud citizen-workers earning living wages.

In coming to accept the necessity of wages, then, workers also redefined wage earning to make it consistent with their vision of a just world. They began to interpret wages not as slavery but as a potential means of escape from slavery. George Gunton, a pamphleteer for the American Federation of Labor (AFL) eight-hour campaign, declared, "Wages are not a badge of slavery, but a necessary and continual part of social progress."[8] While not all labor leaders shared Gunton's utopian vision, almost all of them participated in the redefinition of wage labor from slavish to liberating.

The linchpin of this transformation was the demand for a "living wage," usually defined as remuneration commensurate with a worker's needs as citizen, breadwinner, and consumer. The AFL president Samuel Gompers, for example, declared in a well-publicized 1898 debate that a living wage should be "sufficient to maintain an average-sized family in a manner consistent with whatever the contemporary local civilization recognizes as indispensable to physical and mental health, or as required by the rational self-respect of human beings." Although others put forth very different definitions, all proponents of the living wage shared a new, positive vision of wage labor. Instead of contrasting wage labor with freedom, they contrasted low wages with high ones. The living wage, proponents held, should offer to wage earners in the postwar years what independent proprietorship had promised in the antebellum era: the ability to support families, to maintain self-respect, and to have both the means and the leisure to participate in the civic life of the nation. Far from condemning the wage system, Gompers called the level of wages "the barometer which indicates the social, political and industrial status" of a society.[9] High wages became a benchmark of freedom, independence, and citizenship.

From the start, reformers, politicians, and religious leaders joined labor in debating the meaning of the living wage. By the 1890s, it became impossible for Americans to comment on the "wage question" without invoking the phrase that, according to one observer, had already "found its way in everyday language."[10] The living wage became central to social and political issues of national importance, including Progressive Era minimum wage legislation and New Deal economic policy. For Herbert Croly, a Progressive, "the most important single task of modern democratic social organization" was to determine "if wage earners are to become free men."[11] Workers had wrestled with this question long before Progressives posed it; nonetheless, input from religious leaders, politicians, and social reformers became crucial in shaping the twentieth-century conception of the living wage.

In this book, I explore how the United States became a "wage labor society." I examine changing attitudes toward wage labor in American culture between the Civil War and the 1930s through an analysis of the history of the "living wage" and several related phrases: "wage slavery," "prostitution," "American standard of living," "union label," and "minimum wage." At the beginning of this period few workers could countenance a lifetime of working for wages; at the end, very few could imagine anything else. There was a seismic shift not only in occupational structure but in sensibility—Richard Oestreicher calls it a "profound psychological change"—as the producing classes became the wage-earning class.[12] It was perhaps the most significant ideological development of the late nineteenth century, since it entailed a redefinition of the meaning of freedom, independence, and citizenship.

Explaining changing attitudes toward wage labor in American culture is by no means a simple undertaking. Conceptions varied widely, affected by such variables as class, political persuasion, race, and gender. In addition, the acceptance of wage labor was a process as uneven as the actual proletarianization of the work force. Some in the middle classes trumpeted the promise of wage labor in the antebellum years. Many trade unionists did so shortly after the Civil War. Some continued to reject the legitimacy of the "wage system" well into the twentieth century.

There is also a historiographical difficulty: although labor historians have identified the trend toward wage labor as, after emancipation, the defining event of the nineteenth century, they have tended to focus on opposition to it rather than acceptance.[13] Placed alongside the usual fare of labor history, the living wage demand appears mundane and materialistic. Compared with strikes, organizing campaigns, and political activities, where heroes proliferate, the living wage has been interpreted as a distressing sign of the conservative business unionism that triumphed in the late nineteenth century, "an inclination," as John Bodnar writes, "to seek practical goals . . . rather than the loftier ideals which prevailed in the protest of earlier times."[14]

By deemphasizing demands for living wages, however, historians have neglected an area in which workers demonstrated an abiding political interest.[15] Like the Chicago workers in the 1920s and 1930s, whose concerns, Lizabeth Cohen notes, were both "material and ideological," living wage advocates did not draw a distinction between economics and politics. Samuel Gompers stressed in 1919 that, as political freedom was intimately linked with economic freedom, high wages were necessary for workers "to be free." Conceding that trade unions "have been derided as materialistic and lacking in idealism because they concentrate their forces upon securing higher wages," he responded that "no nation can retain its power when the masses of its citizenship are existing upon inadequate wages." As early as the 1870s, Ira Steward denounced "an atmosphere of cheap labor" as "eminently un-American." Good wages, he claimed, were as integral to the success of American democracy as the "frequency and freedom of elections." A half century later, a union journal maintained that high wages enabled American workers to "become self-respecting citizens in an industrial democracy."[16]

Acceptance of the wage system does not constitute proof of the eclipse of working-class consciousness. Certainly, opponents of the living wage demand from the 1870s through the present have viewed it as a dangerous political threat, a challenge to the laws of the market and an affront to capitalist property relations. "When we resist employers reducing our wages below a living basis," declared Gompers, "we are called Anarchists." Wage labor enabled workers to see themselves as a unified class rather than as a loosely related group of craftspeople, inevitably known for most of the nineteenth century in the plural as the "producing classes." The "modern experience of class," according to David Montgomery, "had its origin in the encounter with wage labor." John Bray noted in 1876 that "the wages class" could for the first time be described as "a unit." A dozen years later, the leaders of the AFL became the first American trade unionists to declare that "wage workers . . . are a distinct and practically permanent class of modern society; and consequently, have distinct and permanently common interests." Few workers, of course, viewed the causes of this newfound unity as an altogether good thing. What brought them together, some believed, was nothing more than the misery of wage labor. The demand for living wages, nonetheless, produced new solidarities since it linked all workers by virtue of their status as wage earners, rather than on the basis of craft or ethnicity. As a British commentator noted in 1913, it was no accident that "permanent wagedom" and "trade unionism" came into existence simultaneously.[17]

"Most Americans once identified themselves as producers whose labor created wealth," Michael Kazin has noted. "Now they see themselves primarily as consumers — or have let themselves be defined that way."[18] This observation, frequently made by historians and contemporary commentators, implies both passivity and defeat. I contend, on the contrary, that workers played an active role in creating a consumerist identity and a consumerist political economy. This "consumerist turn," I believe, occurred in the postbellum years, much earlier than is usually supposed. It was during this period that workers began to think about themselves as consumers and to ponder the power of consumer organizing, while they were developing the idea of the living wage; the two ideas, in fact, developed in tandem.

In late twentieth-century America it may be hard to imagine how a progressive vision could be built around high wages and consumerism.[19] The influence of such critics as Christopher Lasch, who argued that consumer society creates a "restless, bored" populace uninterested in politics, makes it difficult to conceive how such a focus could be anything other than "therapeutic" escapism.[20] The living wage ideology, however, developed in a very different context, when consumer society was nascent and ill defined.

Labor's "consumerist turn" in the late nineteenth century was as much ideological as practical; it reflected new conceptions of identity and economics as well as a new conception of power. Well before most workers were able to enjoy the fruits of mass consumption, living wage advocates theorized about the positive benefits of high wages, consumer activism, purchasing power, and leisure, and they explicitly associated all these with a class-conscious consumerism. They defined what Warren Susman has called "the utopian possibilities in the culture of abundance" in political rather than therapeutic terms.[21] Workers made the new consumer society not just by participating in commercial amusements; far more significant was the consumerist realignment of class consciousness, working-class identity, and, ultimately, economic and social policy.

The consumerist turn did not entail abandonment of "producerism." In order for workers to maintain their special status in the republic, living wage advocates argued, they needed to recognize and empower themselves as consumers because in the new world of wage labor, consumption and production were intimately linked. As an article in the *Journal of United Labor* noted in 1884: "We have been led to suppose that the producer and the consumer were totally separate individuals, with separate and distinct interests, when in reality all producers are consumers."[22] Proponents of the consumerist turn maintained that the productive human being was equal parts *Homo faber* and *Homo consumens*.

For most workers in the period between 1865 and the 1930s, wages sufficient to provide for a well-maintained home, plentiful food, and some discretionary spending money—demands that Gompers grouped under the rubric of "more of the comforts and necessities of life"—were prerequisites for citizenship.[23] Living wage advocates promoted consumption unapologetically, not as a site of embourgeoisement but as a locus of political power. The Boston labor leader George McNeill argued in the 1870s that the class struggle could be reduced to the demand of the capitalists that the worker "produce more." Instead, McNeill declared, "we say make him consume more."[24]

Workers continued to think of economics in moral terms even after they accepted wage labor, but instead of understanding justice and liberty from the perspective of small producers whose class consciousness manifested itself at the point of production, they understood themselves as wage earners, demanded remuneration commensurate with their needs, and articulated a notion of class which centered as much in the realm of consumption as production. While it shared with the eighteenth-century moral economy what E. P. Thompson calls a "highly-sensitive consumer-consciousness," the "social economy" under examination in this book situated itself within, not against, the market.[25] Interpreting spending as productive rather than wasteful, proponents of the living wage renounced thrift and the fetishization of work. Class consciousness moved from the shop floor to the storefront.

The living wage enabled workers to reground a republican morality in the modern world of the wage labor economy. If proprietorship and production had once been the hallmarks of citizenship, living wage advocates reconstructed citizenship around high wages and consumption. In this process, workers helped construct American consumer society. Even as the literal term "living wage" faded from view from the 1930s to the 1970s — only to be revived in the 1980s and 1990s — its underlying ideas became central to the political economy of the New Deal era and beyond.

PART I

FROM WAGE SLAVERY

TO THE LIVING WAGE

Between the Civil War and the 1930s, working-class attitudes toward wage labor shifted from "wage slavery" to the "living wage." In this period, organized labor moved from a deep and defining aversion to wage labor to an equally definitive embrace of particular kinds of wages, usually called "living wages." Although the "living wage" had no single meaning, its appearance signaled a transformation in labor's vision of the just society from a republic of small producers to a republic of wage earners.

Before the Civil War, the idea of a "republic of wage earners" would have seemed a contradiction in terms to most workers. For much of the nineteenth century, wage labor — payment to an employee based on hours or days worked — had posed a fundamental threat to working-class conceptions of liberty. Drawing on two powerful antebellum political discourses, the "free labor" ideology and "artisanal republicanism," most labor leaders, indeed most Americans, defined freedom precisely as the ability to avoid a lifetime of working for wages; the very word "wages" was, to quote one worker in the 1850s, "odious." [1] Langdon Byllesby, a printer, echoed popular sentiment in 1826 when he called wage labor the "very essence of slavery." [2] To earn wages, in the view of these workers, was to depend on another for one's daily bread, and dependence was equivalent to degradation. Working-class men prized independence and the ability to provide for their families above all other manly virtues. As one observer noted in 1871, to "put a man upon wages is to put him in the position of a dependent" and therefore to make him "less of a man." [3] For quite different reasons, wage labor also threatened working-class women, whose gender identity was largely shaped by the uncompensated labor they performed for their families as homemakers and consumers.[4]

Even in the postbellum years, most Americans believed a healthy republic must be made of free men, defined as self-employed small producers.[5] Labor leaders regularly linked wage labor to the erosion of citizenship. In 1877 George McNeill, a labor leader and prominent working-class economic theorist, described the wage system in completely derogatory terms as "a system that encourages cunning above conscience; that robs the producers, and enriches the speculator; that makes the employer a despot, and the employee a slave, — a system that shortens life, engenders disease, enfeebles the mind, corrupts the morals, and thus propagates misery, vice and crime."[6] How could such a system serve a republic, which demanded antithetical values? McNeill saw no easy resolution, and he was not alone.

American workers had long denigrated the "wage system" as the main obstacle to what they thought of as their birthright: freedom, independence, and democratic citizenship. Along with the vast majority of organized workers, McNeill believed that wages and republicanism were on a collision course, with wage labor destroying the possibility of democratic government. In this context, McNeill seemed to be stating the obvious when he declared, in one of the most frequently quoted lines of the Gilded Age labor movement, "There is an inevitable and irresistible conflict between the wage-system of labor and the republican system of government."[7]

Even as wage labor was becoming increasingly common, nineteenth-century workers deemed it acceptable only as a temporary step on the way to self-employment. Abraham Lincoln articulated the expectations of free American workers perfectly when he said, "The man who labored for another last year, this year labors for himself, and next year he will hire others to labor for him." A group of Boston labor reformers agreed in 1872: "During New England's first 200 years, the wage period was the school period of practical life. While working for wages, the young man was looking forward to the time when he would work for himself. . . . The wage period was merely the transition period in labor from youth to maturity." As a stepping stone wage labor was acceptable, but as a permanent condition it was scandalous, the very antithesis of labor's vision of a republic of independent craftsmen. "No wage laborer can be a freeman," declared Jesse Jones, a minister and labor radical, in 1876. "When any body of wage laborers accept, or seem to accept, their wage condition as permanent, and organize themselves as wagemen to contend with their employers as capitalists, without the distinctly announced purpose to end their wage condition, they do thereby organize themselves into a 'caste of serfs,' and the step they thus take tends to make them such forever."[8]

For much of the century, wage laborers fared little better in popular estimation than the nefarious wage system of which they were a part, for in a society that promised independence and mobility to all nonslaves, wage earners had to shoulder the responsibility—and the blame—for their degradation. "If none were willing to work as slaves," declared New York City's most popular labor newspaper in the 1880s, "there would be no wage-system." For most of the century, in fact, labor reformers had expressed little sympathy for lifelong wage earners, blaming them for their own condition, ascribing it to what Horace Greeley described as "their own extravagance and needless ostentation." "If any continue through life in the condition of the hired laborer," said Lincoln, "it is not the fault of the system, but because of either a dependent nature which prefers it, or improvidence, folly or singular misfortune." And the reformer E. L. Godkin insisted that only those exhibiting "vice or misconduct or ignorance or want of self-restraint" would be locked into permanent wage labor; "honest and intelligent and self-denying" workers could reasonably expect to set up on their own. In his Fourth of July oration on the American Centennial, Henry Ward Beecher declared: "The laborer ought to be ashamed of himself who in 20 years does not own the ground on which his house stands . . . who has not in that house provided carpets for the rooms, who has not his China plates, who has not his chromos, who has not some books nestling on the shelf."[9]

As the century progressed, however, wage labor became increasingly common not simply as a way station on the road to independent proprietorship but as a permanent fact of working-class life. In reality, the artisanal ideal had never been entirely congruent with working-class realities.[10] Although independent proprietorship predominated for nonslaves in colonial America, wage labor was already a much-noticed concern at the time of the American Revolution.[11] In the 1780s urban artisans condemned incipient changes in the political economy "that would gradually erode self-sufficiency and remake yeomen, artisans, and their children into workers dependent upon wages."[12]

The uneven but inexorable process of proletarianization continued through the nineteenth century.[13] In an observation that anxious urban commentators would repeat for the next half century, religious reformer Joseph Tuckerman declared in 1829, "The classes are very numerous, of

those who are wholly dependent upon wages" and who "will never be anything but journeymen."[14] By the 1830s, a majority of apprentices worked
for wages, serving as what one printer called in disgust "journeymen
through life," rather than as independent artisans.[15] Philadelphia workers in the 1830s carried picket signs proclaiming "WE ARE NOT DAY LABOR-
ERS" to express their rejection of the increasingly common wage labor
system.[16] Within a generation, however, even their former masters had
become wage earners. By 1850 wage earners outnumbered slaves. Notwithstanding President Lincoln's assurances to Congress in 1861 that "a
large majority are neither hirers nor hired," by that time wage earners
outnumbered independent entrepreneurs.[17] The Civil War accelerated
this process as it both wiped out chattel slavery (turning millions of freedpeople into potential wage earners) and put the final nail in the coffin of
apprenticeship.[18]

Within a few years after armistice, the majority of Americans, male and
female, who labored outside the home did so in exchange for wages.[19]
In 1873 the Massachusetts Bureau of Statistics of Labor reported that
"practically all that the laborer receives is through the wage-system, — a
system more widely diffused than any form of religion, or of government,
or, indeed, of any language." Few workers would have disagreed with the
observation made many years later by Alexander Keyssar that "the era of
the independent artisan had come to a close" as "self-employment became the exception rather than the rule."[20]

Thus, despite their denigration of the wage system, most Americans
earned their daily bread through wages. Even members of the labor aristocracy — white male trade unionists — were forced to sell their labor. As
David Montgomery notes, the fact that "two out of three productively engaged Americans [in the post–Civil War world] were hirelings posed an
ideological dilemma for the free-labor system."[21]

In spite of this dilemma, many workers kept artisanal dreams alive
in their collective memory long after wage labor became commonplace.
Some challenged the unrealistic premises of the expectation that all com-
petent workers would move out of wage labor. Others clung to the myth
that independence was within reach of any hardworking citizen. In 1886
P. M. Arthur, the conservative chief of the Locomotive Brotherhood, un-
realistically proclaimed in language reminiscent of Lincoln's, "The workingman of to-day may be the capitalist of five or ten years from now." To
be free, according to the "free labor" ideology and its later variants, was
to be able to work for oneself, to hire others, and, if necessary, to be
hired — but only temporarily. Even those labor leaders who recognized

1

That Curse of Modern Civilization

Rhetoric linking wage earning to slavery did not originate in nineteenth-century America, but the antebellum United States became, to use David Roediger's words, the "world leader" in the use of the wage slavery metaphor. The term took on tremendous symbolic importance in the first half of the century in popular belief and in the rhetoric of radicals such as Orestes Brownson, Frances Wright, William Heighton, Thomas Skidmore, Langdon Byllesby, and George Henry Evans. Even in the North, Judith Shklar maintains, slavery was "an ever-present anxiety" for workers striving to reach the increasingly difficult goal of independence defined as self-employment. Women in the antebellum North played a crucial role in developing wage slavery rhetoric as well: "American Ladies Will Not Be Slaves," proclaimed the banner of a group of striking New England shoe workers in 1860.[1]

Workers' rejection of wage labor drew from notions of freedom, independence, and citizenship, which they applied to the interconnecting areas of politics, society, economics, and the family. In the political arena, workers thought that equality was possible only if each member of the polity was economically independent. In the guise of the voluntary contract they perceived a compulsion that they believed made it impossible to exercise citizenship. Those who received wages could not possibly participate in civic life as the equals of their employers. Thus, the wage system would promote the formation of an aristocracy. In the late 1870s, for example, the labor editor J. P. McDonnell was discouraged to report: "After a century of political independence, we find that our social system is not better than that of Europe and that labor in this Republic, as in the

European monarchies, is the slave of capitalism, instead of being the master of its own products." In economic terms, they believed that wages inevitably granted employees only a partial payment for their labor, leaving a portion of their work uncompensated. "In what does slavery consist?" asked the *Mechanic's Free Press* in 1830. "In being compelled to work for others so that they may reap the advantage." Finally, within the patriarchal family structure endorsed by male workers, masculine and feminine roles were sharply differentiated; the men were charged with breadwinning and the women with household responsibilities. If freedom was possible only when workers owned their labor, neither men nor women could be free. On all these fronts, wage labor was a form of slavery and the growing army of wage laborers failed to qualify as free.[2]

Most Americans believed independence to be possible only in a society of small producers. Many wondered, as Melvyn Dubofsky has asked, "how could a republican democracy built on the participation of economically independent freeholders and artisans endure in a society composed in the main of dependent wage earners?" Liberty and independence required that each worker receive the "fruits of his labor," that, as Abraham Lincoln declared, workers garner "the whole produce to themselves" and ask "no favors of capital on the one hand, nor of hirelings or slaves on the other." "God intended," said a union broadside of the 1850s, that every man should be "truly independent of his fellow and above the position of mere 'wage slaves.'"[3]

Liberty was defined as complete ownership of one's own labor and, by extension, oneself. The notion of self-ownership was central to antebellum labor rhetoric and important well into the twentieth century. The "identification of the self and property," according to the literary critic Walter Benn Michaels, is "bourgeois." But valorization of self-ownership was not limited to America's middle class: workers too rested their economic understanding on this premise. Ira Steward, a machinist and labor leader from Boston, declared that under a regime of permanent wage labor, "there can be no freedom or self-ownership." Without these "natural and inalienable rights," he believed, the "self is destroyed."[4]

The widespread popularity of the wage slavery metaphor in antebellum America linked disparate groups who shared little common ground other than an antipathy toward the wage system, including both southern defenders of chattel slavery and northern labor radicals. Free laborites and abolitionists considered wage labor acceptable only as a pit stop on the road to independent entrepreneurship and not as a permanent condition. Few antebellum Americans defended permanent wage labor; most agreed that it resembled slavery.[5]

Wage Slavery in the Postbellum Era

The Civil War eliminated chattel slavery, but use of the wage slavery metaphor continued unabated. References abounded in the labor press, and it is hard to find a speech by a labor leader without the phrase. For several decades following the Civil War, as the trend toward wage labor progressed, working-class organizations endeavored to "strike down the whole system of wages for labor" through strikes, worker-owned cooperatives, and political parties. "As long as men work under the wage system there will be slavery," declared *John Swinton's Paper* in 1884. "The wage system is the curse of our time. Away with it." In an address before the 1880 General Assembly of the Knights of Labor in Pittsburgh, Terence Powderly condemned wage labor as "that curse of modern civilization."[6]

Changes in the political and economic climate ultimately transformed the meaning of the wage slavery metaphor, but they did not extinguish the use of the term. Segments of the working class maintained the view that wage earners were slaves well into the twentieth century. The Knights of Labor advocated the replacement of the wage system with an ill-defined but frequently invoked system of cooperation under which all workers would receive their just reward.[7] "Chattel Slavery is dead, but industrial slavery remains," noted the popular political economist and New York City mayoral candidate Henry George in 1886. As late as 1911, Mary E. Marcy, a socialist, implored workers to "sign the death warrant of Wage Slavery!" The Industrial Workers of the World (IWW) made the same demand in equally ardent tones. Indeed, even today the phrase remains popular and compelling. The term "wage slave" has been applied to a host of positions in modern society: from exploited migrant laborers and sweatshop workers, to well-heeled but discontented salarymen and -women, to Generation X slacker tempworkers. One media critic called the television character Homer Simpson a "power-plant wage slave." "At the rate blue collar wages are falling," writes Barbara Ehrenreich, "the U.S. is going to reinvent slavery in the next few decades, only without any of its nice, redeeming features, such as room and board."[8]

Despite its frequent use, the metaphor had neither a stable meaning nor an undifferentiated group of advocates in the postwar years. Wage slavery meant different things to different people.[9] Some invoked it to highlight racial and gender inequality. In 1898, for example, Charlotte Perkins Gilman called housework a form of domestic "slave labor."[10] Others stressed the limitations of "free" contract. Still others focused on workers' lack of political power.[11] Ultimately, however, the bedrock issue — "the fundamental cause of workers' suffering" — was wage labor.[12]

Tracing the changing meanings of the wage slavery metaphor in the late nineteenth century provides new insight into the complex slavery / freedom binary, a staple of American political language and thought. The comparison of wage labor to slavery played a central role in labor's search for the meaning of freedom in the postwar United States. If it seems odd to tease out the shape of freedom by studying the metaphor of slavery, we should keep in mind, as Edmund Morgan, Orlando Patterson, and Eric Foner have demonstrated, that the concepts have developed in close conjunction. "Slavery and freedom," wrote Nathan Irvin Huggins, "are joined at the hip."[13] A study of the wage slavery metaphor in the postbellum years highlights the attempt to reestablish the significance of the comparison after the death of chattel slavery. As the United Mine Workers leader John Mitchell wrote, "The history of the United States from the Declaration of Independence in 1776, to the Emancipation Proclamation in 1863," could be described as "the solution of a labor problem—the problem of slave *versus* free labor."[14] After emancipation, the meaning of free labor could no longer be "not chattel slavery." But could it be "not wage labor"?

Both halves of the slavery / freedom binary radically changed meaning in the post–Civil War world. The revolutionary consequences of emancipation forever altered the symbolic meaning of "slavery"—and not only for freedpeople released from the shackles of bondage. Slavery was for white workers, writes Roediger, "a touchstone against which to weigh their fears and a yardstick to measure their reassurance."[15] But after emancipation, freedom lost its opposite. Hence, labor advocates began to contrast freedom with degrees of unfreedom, rather than with a legally sanctioned absolute unfreedom. White male labor leaders easily discerned a level of unfreedom in the wage relationship, but in tagging it with the absolute term of slavery, they ran the risk of eliding the distinction, crucial to labor ideology and identity, between themselves and other wage-earning workers, particularly women, blacks, and immigrants.[16]

Just as the abolition of chattel slavery forced new distinctions in levels of unfreedom, so too did it lead to a redefinition of the meaning of freedom, especially in regard to the ideal of free labor. Emancipated black workers entered a world in which the meanings of wage labor were still being ironed out.[17] While both they and their white counterparts had prior experience earning wages, only after the Civil War did most workers face wage labor as a permanent condition. A double shift occurred simultaneously: as the percentage of wage earners in the economy grew, the meaning of wage labor itself was increasingly contested. The system of wage labor was anything but stable. After the Civil War it would become narrowly defined in ideology and even at law not as a step toward freedom but as freedom itself. Freedom for wage laborers came to be understood as pure contractual freedom, the unfettered ability to sell the self.[18] No consideration was given to the tangible benefits, if any, such a sale brought the worker.

Many workers, increasingly diverging from their employers, believed it was wrong to equate the abolition of chattel slavery with the elimination of enslaved and unfree labor. Prior to the Civil War, the free labor ideology had united northern workers and their employers as it promoted both a hatred of slavery and an equally strong faith in mobility out of wage labor. In the absence of their common enemy, workers and their employers developed radically different assessments of wage labor. Far from uniting the disparate classes of the North in a "free labor" consensus, attitudes toward wage labor diverged sharply by class after the Civil War. This new class conflict played itself out in the language of wage slavery, which articulated distinctions among "free" workers.

It galled workers that many middle-class Americans complacently celebrated wage labor as a sign of freedom. The abolitionist Charles Sumner had defined slavery in 1860 as "labor without wages," implying that wages were a hallmark of freedom. "We cannot see what is wrong to give or receive wages," declared his fellow abolitionist William Lloyd Garrison, who condemned labor's use of the metaphor of wage slavery as "an abuse of language." But postwar workers thought it perverse to assume that wages automatically conferred freedom. Wage workers, wrote Henry George, were "mocked with the titles and insignias of freedom" while being forced into a condition "virtually that of slavery." Some workers considered wage slavery more dehumanizing than chattel slavery because employers, unlike slaveholders, did not have to provide even basic subsistence. In 1897 G. B. De Bernardi described chattel slavery as "a system in which the master has the burden to care for men, material, and products," but under the wage system, "the employer has no care whatever of the workers. Live or perish, they are none of his concern."[19]

In this view, wage labor fell below chattel slavery on the hierarchy of freedom, since the market refused to recognize the power imbalances that made workers dependent. A letter writer to a labor newspaper in 1885 claimed to know of "a man well-known in the labor movement" who "announced . . . that he would willingly be a bond slave for the rest of his life to any man who would provide for himself, his wife and family sufficient to live on with clothing and rent."[20] Under the wage system, he argued, the only way to provide for one's family was to enslave oneself. Wage labor made manhood so unreachable that those forced into it longed for the paternalism of chattel slavery. The system of wage labor deprived men of the ability to provide for their families; how could it represent freedom?[21]

Although few workers went to the extreme of ranking wages below slavery on the hierarchy of unfreedom, a majority identified the workings of the "free market" as the cause of modern wage slavery. Being forced to sell one's labor was a form of slavery in George McNeill's view. "Men who are compelled to sell their time are slaves to the purchaser," he told the International Labor Congress in 1893.[22] Where human labor seemed no different from any other commodity, slavery would inevitably reign.

This critique of wages, what one labor journalist called "the slavery of the present," was not developed exclusively by white workers. For black workers too, including ex-slaves, as Foner notes, "freedom meant more than simply receiving wages." A wartime journalist in Port Royal, South Carolina, noted, "Labor for wages . . . is but a modified servitude," and Richard L. Davis, a black miner agreed: "None of us who toil for our daily bread are free. At one time . . . we were chattel slaves; today we are, one and all, white and black, wage slaves." Indeed, rather than work for the low and irregular wages that characterized the postbellum southern labor system, most freedpeople wanted the opportunity to own land, to serve in effect as their own employers. Joseph Reidy describes the wage slavery critique developed by the freedpeople of central Georgia: "Freedpeople who prized their independence had grave misgivings about a labor system resting solely upon cash wages. They specifically resented the equation of the wage laborer with a hireling—a virtual automaton, devoid of volition and unquestioningly obedient to the employer." A generation later some black workers concurred, noting that the "Negro worker is no better off under the freedom he has gained than the slavery from which he has escaped."[23]

Transformation of the Wage Slavery Critique

What compelled so many workers in the postbellum years to assert a deep affinity between chattel slavery and wage labor? A telling clue can be found in a defense of the rhetoric of wage slavery which appeared in the newspaper of the Knights of Labor in 1883. In response to some union members who had "sharply criticized" the newspaper's use of the expression, the editors of the *Journal of United Labor* explained its relevance. The critics claimed that "wage slavery" rhetoric had outlived its usefulness in the postwar years as overuse and exaggeration had drained the term of all meaning. The editors responded that slavery should be properly thought of not as a specific legal condition of the historical past but as an ever-present multifarious threat to wage earners. This flexible conception had great appeal to workers. "By the phrase wage slavery is usually meant a condition of practical enslavement," explained John Mitchell in 1903, "brought about, not by legal, but by economic subjection, a slavery enforced not by the lash, but by pangs of hunger."[24]

Slavery, on this view, was not a monolith but a continually shifting field of exploitation. By detaching wage slavery from the recently defeated system of racially based chattel slavery, the newspaper defined it as a fact of life for all American workers. An inability, it said, to gain "an exact equivalent, is and always will be slavery, without regard to color, race, location or position." The difference was one of "degree only and not in kind as neither the wage slave nor the chattel slave were in a position to arrange the terms of competence for labor performed." Slavery, the editors concluded, "simply consists in placing oneself in that condition where he is powerless to exact an equivalent for services rendered."[25] Following this logic, there was no question of the utility of the wage slavery discourse for the nation's producers, who consistently complained that the wage system had rendered such an "equivalence" unreachable.

Although most who spoke of wage slavery described it as primarily an economic condition, they believed that the inability to garner the full fruits of one's labor extended slavery's reach beyond the purely economic realm into both personal and political life. In this view, the servility produced by wage labor undermined the independence that lay at the root of republican manhood and republican citizenship. Under "wage labor," wrote Justus O. Woods in 1883, "the workers will be in a servile position." Self-employment was the only way to "place workers in their natural relations with each other and upon a basis of true manliness."[26] The implication was clear; wage labor would lead to both "unnatural relations" among men and to emasculation.

Many workers echoed Woods in condemning the emasculating effects of the dependency that seemed inherent to the wage relationship. Whereas artisanship had produced a class of hardy, independent, virtuous, and above all, virile craftsmen, the new organization of work threatened to produce the antithesis. Manhood and independence, the hallmarks of producerism, seemed out of the reach of "12 hour wage slaves."[27]

Nineteenth-century workers consistently understood the personal affronts of the wage system in political terms. For them, the personal was political: dependence threatened not only to destroy the manhood of the nation's breadwinners but also to subvert the egalitarian social basis of the republic. As the editor E. L. Godkin wrote in 1867, "Workingmen . . . will never cease agitating and combining until the regime of wages, or, as we might perhaps better call it, the servile regime, has passed away as completely as slavery or serfdom, and until in no free country shall any men be found in the condition of mere hirelings."[28] Since the abolition of wage labor was unlikely, workers feared the personal and political degradation of servile employment. Many others took up the theme that wages endangered social equality, the cement of the republic. The Boston Conference of Labor Reformers invoked contrasting images of royalty and vassalage to indicate the extent to which the wage system violated republican values: "The whole spirit and structure of the system, requires, yea, compels that a thousand men be kept as wage serfs, in order that one merchant prince may reign." The group concluded in 1872 that the "wage system is a crime" that destroys "the body," "the vital forces," and "the moral life" of the wage laborer. In the same year, the abolitionist and labor reformer Wendell Phillips gave a speech whose martial language evoked Jacksonian labor rhetoric: "We declare war with the wages system, which demoralizes alike the hirer and the hired, cheats both, and enslaves the working man." Few argued with this gloomy assessment. Many workers continued to demand what Uriah Stephens, founder of the Knights of Labor, called "the complete emancipation of the wealth producers from the thraldom and loss of wage slavery."[29]

Producerist and Consumerist Forms

Defenders of the wage slavery metaphor argued that economic deprivation inevitably damaged both the person and the polity and that wages necessarily produced economic injustice, usually conceived as a kind of robbery. But what exactly was the nature of this injustice? Were all wages inherently unjust or only particular kinds of wages? The vocabulary employed suggested a consensus about the immoral economics of wages. The wage system, critics railed, did not provide an "exact equivalent," a "just return," the "full fruits of one's labor," "fair remuneration," or simply, "one's worth." Most used these terms interchangeably; few actually defined them. Ultimately, however, the crucial differences among them reveal fissures in the seemingly monolithic edifice of opposition to wage slavery. The persistence of the slavery metaphor masked the fact that the meaning of the term had changed significantly since the Civil War.

There were, in fact, two related but fundamentally distinct ways of thinking about wage slavery and the worth of labor: producerism and consumerism. According to the producerist argument, wage slavery resulted from the difference in value between what workers produced and what they earned in wages, which was often said to have been stolen from them. The consumerists were more concerned about the inadequacy of wages that did not meet the needs of workers as family supporters, citizens, and consumers, and they condemned the wage system for its seeming inability to reward the nation's producers with a comfortable republican lifestyle. This distinction is critical. The producerist rhetoric predominated during the first years after the Civil War, but as the nineteenth century waned and workers redefined and ultimately accepted wage labor, the critique shifted from the producerist to the consumerist version.

The producerist critique conveyed the commonsense meaning of the metaphor for much of the nineteenth century. The language used by the *Journal of United Labor* in 1884 was most familiar: "The real essence of slavery is the coercing of one man by another in such a way as shall compel him to yield up the fruits of his labor . . . without the power or opportunity or freedom to extract a return which shall be a just equivalent for such service." On this definition, since the wage system could not possibly accord workers the full productive value of their labor, a "just equivalent" in wages was not simply unlikely but altogether unreachable. Accordingly, the "system of paying wages to workers is a system of slavery." In a 1904 letter to the editor of the *Railroad Telegrapher*, "Alphega," extending this producerist argument, suggested that the extent of inequivalence marked the degree of enslavement: "If you produce wealth equivalent to $1,000 per year and receive a wage of $500, then you are one-half a slave. If a profit of 10% is made on your labor, then you are one tenth a slave. If you get only your living out of a year's continuous toil, then you are as much a slave as ever a black man in the antebellum days." By this standard of equivalence, the key to the producerist definition of wage slavery, workers could never be fully rewarded and therefore would always be at least partial slaves. No "considerable improvement can take place in [workers'] circumstances as long as they remain simply wage workers," announced Charles Pope, secretary of the Shoe Makers

Union of San Francisco, in 1879. For Pope, robbery was an inherent aspect of wage labor, since "the producers receive but a portion of their earnings in the form of wages."[30] Wage slavery, on this view, was an inevitable concomitant of wage labor.

The consumerist view, which eventually displaced the producerist view, was in many ways more relevant to a republic of wage earners. Its defining concept was the notion of a "just reward," rather than "exact equivalence." Although superficially similar, the concepts turned out to be crucially different. Unlike the producerist schema, which insisted that anything less than exact equivalence was inherently unfair, the consumerist idea of just reward implied, at least theoretically, that workers under the wage system could be free and fairly remunerated. It required only a short leap from the concept of the "just reward" to "just wages," and from "just wages" to "living wages."

One of the first hints of the consumerist argument came in an 1870 report by the Massachusetts Bureau of Statistics of Labor, which denounced wage slavery in the strongest possible terms: "Not a single workman working at day wages has acquired a competence." Only by "thrift and injustice," by denying himself and his family the "necessaries of life" could a worker survive. The "wage system," the report concluded, "has proved to be adverse to the general good."[31] While the report employed the prevailing producerist wage slavery metaphor, it used the term in a new way, condemning the wage system not because it robbed workers of an equivalence but because it denied them what they needed to live as family men and citizens. The focus was shifting from equivalence to needs, from production to consumption.

No one in the labor movement did more than Ira Steward to promote the view that it was inability to consume rather than failure to receive an exact equivalence which constituted wage slavery. Raised in antebellum Massachusetts, Steward retained the abolitionist spirit of reform. Even after the Civil War abolition remained a leitmotif in his writings, guiding his vision of political economy, especially with respect to wage labor. Arguing that American workers had uniquely cultivated wants and needs, Steward believed that a denial of these lay at the heart of this new slavery. "To surround a very poor man with what seems to him abundance is to surround him with temptations," he noted. "The only safety therefore when the laboring classes are limited to the most barren, dreary and cheerless physical necessities is chattel slavery."[32]

Another New Englander, the young reformer Edward Bellamy, articulated a consumerist understanding of wage slavery in an address at the Chicopee Falls Village Lyceum in 1871. After condemning the payment to workers of a "bare subsistence" for their "painful labors," he went on to describe as slavery the perpetuation of a system in which the few enjoy the consumerist benefits of "the abundance created by labor."[33] For Bellamy, lack of leisure and wages too low to meet family needs and workers' wants constituted slavery.

The consumerist emphasis on needs did not entirely supplant the producerist focus on equivalence, however. The two strands coexisted throughout the late nineteenth century. In an 1886 article titled "Wants," for example, the *Journal of United Labor* posited a natural connection between "the full fruits of their toil" and "legitimate wants."[34] A "just wage" represented both the value of labor and the needs of the worker.

The shift from a producerist to a consumerist critique of wage slavery registered a significant change in the relation between economics and politics. For producerists, rewards could be fair only if they amounted to the full fruits of one's labor; for consumerists, rewards could be just if they met one's needs. Equivalence called for productive payment. Wants and needs required consumerist payment. Both versions linked economic autonomy to political freedom; but whereas for producerists, an economic concept — equivalence — was inextricably tied to a political vision, for consumerists, a political concept — justice — informed the economic.

An instructive example of the transformation of the idea of wage slavery can be found in an unlikely source, a 1911 advertisement in the *International Socialist Review* (Fig. 1). The bold headline "Don't Be A Wage Slave" announces not a trenchant article denouncing wage labor but an advertisement for a pamphlet titled *How to Become a Mechano-Therapist*. This vocation, the copy trumpeted, would provide "wonderful money-making possibilities." The "wage slavery" targeted by this advertisement was the system that prevented a healthy level of consumption. The ad cleverly supplemented the producerist insistence on the dignity of labor with a consumerist vision of social mobility through high wages. Higher wages would make for dignified labor, and in turn, dignified labor — hence respected citizenship — depended on the consuming powers such labor afforded. As a doctor of mechano-therapy one could make very good pay, provided that the worker had "a spark of manhood or womanhood left." While the idea of "going into business for yourself" was consonant with a long line of labor ideology, the ad emphasized "earning big money" as much as being a productive worker. What mechano-therapists actually

Don't Be a Wage Slave

Make $3,000.00 to $5,000.00 a Year
Be a Doctor of Mechano-Therapy
We Teach You By Mail or In Class

Are you tired of working for wages which barely keep body and soul together? Have you the ambition to enjoy the profits of your own labor? To gain social prominence and financial independence? To go forth among your fellow men with your head up—an honored and respected citizen of your locality?

THEN SEND FOR OUR FREE BOOK

Entitled "How to Become a Mechano-Therapist." It tells how every man and woman, with an ordinary, common school education. can acquire a profession within a few months which will insure financial independence for life. GET OUR BOOK—i* costs you nothing.

What is Mechano-Therapy?

Mechano-Therapy is the art, or science, of treating disease without drugs. It is similar to Osteopathy, but far superior, being the latest, up-to-date method of treating disease by the Natural Method. It heals as Nature heals—in accordance with Nature's laws.

The Mechano-Therapist is a drugless physician and a bloodless surgeon. His medicines are not drugs, but scientific combinations of food, circumstance, idea, water and motion.

The Mechano-Therapist is skilled in compelling the body TO DO ITS OWN HEALING with its own force, rather than with poisonous drugs of the old school practitioner.

CAN I LEARN IT?

Have you asked yourself this question? We answer, unhesitatingly, YES.

If you have so much as an ordinary, common school education, you can learn.

If you have the ambition to better your condition—to earn more money—to have more leisure—you can learn.

Nor does this require years of patient study to learn Mechano-Therapy—we can teach you in a very short time, so that you may enter this profession—and when you do, you begin to make money. No text books are required, beyond those furnished by us. We supply all lessons and necessary text books free of cost to you. No apparatus is used. You do not even need a place to work. All you require is your two hands.

A Personal Word
From the President of the College.

Have you ever thought of going into business for yourself?

Then send for my FREE book. It will tell you how others are enjoying a life of luxury, while putting money away in the bank. How YOU can not only gain independence, but be a benefit to humanity and a highly respected citizen with an income of $3,000 to $5,000 a year.

All I ask is that you send me the coupon below for my FREE book. You can then decide, in the privacy of your own home whether you wish to embrace the opportunity which I offer you, or whether you will continue to plod along the balance of your days slaving for others.

Wonderful Money-Making Possibilities
FOR MEN AND WOMEN

No matter what your occupation may be, Mechano-Therapy offers a new field for improving your social and financial condition. Hundreds of men and women have taken up Mechano-Therapy and many are today independent and earning big money.

READ WHAT OUR GRADUATES SAY

Statements of our graduates below verify every claim we make. What these men and women have done you may do. We do not give addresses of people whose testimonials we print. If you are interested we furnish them on request.

I Make $10 to $15 Per Day and Work Seven Days a Week
Dr. W. F. Leslie, M. T., writes: I am making from $10 to $15 a day and work seven days a week. I am busy all the time.

Makes $25 to $30 Per Day
F. L. Stout, M. T. D., writes: I now make as high as $25 to $30 per day. I feel that in Mechano-Therapy there is financial success for all who will put forth the necessary energy.

$2.50 to $5 for a Single Treatment
P. W. Dyment, M. T., writes: In my year's practice I have never given a single treatment for less than $2.50 and the most was $5

Income $15 a Day; Formerly a Blacksmith
W. S. McClure writes: The possibilities of the Mechano-Therapist are almost unlimited. The man who induced me to take a course in Mechano-Therapy was formerly a blacksmith with an ordinary education. Today he is practicing drugless healing with an average income of $15 per day.

One of our most Successful Graduates, located in New York City, writes:—I cleared $80 above all expenses in four days' time.

We Teach You in Your Own Home

We can teach you an honorable and profitable profession in a few months, which will insure your financial independence for life. We can make you master of your own time—to come and go as you will—an honored and respected citizen, with an income of $3,000 to $5,000 a year. We teach you this pleasant, profitable profession by mail, right in your own home, at your own convenience, and without interfering with your present duties. It makes no difference how old you are, any person—man or woman—with just an ordinary common school education, can learn Mechano-Therapy. It is easy to learn and results are sure.

It is simply drugless healing. A common-sense method of treating human ills without dosing the system with poisonous drugs—that's all. We have taught hundreds of men and women who were formerly clerks—farmers—stenographers—telegraph operators—insurance agents—railway employes—in fact, of nearly every known occupation—old men of 70 years who felt discouraged and hopeless—young men of 20 years, who never had a day's business experience—salaried men, who could see nothing in the future but to become Osierized—laboring men, who never realized that they had within themselves the ability to better their conditions. Write for our FREE book, which explains all—today.

Cut Out This Coupon and Mail It Today

AMERICAN COLLEGE OF MECHANO-THERAPY,
Dept. 407, 120-122 Randolph Street, Chicago, Ill.

GENTLEMEN:— Please send your book, "How to become a Mechano-Therapist," free of cost to me.

My Name...

My Post Office...

R. F. D. or St. No......................................State..........
(Write name, town and state very plain)

SIMPLY SEND THE COUPON FOR THIS FREE BOOK

Illustrated BOOK
How To Become A
Mechano-Therapist
Sent To Any A.
FREE

Try to realize what this opportunity means TO YOU. If you are contented, and willing to drudge for others all your life for a mere pittance, our proposition may not interest you. But if you have a spark of manhood or womanhood left—any ambition whatsoever to improve your condition socially and financially, learn this pleasant profession. It will make you independent for life. It is so easy—so VERY easy—to get all the details—without trouble or expense. Simply sign and send us the coupon now.

AMERICAN COLLEGE OF MECHANO-THERAPY
Dept. 407, 120-122 Randolph St., Chicago, Ill.

Figure 1. "Don't Be a Wage Slave," *International Socialist Review* (August 1911), 128. Courtesy Charles H. Kerr and Company

did was not discussed; the emphasis was on what they earned. The changing context of the postwar years transformed the "wage slavery" critique from condemnation of wage labor to condemnation of low wages.

Toward the Living Wage

Negotiating the postbellum definition of freedom, which was central to the wage slavery metaphor, necessitated coming to terms with wage labor and challenging the conception that subsumed all wage earners under the rubric of wage slavery. This negotiation had several components.

First, in an increasingly market-oriented and market-dominated country, it became difficult to maintain a definition of slavery that included wage workers. In late nineteenth-century America almost no one existed outside the market, and such existence had come to seem a sign not of independence but of isolation from the benefits of freedom. Many workers, stressing the allure of the market, claimed that withdrawal from it led to stagnation and depression and that the attempt to avoid it signaled savagery. Even George McNeill, who in 1877 famously denounced the selling of labor as slavery, put forth a much more positive view of wage labor in his eight-hour pamphlet a decade later. Employing the rhetoric of the market, he described wage earners as "the merchants of time," marking as the key issue not the sale of human labor as such but the price that could be extracted.[35]

Second, rhetoric consigned almost all wage earners to the category of "slave." This was a position that even vociferous advocates of the term preferred to view as a worst-case scenario, a benchmark rather than a self-description. The rhetoric was used most effectively by those who believed that they were not yet slaves. Organized workers, especially, treated slavery as a degraded status toward which they might be heading but at which they had not yet arrived. White male workers, who constituted the heart of the organized labor movement, put workers on the margins of the trade union movement—women, blacks, and recent immigrants—in the ranks of the wage slaves.[36] Although denying the relevance of wage slavery for trade unionists, John Mitchell conceded in 1903 that it remained an important issue for some workers, since "in certain sections of the country and in certain industries, the wage earners, especially women and children, are in a condition so debased and degraded, and are so subject to oppression and exploitation, that it practically amounts to slavery."[37] Versions of wage slavery which placed all workers in the same category elided distinctions essential to white male working-class identity.

Third, the consumerist formulation of "wage slavery" narrowed the object of criticism from the entire wage system to the issue of low wages. Some working-class leaders began to question the usefulness of the metaphor. Trade unionists claimed that it did not accurately describe the reality of modern working-class life in which wage earners predominated even among the labor aristocracy and that it was harmful to perpetuate such an antiquated worldview. Writing in the *Tobacco Worker* in 1902, James Ellison dismissed the term as an irrelevant vestige of antebellum labor radicalism: "Almost all the early American unions, in the thirties and forties, demanded the 'abolition of wage slavery' and the 'full product of our toil.'" Although these phrases "sounded well," they "were not very clear," Ellison complained. The imprecision, he believed, followed from its outmoded producerist call for the full fruits of one's toil. A year later, John Mitchell concurred that the term hid as much as it revealed, since trade unionism did not oppose the wage system, only low wages: "Trade unionism is not based upon a necessary opposition to the so-called 'wage slavery' of the present time. . . . Where . . . slavery exists . . . trade unionism is opposed to the slavery as such, and not to the wages as such." Mitchell disclaimed any necessary link between wages and slavery.[38]

The blanket critique of the wage system implied by the producerist sense of the term became increasingly problematic even for those who continued to invoke the threat of wage slavery. Writing in the *Machinists Monthly Journal* in 1901, John Allen Motte declared that the worker who "must take what his master gives him" and who is "compelled to work for a mere subsistence" thereby "degenerates into a wage slave."[39] Motte's nonproducerist critique centered on the issues of compulsion and subsistence, not wage labor itself. Many agreed with him that an inability to demand and receive high wages was enslaving. But this was different from the view that slavery inhered in wage labor itself: workers who gained good wages rather than subsistence were not wage slaves.

Consumerists who condemned wages as enslaving painted a positive picture of the potential, if not the actuality, of wages. They suggested that wage labor properly conceived could undergird modern citizenship rather than undermine it. "He is not really free who is forced to work unduly long hours for wages so low he cannot provide the necessaries of life for himself and his family," wrote John Mitchell. "To have freedom a man must be free from the harrowing fear of hunger and want."[40] By calling slavery a function of unmet need, he defined underconsumption as a form of slavery, and as a corollary, he'suggested that wages that met people's needs ensured freedom.

As workers abandoned the notion that wages necessarily enslaved, the criterion for determining wage slavery changed: the issue became not whether one worked for wages but the kind of wages one received. At an 1899 lecture by Ira Steward's protégé George Gunton, an AFL pamphleteer and political economist, a member of the audience challenged Gunton's contention that high wages would entirely eliminate the dangers of wage slavery. While conceding that the "factory system has enlarged the capacity of the people to consume more products and have a broader social life," the questioner argued that the concomitant loss of workplace autonomy inherent to the wage system offset these gains: "Has it not in reality degraded the workingman by discarding his individuality as a producer, and taking out all his personal interest or pride at work? He becomes a wage slave, with little or no opportunity to rise." Wage slavery, Gunton responded, had nothing to do with wages in themselves and everything to do with narrowed opportunities. "Higher wages," he declared, led to "increased demands" as well as "new varieties of satisfaction." Since good wages created new needs and new opportunities, they contradicted the nature of wage slavery.[41]

The consumerist discourse quietly but effectively redefined the meaning of wage slavery. While condemning low wages as enslaving, it stressed that wage labor and freedom went hand in hand. By 1916 the *Stone Cutters Journal* suggested that good wages marked the very opposite of servitude: "A slave is indeed he who works for no wages and what food, shelter, and clothing his owners will dole out to him. Conversely, then it is the good wages and conditions that make a man really free."[42] In less than half a century wage labor had metamorphosed from a mark of servitude to a sign of freedom.

The Appeal of Emancipation

Despite these developments, the wage slavery metaphor did not disappear. The producerist meaning fell to the side in the post–Civil War years, but the term was revitalized as a marker of consumption, signaling a new kind of connection between wages and freedom. "I think a man should be paid enough wages for eight hours' work to enable him to live comfortable like a free man, and not like a slave toiling every hour that he is awake," declared John Kelly, a member of the Knights of Labor, in 1886. That is, freedom was a product of wage labor, provided that wages were adequate.[43] Even as the wage slavery metaphor changed meaning, then, the slavery/freedom dichotomy, the key to the antebellum republican and free labor discourses, retained centrality.

If the consumerist view made wage labor acceptable, it did not eliminate use of the slavery metaphor to distinguish worthy from unworthy workers. The consumerist interpretation of wage labor opened up possibilities of freedom for some, but it also allowed for new "slaves." This perspective was sometimes used to evoke the sympathy of skilled workers for their less powerful brothers and sisters. More frequently, however, skilled workers blamed these "slaves" for perpetuating their own enslavement.

Racialized understandings of wage slavery were reframed in consumerist terms. In 1886, for example, Terence Powderly, the leader of the Knights of Labor, condemned the "mental slavery" of "able-bodied colored men in the South who do not know enough to ask for living wages," who "work for starvation wages." He declared: "The colored laborers can and do exist on an amount that would not pay for a single meal for a northern white laborer. The colored man lives with his family in a hovel but little better than the quarters of the slaves prior to the war, and upon food practically the same as was issued to the slaves."[44] Powderly thus rearticulated wage slavery not as working for wages as such, but as failing to demand wages high enough to support a sufficient standard of living. The new freedom, it seemed, involved a cultural disposition to demand good wages and to consume properly; the new slavery its opposite. This discourse, as we will see in Part II, evolved into the often racially motivated "American standard of living" discourse.

Even more striking use of the rhetoric of slavery and freedom can be seen in a statement by the Cleveland labor leader Luke McKenny in the midst of a streetcar workers strike in 1898. McKenny, secretary of the Brotherhood of Wood, Wire, and Metal Lathers, claimed that the "colored race" predominated among those who continued to ride the streetcars in spite of the strike:

> I contend that the negro, who owes his freedom and right of suffrage to the working class more than to any other, should stand shoulder to shoulder with those that have befriended him in the past. The wage slavery that now enthralls both black and white is every bit as galling as was the chattel slavery which the black race endured so long. I have been pondering to myself . . . on what would have been the result had

the conditions of the black and white races been reversed in '61. Would the negro take the same stand to abolish white slavery that the white men of the north did to free the blacks? Well, in view of the attitude of the Cleveland colored people in this emergency, I am rather inclined to think that white slavery would exist forever.[45]

Not only did black workers contribute to their own enslavement, according to McKenny, they also threatened to enslave whites through their irresponsible patterns of consumption.

But to end the story of wage slavery on this note would not be entirely accurate. The racist cast of the metaphor in the postbellum years can not be denied, but there is also no question that emancipation fundamentally affected conceptions of slavery and freedom. While deemphasizing the slavery aspect of the freedom/slavery dichotomy, more and more workers pointed to the model of emancipation and suggested that with the end of chattel slavery "all kinds of slavery" should be "buried . . . forever." Terence Powderly declared the project of the Knights of Labor to be "industrial emancipation."[46]

For many ex-slaves, emancipation meant that they had finally gained the right to demand that their labor be treated with dignity and fairly compensated, but African Americans were not alone in making use of the metaphor of emancipation.[47] Although the defeat of chattel slavery did not free the "wage slave," it provided a model of liberation for wage workers, white and black. Notwithstanding W. E. B. Du Bois's comment that white labor, to its detriment, never saw in "black slavery and Reconstruction the kernel and meaning of the labor movement in the U.S.," workers of all races invoked emancipation in the context of their battle against the ever-present danger of wage slavery. The "trade union movement," according to a labor newspaper in 1905, had, in a process analogous to emancipation, transformed "the wage earner from a practical slave wage" into a republican citizen. John Mitchell deemed living wages essential to a "second emancipation" for American workers.[48]

Although the United States had legally moved beyond slavery, the issues of freedom and bondage were very much alive and relevant to American workers. Ira Steward invested the spirit of abolition in his work as a proponent of the eight-hour movement. Steward believed that the crux of slavery was poverty, and poverty, however frequently it accompanied wage labor, did not inhere in it.[49] "The practical question for an American . . . is not between freedom and slavery, but between wealth and poverty," Steward declared in 1879. By contrasting a political dichotomy to an economic dichotomy (and seemingly subsuming the political under the economic), Steward was arguing that the economic order shaped the political order. Wealth in the form of good wages would produce the conditions necessary for freedom, but poverty would lead, in effect, to slavery, since "when the working classes are denied everything but the barest necessities of life, they have no decent use for liberty."[50]

Steward continued to speak of freedom along with wages and wealth as goals for the American worker, and he framed political questions in economic terms. "Slavery is . . . the child of poverty, instead of poverty the child of slavery; and freedom is the child of wealth, instead of wealth the child of freedom," he declared in a Fourth of July address. Liberty for Steward was rooted in economics and politics. Emancipation was impossible without just wages, and Steward called on all workers to apply the spirit of emancipation to the new world of wage labor, to move, as he wrote, "out of the slavery of poverty into the freedom of wealth."[51]

Other labor leaders drew analogies between the labor struggle and emancipation. William Mullen, a labor leader from Richmond, told a Knights of Labor assembly in 1885: "There still remains a battle to be fought for the establishment of universal freedom. Can those who are now the slaves of monopoly and oppression be liberated as easily as was the African race in America? Yea, even more easily! . . . two grand principles — a fair day's pay for a fair day's work, and an injury to one is the concern of all."[52] Fittingly, Mullen, a southerner, linked the goals of the labor movement to the spirit of emancipation. Other labor leaders stressed the need for the nation's "wage slaves" to explore the meaning of freedom through the model of emancipation. "While the Declaration of Independence established civil and political liberty," wrote John Mitchell in 1910, "it did not . . . establish industrial liberty." Indeed, noted Mitchell, "real industrial liberty was not even established with the abolition of chattel slavery," since "he is not a free man whose family must buy food today with money that is earned tomorrow." Ira Steward, years before, had similarly suggested that workers should be emancipated through wages, not from them: "The repeal of . . . slavery . . . was an indirect way of deciding, that laborers should have some more wealth. How much more is the great unanswered question."[53] This consumerist reading of emancipation went hand in hand with a view of slavery as poverty and poverty as enslaving. In this vision, living wages marked a kind of eternal emancipation.

2

Idle Men and Fallen Women

American workers, labor leaders, and reformers expressed acute anxiety about the dangers of the encroaching market in the years between the Civil War and World War I. Wage labor, they feared, threatened to turn everything into a commodity, with dangerous ramifications for the republic and the working people who constituted it. "As a rule everything a poor man has is for sale," wrote Ira Steward, who filled his voluminous writings with incessant worries about America's growing army of poorly paid wage laborers. When "bread and employment is not secure," he concluded, "principles, votes and honor have each their unknown price." Poverty made even upstanding citizens vulnerable to attacks on their "virtue"; as Steward noted, "Higher prices are sometimes successful when lower ones fail."[1] Low wages, he believed, threatened the male worker's ability to own himself, thus calling into question his ability to fulfill his political and familial duties.

Labor reformers expressed similar fears in relation to women workers. In 1911 Margaret Dreier Robins asked: "Why must young girls pay the price of their youth and forfeit their right to motherhood at the machine — why must thousands of men and women endure hardships and sufferings to secure the primitive demands of a living wage and the right to self-government, to which as a people we stand pledged?" Like Steward, Robins linked economic independence with democracy, the term "self-government" registering at both personal and political levels.[2]

The interpretation of poverty as the loss of self in the market economy, merged frequently in labor and reform discourse with images of prostitution, which — along with slavery — represented the quintessential example of the immoral implications of the sale of the self. Slavery and prostitution were widely used to describe the ultimate humiliation of a liberal capitalist society: the self *as* property rather than that which *owns* property. Both slavery and prostitution involved being sold or selling oneself on the market and hence losing control of bodily activities related to production and reproduction which rightfully belonged to the free individual. To those who feared wage labor, prostitution represented both the inevitable outcome of its logic and a worst-case scenario. Steward, who frequently referred to prostitution as a subset of the problem of wage labor, was not the first to make this connection. Karl Marx declared that "prostitution is only a specific expression of the general prostitution of labor."[3]

Although the languages of slavery and prostitution performed different kinds of rhetorical work, there were significant parallels between them. Both were used to critique the wage system and to delimit the boundaries of the acceptable sale of the self. Just as "wage slavery" reveals the deep anxieties of workers about the degree of their freedom, so too does "prostitution" shed light on anxieties about their sexuality and sex roles. By expressing a vision of the proper relationship among gender, wage labor, and citizenship, the rhetoric of prostitution demonstrated the central role of wage earning and market behavior in constituting sex roles. My job in this chapter is to trace how anxieties about the new predominance of wage labor were displaced onto gender and to demonstrate the role of the living wage in the resolution of these anxieties. Understanding the "prostitution" discourse helps to explain the rhetorical path to the living wage.

Unlike chattel slavery, prostitution represented a continuing problem in reality as well as metaphor. Yet labor's prostitution discourse was surprisingly disembodied, rarely referring to real prostitutes or, surprisingly, even to women. It was, in fact, a discourse about masculinity. Reconciling wage labor with normative gender roles, it shed light on the conditions under which wages would be accepted: namely, when they permitted inherited notions of masculinity and femininity to be maintained in a market economy. Workers and reformers employed prostitution for two distinct rhetorical uses: metaphor and narrative. Those who invoked the metaphor directly compared wage work to prostitution, and those who used the narrative made prostitution part of a chain of related events set off by low wages and threats to the gender system.[4] The metaphor left little room for rhetorical escape from "prostitution." If workers were like prostitutes simply because they earned wages, little could be done about it. But the narrative of prostitution was more flexible; it opened possibilities to solve the problem of prostitution within the wage system itself, notably through the living wage. Whereas the metaphor emphasized the shame of wage labor, the narrative suggested remedies for the shame within a regime of wage labor, and, for this reason, ultimately became the more common way to invoke the language of prostitution.

The metaphor/narrative distinction in the prostitution discourse closely parallels the producerist/consumerist distinction in the wage slavery discourse. In each case, the first term suggests that only the abolition of the wage system will suffice. The latter terms suggest amelioration within the wage system. Thus the prostitution narrative, together with the consumerist version of wage slavery, became a building block of the living wage discourse.

The competing uses of prostitution as metaphor and narrative illuminate a debate about working-class gender roles, particularly masculinity, in the age of wage labor. Those who invoked the metaphor to condemn all wage earning as the moral equivalent of prostitution suggested that wage labor was incompatible with working-class manhood. Preserving manhood meant avoiding wages. Manhood was equally challenged when women worked for wages, since working women were taken as evidence of the failure of the male breadwinner.[5]

The prostitution narrative, by contrast, suggested that wage labor was like prostitution only in specific cases — as, for example, when wages were low. This view defined modern manhood by its relation to the market. Within the market mentality, manhood had to be redefined in terms of the worker's ability to earn a "living wage." As long as men earned such a wage, they could not be legitimately compared with prostitutes and manhood could be salvaged. According to the prostitution narrative, the sale of the self in exchange for living wages became a paradigm of self-ownership and symbol of modern masculinity.[6] Selling one's labor under a regime that offered living wages ceased to be the same as selling one's virtue.

There was more ambivalence about the relation of femininity to the market. If the recognition that many working-class families needed the income of women workers and that there were increasing numbers of single "women adrift" led to calls for living wages for women as "the only social foundation for a decent industrial system," many men still considered having a female relative at waged work to be a sign of a man's moral failure.[7] In addition to patriarchal humiliation, working women felt the pall that prostitution cast over even legitimate jobs. If the prostitution narrative had opened the way for an endorsement of wage labor for men, it did so by relegating women to the role assigned to men in the metaphoric use of prostitution. Labor reformers and the popular press compared virtually any form of female employment to prostitution. Women could "earn a fair or even an abundant living," Clara Ruge wrote, "only at the risk of losing their characters and their higher self." She grouped all jobs under the rubric of prostitution, which she defined quite broadly: "I do not mean only that which is strictly so called, but all grades of earning . . . good wages, in which the sensual attraction of the women rather than her special fitness for the work counts."[8] Women workers faced a double bind: low-wage jobs were said to lead inevitably to actual prostitution, but well-compensated labor was called a form of prostitution.

The Wages of Sin and the Sin of Wages

Workers had long made the connection between selling their labor as wage earners and selling their bodies as prostitutes. Like slavery, prostitution was a way of selling the self on the "free market." In a society that closely linked personal identity to work, selling one's services to an employer struck many workers as analogous to prostitution. An antebellum dictionary, for example, listed "hireling" as a synonym for prostitute.[9] For many workers, there was no meaningful difference between the wages of sin and the sin of wages.

The prostitution metaphor gained particular salience in the late nineteenth and early twentieth centuries, a time when the seemingly inexorable expansion of wage labor raised anxieties about the implications of a society bound in every way by market principles. Some reformers argued that prostitution itself had entered a new stage as a deep-rooted social problem rather than an individual lapse of morality; they feared it might be a structural fixture of modern capitalism. Shortly after the Civil War, for example, the reformer Caroline Dall maintained that modern prostitution was distinctive for having achieved a "permanent position" in the American economy.[10] Progressives later echoed this argument in their "white slavery" investigations, as they shifted the focus from the morality of individual prostitutes to the economic system that seemed to produce them in large numbers.[11]

Those who invoked this language to denounce wage labor, however, rarely condemned prostitution itself, or even expressed concern about the wages or working conditions of prostitutes. Far more often, they used the metaphor to critique the deleterious effect of the wage system on social and economic relations. The logic of capitalism, in this view, threatened to turn all commercial activity, most obviously wage labor, into prostitution.[12] If the metaphor did not necessarily equate workers with prostitutes, it suggested an uncomfortably strong resemblance. The *New York Call*, for example, suggested in the early twentieth century that prostitution exposed the "real nature of the wage system," which it identified as the "original graft of all grafts."[13] Both wage labor and prostitution required the immoral sale of the self, which could be preserved only if it stood outside the market. Both stripped away the essential elements of freedom, independence, and citizenship.

Although both male and female workers compared wage work with prostitution, the comparison had particular salience for working-class women, since they, not men, formed the pool of potential prostitutes. One working woman told a Progressive Era factory investigating committee that she and her peers had trouble deciding "whether there is any difference between selling yourself for $6 a week or $5 a night."[14] Working-class women had special license to use the prostitution metaphor, especially given the permeable boundary between low-wage jobs and prostitution.[15]

But they did not have exclusive claim to it. Male workers made full use of a metaphor that worked by analogy rather than synonymy. Unlike their working-class sisters, they were unlikely to become prostitutes in a literal sense; indeed, the rhetorical power of this comparison rested precisely in its unlikeliness.[16] By comparing themselves to prostitutes, working-class men, who made independence and masculinity a cornerstone of their identity, criticized the social order. In an ironic twist, the language of prostitution became primarily a male discourse about the reproduction of masculinity in a wage-labor regime.

Prostitution as Narrative

Despite its rhetorical power, the prostitution metaphor was difficult to maintain in an era in which wage labor was no longer the exception but the norm. Just as the language of wage slavery changed as the economy became dominated by wage laborers, so too did the language of prostitution. Beginning in the late nineteenth century, another strand emerged, and workers developed a narrative of prostitution.

The narrative replaced the one-to-one correspondence between wage labor and prostitution with a series of events. Instead of idealizing a non-market world, the prostitution narrative accepted the market mentality and ensconced workers squarely within the world of buying and selling, wage labor and consumption. The way to avoid prostitution was not to escape the market but to embrace it more effectively.[17] Prostitution came to be seen as a lack of working-class control over the wage labor market, not as mere participation in that market.

The narrative narrowed the focus from a blanket condemnation of the wage system to specific instances in which the system had gone awry. Wages were unacceptable if they undermined the possibility of family life, subverted gender roles, and made self-ownership impossible. The narrative was better suited to talking about the nuances of gender. In the narrative of prostitution, thus, a well-wrought wage labor system that preserved gender roles, far from encouraging prostitution, would make it all but impossible. The narratives presented two poles: prostitution symbolized incongruence between economic activity and gender roles, and living wages represented harmony between economics and gender. Prostitution narratives thus provided a way to describe, critique, and reformulate the relation between wage labor and gender.

Prostitution figured variously in these narratives, but it always involved a transgression against the gender system. Labor leaders both criticized wage labor and reconciled themselves to it through the language of gender and the family. To them, the family represented the essential building block of society.[18] They viewed the patriarchal family of the male breadwinner and the female homemaker as central to preserving the republic and the self-worth of men and women. The motto of the National Women's Trade Union League expressed the connection among wages, leisure, and domestic life in its motto, "The Eight Hour Day / A Living Wage / To Guard the Home." Any attack on family and home threatened the very fabric of working-class life and, by extension, the republic itself (see fig. 2).

Critics of wage labor developed a narrative of the embattled family threatened by the market. Just as wage labor had destroyed artisanal work practices, it threatened to destroy the family. In his study of the family life of the English proletariat, Frederick Engels maintained that capitalist wage relations rendered a normal family life "almost impossible." Similarly, *John Swinton's Paper* criticized forms of labor that destroyed traditional gender roles: "The present industrial system under capitalist rule is destructive of family ties and has already succeeded in forcing women out of their natural positions at home." "Capital thrives not upon the peaceful, united, contented family circle," thundered the

Figure 2. Joseph Keppler, "The Overcrowded Raft," *Puck*, April 2, 1913, Print Collection, Miriam and Ira D. Wallach Division of Arts, Prints, and Photographs, New York Public Library, Astor, Lenox, and Tilden Foundations. Courtesy New York Public Library

AFL official Edward O'Donnell in 1897.[19] The wage labor regime, characterized by its underpayment of men and its enticement of women, seemed at odds with working-class conceptions of family life.

Workers routinely invoked the family in their pleas for living wages. To the Workingmen's Party of Illinois just recompense meant wages sufficient to hold the patriarchal family together: "We have asked in the name of humanity, for the sake of our starving wives and children and our own manhood, only a fair allowance of life's necessities." Workers defined disruption of the family as the most humiliating effect of low wages. "Wherever the compensation of labor falls below the cost of living . . . disastrous results will follow," noted B. W. Williams in 1887. Disruption of gender roles, especially that of the breadwinner, was the most crushing consequence: "Able bodied men will be reduced to pauperism; their wives and children will be on the verge of starvation." Samuel Gompers expressed fear in 1902 of an ill-paid and, thus, "a degraded, a debased, or a demoralized manhood."[20]

The wage system threatened to subvert and reverse sex roles that critics deemed to be natural. Although masculinity and femininity were supposed to be complementary, the market threatened to make men and women antagonists by promulgating an unnatural society consisting of feminized men and manly women. Congressman Martin A. Foran, former president of the Coopers' International Union and a leading proponent of protective labor legislation, stressed the causal connection between low wages and gender subversion, family disruption, and finally, prostitution: "Low wages sends the pregnant mother into the factory. . . . low wages sends children into the shop, low wages prevents marriage and increases bastardy; low wages fills the brothel as well as the jail."[21] Prostitution was the ultimate product of topsy-turvy gender roles resulting from a poorly tuned wage system.

The following eight episodes demonstrate how the prostitution narratives inscribed gender in relation to the world of wage labor. Behind each of these stories lay the specter of prostitution or the marking of its absence, which is no less significant, inasmuch as it signals the acceptable role for women in this gendered economy, that of housewife and helpmate.

Sex Roles in the Age of Wage Labor

American labor historians have long argued for the centrality of "manhood" to working-class culture. David Montgomery suggests that "few words enjoyed more popularity in the nineteenth century than this honorific, with all its connotations of dignity, respectability, defiant egalitarianism, and patriarchal male supremacy."[22] Nick Salvatore describes the breadwinner as the "active participant in the world," whose "duty and responsibility demanded he provide for his wife and children in a material way," and whose manhood "required an active political participation and the fulfillment of one's duty as a citizen." Fundamentally tied to control of the market in general and good wages in particular, modern manhood required striking a bargain with the wage system which would permit the patriarchal family to be kept intact. It was an important transformation in the history of American masculinity: rather than working for oneself, working for living wages became the hallmark of manhood.[23]

One aspect of working-class manhood involved a display of physicality. Labor newspapers emphasized this attribute well before "muscular Christianity" (a term used by Ira Steward in the 1870s) became a middle-class obsession in the 1890s.[24] In 1887, for example, *John Swinton's Paper* described a national convention of workingmen's parties as an assertion of virility. "All kinds there were," the article began, "men of herculean build from the ever bountiful West; tall, gaunt natives of the sunlit South; good-looking business men; men of the farm and workshop, with muscles inured to toil; men of the mines and the frontier, keen-eyed, swarthy and slouch-hatted; men who fought Indians and grizzlies; men who had worn the blue and the gray and bore the marks of conflict on their bodies."[25] The article did more than simply applaud the varieties of manhood: it connected manhood to political economy. Muscularity made men strong and independent citizens who, according to the paper, were "all united against a common enemy," that is, "monopoly!" Manhood encompassed the related virtues of physical strength and moral responsibility. Industrial capitalism and wage labor—"monopoly" in the patois of the labor press—threatened both. Hence there was a need to affirm physical manhood and the values associated with it: independence, patriarchy, virtue.

Labor rhetoric closely linked the physical dimension of masculinity to the political economy of the family, especially to breadwinning, the defining characteristic of manhood for the late nineteenth-century working man. Men had a responsibility to support "dependent" women and children. William Sylvis, a leader of the post–Civil War labor movement, criticized male "non-producers" as "effeminate" precisely because they shirked this responsibility.[26] Transformations in the organization of work, especially the widespread growth of wage labor, posed a direct threat to working-class culture because such changes challenged the sexual division of labor.

The meaning of working-class manhood could be understood only in relation to its necessary complement, working-class womanhood. If labor ideology defined men as providers, it placed women in charge of all facets of reproduction and domestic life. Family responsibilities, divided by gender, were mutually reinforcing. J. Pickering Putnam noted in a study of working-class life that "the work of men and women are distinct from, and supplementary to each other," and "the work of each is equally necessary for the perfect health of the social state."[27] In this working-class masculinist ideology, women not only fulfilled necessary reproductive and domestic functions; they also demarcated a dependence whose absence defined manhood. Femininity, then, represented both the complement to and the negation of masculinity. Although male and female functions were equally important to the perpetuation of working-class life, woman's essential function was to preserve rather than challenge manhood.

Defining women as men's complement circumscribed the definition of liberty for women. Although both sexes equally deserved it, liberty consisted of serving one's "natural" function, whether as a man or as a woman. William Sylvis could call for "universal liberty and universal suffrage, regardless of sex or color," while arguing that women should stay at home. "I am not in favor of women working at all," he wrote. "I believe that every man should be able to derive enough profit from his toil to enable him to support his wife, daughter, or mother. I do not believe that woman was intended to live by the sweat of her brow."[28] "Universal liberty," for Sylvis, had a different meaning for each sex. It did not entail complete equality. Women gained their liberty by nurturing men; men achieved theirs by bringing home the bacon for their family.[29] The view that what women did qualified not as work but as nurturing was central to the developing ideology of masculine breadwinning that "pastoralized" women's work, thus naturalizing sexual inequality.[30]

The Fear of Gender Subversion

Despite the seeming fixity of sex roles, many workers expressed a fear of gender subversion. At the root of this fear was the spread of wage labor, which, in the rhetoric of the labor movement, led to a chain reaction of developments culminating in the breakdown of the working-class family. If stable sexual roles signified social stability, fear of gender instability marked problems in the social order. In the critique of low wages, well-established images of gender were typically invoked and then shown to be under siege.

An article in the *Journal of United Labor* described, with a mixture of joviality and gravity, a case of gender masquerade at an 1887 meeting of a local assembly of the Knights of Labor in Buffalo. The article began on a note of carnivalesque sexual innuendo: "Some Buffalo girls . . . wished to initiate the young men into [the order's] mysteries." Women unionists blindfolded male initiates and led them into another room, where the blindfolded men received a big kiss on the lips. When the men took off their blindfolds, they discovered that they had been kissed not by the women who led them into the room but by a man who had entered previously. Instead of protesting, the men played along with the game, giving the next group of men the requisite kiss.[31] The newspaper reported this event as a joke, but its humor was tinged with the anxiety that male and female roles were no longer securely fixed.

Fears of gender instability in the working-class family were expressed in a variety of ways. Often, reformers invoked a distinction between contemporary reality, which forced many working-class women into wage labor, and the ideal, in which women fulfilled their domestic duties sequestered from wage earning. "Uncounted mothers who have a right to be home stayers, are denied that right by the wages system, and are driven into the factory with the husbands whose incomes cannot support homes," wrote Lyman Abbott in 1890. The gap between theory and practice was widely emphasized in articles about working women in the labor press. "In theory women live a protected home life," wrote Florence C. Thorne. "In reality many earn their own livelihood and provide for those dependent upon them."[32]

This trope allowed organized labor and its supporters to make claims on behalf of working women while criticizing the circumstances that led women to work. "Under justly ordered social and industrial conditions women would not become wage-earners at all, except from choice; and their great and increasing number in the industrial ranks at the present time is an additional evidence of the disordered and anarchic state of society," declared Ida Van Etten in an 1890 address before the AFL. "But since, under the *present* industrial system, they have become a permanent factor in industry, their condition, wages, hours and physical fitness for the different kinds of work in which they are employed . . . is one of the most vitally important questions of the time." The "normal place of women is in the home," wrote Eva McDonald Valesh, a labor organizer and managing editor of the *American Federationist*; "yet the fact remains that for some generations to come the wage-working woman is likely to be in evidence in even greater numbers in the industrial world than today."[33]

Working women threatened the sexual division of labor and challenged gender roles.

The Threat to Manhood

In selling his labor on the market, a man who earned wages lost owner-ship of himself and his product and was owned by somebody else with great power over his life. This transaction subverted the working-class gender system because it made men dependent on their bosses in a way that was analogous to the dependence of the women in the patriarchal family. Engels had written that "within the family the husband repre-sents the bourgeois and the wife represents the proletariat."[34] He, like other critics, charged the wage system with putting men in the properly feminine position.

The wage earner, forced to face the employer as a wife would a husband in a well-ordered patriarchal society, could no more display "manhood" than the prostitute could display "womanhood." An 1885 letter to a labor newspaper condemned the type of men rewarded by the wage system. According to the writer, a self-described "Nobody," these emasculated men displayed none of the virtues of artisanal masculinity: "Who are the men often raised to positions of prominence in factories, workshops, offices . . . ? Are they the bold . . . independent workmen? . . . He who is a thorough workman, quiet, firm, and independent, the boss looks on as his most dangerous enemy . . . but he who is most sycophantic, pander-ing to all the whims of his boss, the boss looks upon as an ideal work-man."[35] Manhood conflicted with the perceived feminine behavior de-manded of wage earners.

The Free Market and Gender

Labor leaders often condemned the "free market" for ignoring sexual dif-ference. The "invisible hand," they complained, did not adequately rec-ognize gender. "Capital is just as ready to crunch up the bones, brains, hearts and souls of women as of men," noted *John Swinton's Paper* in 1885. "It knows no sex; it has no chivalry." Employers, in their blindness to gender differences, threatened to emasculate men, defeminize women, and destroy the family. "Many if not most employers do not care how or where you get enough to live on when your wage is $5 a week and it costs $10.00 to live," declared the suffragist Raymond Phelan in 1913. "Some suggest, others force, their girl employes to live immoral, indecent lives in order to subsist." Similarly, another reformer accused bosses "of pay-ing girls such low wages that many were forced on the streets to earn their living by a life of shame." The result of the unfettered market in which women could so easily undersell the labor of men would be to force women, "the cheapest commodity on the market," as one radical journal described them, into the unnatural position of breadwinners. Ira Steward argued that women underselling men was merely an instance of capitalism's preference for "the cheaper over the dearer." Because women could not succeed as breadwinners in a market that did not pay them living wages, prostitution was sure to follow. "Why do lewd women walk the streets?" "A Working Woman" asked businessmen. "Is it not because unable to live upon the wages you offer that their souls were bought with the rich man's gold? Think of this, brother men. When you hire cheap labor; think of it when you reduce the wages of the women in your employ!!!"[36] A just economy, labor leaders contended, would respect and reinforce, not elide, gender differences. Out of this recognition would come solutions for men to the problem of low wages.

The Actions of Women

The market was not the only culprit; these narratives assigned working women a critical role in the simultaneous destruction of the working-class economy and family. Working, it was claimed, threatened both their morals and the ability of men to support families. Samuel Gompers called on women to remove themselves from the labor market, since "the wife as a wage-earner is a disadvantage economically considered, and socially is unnecessary." Critics of low wages blamed women for taking jobs away from men. "There are many women today taking men's places, working for less pay," noted a member of a women's local of the Knights of Labor. "I do not question their right to work . . . but I do object to them working at reduced rates." In arguing that women had no "moral right" to reduce wages, Ida Van Etten of the AFL implied that they did so by choice.[37] Although not everyone criticized women for working, many echoed the notion that women's labor had dangerous repercussions. Gompers was less concerned about the threat of prostitution for "defenseless" women than that the "competition of the unorganized defenseless woman worker . . . tends to reduce the wages of the father and the husband."[38] Gompers described these women as victims, but he also condemned them as threateners of manhood.

Gender Difference Naturalized

Compounding the erosion of gender under the regime of wage labor was the widely held view that men and women responded to low wages in different but analogous ways. Biology it was thought would drive poor women to prostitution but impoverished men to theft. "There are in San

Francisco 2,800 boys and girls aged from 15 to 21 years mostly unemployed who will become thieves and prostitutes," noted the *Journal of United Labor* in 1882. "Give a man a chance to earn a good living and you may save his life," wrote Wendell Phillips in 1884. "So it is with women in prostitution. . . . Give a hundred men in this country good wages and eight hours work, and ninety-nine will disdain to steal. Give a hundred women a good chance to get a good living, and ninety-nine will disdain to barter their virtue for gold."[39] The analogy: man is to woman as thief is to prostitute.

Some took an emphasis on sexual difference to essentialist extremes, arguing that because women possessed the option of prostitution (they overlooked the fact that in urban areas, at least, men had this option as well), their wages would necessarily be lower than men's wages. "As wage earners women can at present only be regarded as detrimental to the prosperity of the country," explained Alice L. Woodbridge in 1894, because "the wages of men can never fall below the limit upon which they can live while the wages of women can have no limit since the paths of shame are always open to them."[40] In the realm of wage labor, according to Woodbridge, biology was destiny. Connected with this biological essentialism was the belief that a male breadwinner's natural minimum wage should support all his dependents. Women's minimum wages, on the other hand, need be sufficient to support only themselves.[41] Biology was thus taken to support gender constructions.

The Gendering of Desire

In narratives of prostitution, not only wages but desires were gendered. It is not surprising that they were, given the close connection many workers posited between desires and wages. New theories promulgated by working-class leaders held that masculine desires formed the basis of wages, and these desires, provided they fell within respectable boundaries, lay at the root of manhood and republican citizenship.

Labor advocates treated women's desires quite differently. These were usually defined as unreasonable, insatiable, and they were said to lead not to high wages but to "lives of shame." It was what one writer called women's "merciless temptation" for the fruits of consumer society as much as inadequate wages which led to prostitution.[42] "The White Slave," an ostensibly sympathetic song by the IWW balladeer Joe Hill, reflected the view common in labor ideology that women's desire was dangerous. In the song, a "little girl, fair as a pearl," who works as a laundress, becomes a prostitute. Although Hill's account is sympathetic, it is clear that the laundress is drawn, not driven, into prostitution because of her relative sense of poverty rather than absolute need. Her tempter persuades her to prostitute herself by offering not basic necessities such as food and shelter but "fame and gold," "automobiles to ride in," and "diamonds and silks to wear." To be sure, the song holds to the Wobblies' line and blames the boss, but it also implies that inappropriate desires played a large part.[43] A 1913 report on Kansas City working-class women noted: "It is clear that girls who receive insufficient wages to pay for the bare necessities of life . . . are subjected to great temptation" because of their inability to "secure not only the necessaries of life, but also nice clothes and amusements desired by every normal girl."[44]

In this version of the prostitution narrative, women's desire for the wonders of consumer society conflicted with their inability to earn decent wages. An 1883 article in *John Swinton's Paper* described the plight of a woman who worked in an opulent department store but could not afford to sample the cornucopia surrounding her. Raising the metaphor of tuberculosis, the wasting disease, it declared that she was "dying of consumption." It was an apt expression of the dangers of working women's desires.[45]

Just as women's biology dictated low wages, it also seemed to tempt them to overconsumption. In 1886 Otis Stuart drew upon both of these views to explain the "appalling" spread of prostitution in America. That "blackest spot upon our civilization," Stuart maintained, was "largely resultant from the low wages of women," but their own natures were also at fault. Women, said Stuart, wanted to participate in popular entertainment. "The nature of woman — lively, sympathetic, shrinking — craves protection and companionship and entertainment. Low wages [deprive a woman of these]. She is starved, body and soul, for want of money. . . . But if the wages of labor will not bring her companionship and amusement, the wages of sin will, and woman, in utter desperation from selling her labor, stoops to selling herself." While acknowledging that "hundreds of young women employed in factories and stores are paid such a low wage that they are driven into prostitution," Frank Copley suggested that the real cause was the inability of working women to live within their means. For organized male workers this inability was a sign of their need for higher wages; but for women it was taken as a sign of depravity.[46] Desire, it seems, gained men manhood and women whoredom.

Tramps

Low wages brought shame to both men and women, but the nature of the humiliation varied according to sex. In labor rhetoric women faced prostitution but men faced a far worse possibility: the loss of the breadwinner's status. "Are prices to be paid to females for man's work which necessitates the poor house, suicide, or the house of prostitution?" asked one worker, laying out the grim alternatives. Although "the mantle of shame" rested on both men and women, male breadwinners bore the brunt of this humiliation and women bore the blame for it. "Have you considered that your daughter, when working for less than a living wage, is . . . in many instances competing with your son, and will bring down his wages to a lower standard?" asked "A Union Man's Wife."[47]

The most tragic product of the same forces that turned women into prostitutes was the idling of men. Working men saw idleness as a pernicious form of emasculation. Witness Labor Secretary James J. Davis's comment, "I have no more desire to be idle . . . than I do to wear women's clothes." Low wages resulting from women's competition threatened manhood, according to the *American Federationist*: "It is an economic fact . . . that in industries where the wives and children toil, the man is often idle because he has been supplanted, or because the aggregate wages of the family are no higher than the wages of the adult man — the husband and father of the family."[48]

In an 1887 letter to a labor newspaper, J. P. Kohler described emasculation and prostitution as two sides of the same coin. Obliged to "sacrifice their manliness," men lost their breadwinning powers to a "disgraceful" degree, burdening women with the task. Low wages, Kohler complained, bred a "labor market so overrun with all manner of artisans that men crawl and cringe to earn an honest living and women run the streets and sell their bodies and souls to supplement the miserable pittance they get for their work."[49] This equivalence between the images of men crawling and women selling themselves became a staple of labor narratives. Workers depicted a future in which both sexes became tramps, but tramps of different kinds. Male tramps did not work; they were idlers. Female tramps did precisely the wrong kind of work; they were prostitutes.

Male workers argued that low wages would cause both female prostitution and emasculation. W. Whitworth, a Cleveland worker, wrote in 1884 that women, by accepting low pay, produced male idlers and tramps, dealing a severe blow to masculinity. The subheading of the letter highlighted his point: "Women Underworking the Men, Whom They Turn into Tramps." Whitworth deemed idleness the male equivalent of prostitution but considered it even more harmful to the working-class family since it was the male breadwinner who held the family together. "Wherever a half-priced woman can thrust aside a better-paid workman, she is employed, until . . . the men they have supplanted are sinking to trampdom. In scores of shops in this city, they have thrust out men." Whitworth described one printing shop in which "the women and boys, by the aid of machinery, do men's work for boy's pay." As a result, "able-bodied and skilled men [are] idle."[50] The path of gender subversion was strewn with idle men and fallen women; both men and women were being reduced to the status of tramps.

The market held the key to this sexual division. The worst case for women was being forced to sell themselves; for men it was being unable to sell their labor at all. Both tramps and whores walked the streets to bad effect. The idleness of aimlessly wandering the streets represented the opposite of masculine leisure, which could be enjoyed only in the context of a job in the commercialized world of wage labor. The ability to consume invested free time with value, making it something more than idle time.

Edward O'Donnell took the collapse of male breadwinning as the portent of a general gender crisis. In "Woman as Bread Winners — the Error of the Age," O'Donnell contrasted the ideal family consisting of breadwinner and homemaker with what he took to be its mirror image: a nonfamily composed of the idler and the prostitute. O'Donnell agreed that low wages led women into "lives of shame," but his main concern was the more serious danger that such wages posed to working-class masculinity. He condemned the "rapid displacement of men by women in the factory and workshop" as an "evolutionary backslide" in which "the father, the brother and the son [are] displaced as the bread winner by the mother, sister and daughter." The growing demand for female labor was "an insidious assault upon the home" which would destroy both masculinity and femininity, making men like women and women like men. "The wholesale employment of women . . . must gradually unsex them, as it most assuredly is demoralizing them . . . while it numerically strengthens the multitudinous army of loafers," he noted, using the characteristic dichotomy of the prostitution narrative. "As masculine labor destroys the finer promptings and feelings of the sex, the necessary factors to happiness and prosperity, under the conjugal knot, are undermined or they become totally undesirous of assuming domestic responsibility."[51] The result of this gender confusion caused by low wages was a world filled with tramps: female prostitutes and male idlers.

The Living Wage Solution

The grim scenarios of the prostitution narrative supported the advocacy of a way to reconcile manhood with wage earning: the living wage. Proponents maintained that the twin problems of prostitution and emasculation could be solved within the wage system if two problems were corrected: the "free" market's refusal to recognize gender difference and the unwitting complicity of working women in lowering wages. Living wages would enable gender to be reproduced within the wage system.

According to living wage narratives, the problem was not buying and selling but the inability to gain proper remuneration. Living wages would protect women from prostitution and preserve their femininity; they would promote the employment of men and fend off the threat of emasculating idleness. Male and female versions were proposed: an expansive living wage for men and a subsistence one for women, what Margaret Dreier Robins called a "primitive living wage."[52] These would keep idlers and whores off the streets and return men and women to their proper gender roles.

Though the living wage resolved the main problems exposed by the prostitution narratives, it also developed as a positive concept for men and a negative one for women. While it would uphold manly virtues, it would prevent women from debasement. Male workers would be able to reassert wage differentials on the basis of their different needs. As breadwinners, men deserved wages sufficient to supply the needs of their entire family.

Those who demanded living wages for women concerned themselves solely with what would be required to keep women from prostitution. Edward Janney's study of the "white slave" traffic followed the conventional wisdom in noting that "when the wages of girls and women are low, the traffic in women flourishes," and in promoting a subsistence living wage for "a self-supporting, self-respecting woman." A 1913 editorial in the *American Federationist* claimed that "the relation between wages and entrance into that dreadful life" was "clearly established," and the solution was living wages. Noting that "there is little connection between value of services and wages paid," the *Federationist* called for a new standard of wage payment outside the realm of production.[53]

Although, as Emilie Hutchinson noted, there was "no logical reason for fixing [the minimum wage] only for women . . . in the United States the minimum-wage movement has been connected with the question of wages not primarily as a labor problem but as a sex problem." In 1915 the Brooklyn Central Labor Union argued that minimum wages should "only apply to low paid industries where the majority of the workers are women and minors whose wages now are less than the actual cost of living." Women's minimum wages were a matter of subsistence, not consumption.[54]

Even those labor leaders who claimed to be supporting a universal living wage suggested male and female variations. The labor reformer Alice Henry called for "a living wage for everyone" in an article on the "vice problem," but it was clearly the living wage for women which concerned her. It would "remove temptation," she wrote, and "open the way towards self-respecting marriage relations." Henry Abrahams of the Boston Central Labor Union suggested in 1913 that there were in fact two minimum wages, one for each sex. For men, the minimum wage was merely a synonym for an expansive living wage, "which will enable the worker to support himself, his wife, and their children, and to lay by something for old age." Abrahams defined the minimum for women in distinctly narrower terms; it should "give a girl enough to pay her board, clothe herself, lay by something for sickness and still have something to pay for amusements and literature." Abrahams made different assumptions about the level of need for working men and working women, but some male workers simply made the tautological claim that they should earn more than women because they were men.[55]

As it minimized the ignominy associated with the sale of the self, the living wage allayed anxieties expressed in the prostitution narrative by preserving gender roles within the wage system. Living wages for men would incorporate their families' needs as well as their ever-growing desires. Women, however, were excluded from this version of the living wage. Although the prostitution narrative brought the question of female desire to the fore, the problem of prostitution was resolved in the discourse of the living wage not by calling for wages to meet women's desires but by advocating sufficient pay for men to support their families.

The consumerist living wage discourse and the narrative of prostitution worked in tandem to make wage labor acceptable to working people. They did so by distinguishing good from bad wages and by locating the dividing line between the two in the realm of consumption. By late in the nineteenth century, workers and labor reformers, having redefined wage labor to be consistent with both freedom and the preservation of sex roles, had laid the foundations for the living wage discourse and the consumerist turn in labor ideology.

PART II

THE SOCIAL ECONOMY

"The first economic theory that came under my eyes was not calculated to make me think highly of economists," Samuel Gompers once declared. "My mind intuitively rejected the iron law of wages, the immutable law of supply and demand, and similar so-called natural laws." Gompers's disdain for economists did not extend to their field of study, however. When asked at an 1898 lecture whether he opposed "the study of political economy by laboringmen," Gompers responded huffily, "I would consider myself a fit subject for the insane asylum had I been guilty of such a thought." "Political economy is the science of life," he concluded, "and why shouldn't laboringmen study it?" [1]

George McNeill conveyed the same mixture of respect for the field and loathing for its practitioners in his testimony before a Senate labor committee in 1901. When workers "commenced to study political economy," the veteran Boston labor leader declared, "we discovered that the science of political economy had never been written." McNeill did not mean for the senators to take him literally; like most labor intellectuals of his time, he demonstrated an easy familiarity with the classic works of political economy.[2] Instead, he suggested that working-class conceptions of the relationship between economy and society were no longer part of mainstream economic discourse.

In combining a disdain for economists with a keen interest in political economy, Gompers and McNeill articulated a view held by labor leaders of all stripes.[3] To emphasize their differences with the economists, many workers rejected the term "political economy" and demanded instead what they called "social economy."[4] Reflecting this trend, George Gunton founded a journal called the *Social Economist*.[5]

In reclaiming rather than rejecting political economy, working-class economic thinkers and labor reformers saw themselves not as interlopers into an arcane science but as the true inheritors of its original spirit, as embodied by its founding thinkers. In demanding the living wage, Henry Demarest Lloyd wrote, workers "stood for no more than what Mill, Ricardo and all the great economists have declared to be the true law of wages." Carroll Wright, a pioneering labor statistician, suggested in 1882 that the true spirit of political economy was an "ethicopolitical economy" rather than coldhearted market calculations. Modern political economy had come unhinged from this moral vision and needed the injection of "a new life, a warmer blood" in order to reclaim its proper role as both "a moral philosophy" and a "science."[6] Workers saw the "substitution of a moral for a purely economic law" as the essence of political economy.[7]

Just as labor leaders condemned corporate capitalists as the true revolutionaries and identified themselves as conservers of republican values, so too did they blame the new professional economists for turning the field on its head and loosing it from its ethical moorings.[8] This critique accords with Dorothy Ross's analysis of the republican roots of antebellum political economy. Even in the late nineteenth century, she notes, a school of historical political economists, including Henry Carter Adams, Richard Ely, and John R. Commons, expressed sympathy for the labor movement.[9] As economics professionalized, however, its practitioners rejected ethics and history. Attempting to transform economics into a "positive" science, Francis Amassa Walker "urged the economist to have nothing to do with ethics and keep sentiment altogether out of sight." This was a far cry from Wright's insistence that "we must . . . view the whole superstructure in looking at the labor question, and not merely the economical shingles of the edifice."[10]

Although they rejected the positivism of contemporary political economy and challenged the view that only credentialed economists were qualified to study these things, labor leaders recognized the fundamental importance of understanding the structures of economic life. Political economy was too important to be left to the professional economists. As early as the 1820s the British labor radical Francis Place proclaimed that "political economy is the science of the working people," expressing a sentiment similar to that of the artisans across the Atlantic who sought to develop what one antebellum journeyman's committee called a "true system of political economy."[11]

Late nineteenth-century workers continued to make such claims. A

Boston eight-hour organization declared that "the Trade Union is, in most cases, the only school where the working man learns what he knows of Social Science and Political Economy." Political economy, wrote Henry George, was of all the sciences "that which . . . is of most practical importance." Echoing working-class leaders, the popular political economist declared that no special expertise or academic training was required. Since economic "laws of nature" were best apprehended through common sense and lived experience, political economy "is . . . the science which the ordinary man may most easily study. It requires no tools, no apparatus, no special learning. The phenomena which it investigates need not be sought for in laboratories or libraries; they lie about us and are constantly thrust upon us." William Cunningham agreed: "Advocates of the living wage need not fear political economy." [12]

George and others perceived a disjunction between the economic "laws" propounded by economists and the realities of economic life for ordinary people. Typical was the criticism of one letter writer to *John Swinton's Paper*, who denounced the "old fashioned . . . dismal science of wages-and-capital-supply-and-demand political economy," as a system of thought which justified the inequalities of the economic status quo. Economists, said George Gunton, were blind to the real world, and "one-eyed political economy" failed to place economic questions in their proper social context. [13]

Advocates of the "social economy" criticized the mainstream political economists of the day on other grounds as well, including their use of a disembodied and scientific language—what Gompers dismissed as "dreary columns of statistics"—to justify treating workers as commodities. [14] Yet the social economists did not eschew the language of economics. As Robert Blatchford explained in 1895, while there was indeed a "moral" right to a living wage, there was also an "economic" right; living wages, he claimed, were consistent with the science of political economy:

> Whenever you hear a speech or read a paper which tells you that the "living wage" is against an "economic law," ask the speaker or writer these questions: —
> 1. What is the actual working of the economic law?
> 2. In what book on political economy can that law be found?
> . . . in every case . . . the speaker will be unable to tell you. [15]

Remolding mainstream economic vocabulary, social economists applied the central concepts of capitalist apologists—wages, consumption, and the market — to very different ends; for social economists these terms reflected an overlap between the moral and the economic. Just as ante-bellum labor radicals "interpreted liberal precepts in ways diametrically opposed to those of their employers," living wage advocates contested the orthodox political economists not by developing a completely new language but by reclaiming and reinterpreting the older one.[16]

This reinterpretation of political economy manifested itself in a shift of emphasis from production to consumption. Social economists were particularly keen to resuscitate what they claimed was once a central tenet of political economy, that working-class consumption was vital to the health of the nation. "The fact that in the end the toilers must be the great body of the consumers," Gompers noted, "has been given little or no consideration at all." Similarly, Gunton decried the view "which sees the laborer as a factor in production, but not as a factor in consumption." Claiming that an emphasis on consumption and wages did not mark a radical break in economic thinking, Wright approvingly quoted Thomas Chalmers, who in 1832 had identified as the aim of political economy "the diffusion of sufficiency and comfort throughout the mass of the pop ulation by a multiplication or enlargement of the outward means and materials of human enjoyment." Noting the continuity between their emphasis on consumption and that of earlier political economists, some labor leaders depicted Adam Smith as a republican moral philosopher rather than as the father of liberal individualism. Smith was widely recognized in the nineteenth century as a proponent of high wages and healthy consumption for workers. So often did labor leaders quote his remark that consumption was "the sole end and purpose of all production" that it amounted to a virtual mantra.[17] The following chapters trace the consumerist reconceptualization of wage labor by examining working-class interest in the market as manifested by the development of the concepts of the living wage and American standard of living.

3

Defining the Living Wage

In *The Wage Slaves of New York*, Roy McCardell's popular novel, serialized in the *New York Evening World* in the late 1890s, the self-described wage slaves demand "just recompense" as a way to escape their degradation.[1] Although, as we will see, McCardell's "Wage Slaves" proposed a new way to achieve the goal of just recompense, there was nothing unusual about the demand itself, which in its evocation of the labor theory of value echoed long-standing labor rhetoric.[2] But what exactly did just recompense mean in an age of wage labor? This was the vexing issue at the root of the much-discussed "labor question." B. W. Williams described the problem in 1887: all Americans agreed that workers deserved "fair remuneration," he said. "The difficulty arises when we come to consider the question as to what constitutes fair and honest remuneration for labor."[3]

For most of the nineteenth century, we have seen, labor had an unvarying response to this question: fair and honest remuneration amounted to the "full fruits" of one's labor.[4] If it was legitimate on occasion to determine this figure in wages, as for example in the case of apprentices or journeymen, as a general rule only ownership of the means of production made honest remuneration possible. From the perspective of antebellum workers, wage earning was inherently problematic since it entailed the sale of one's person rather than the product of one's labor. In his poem "Chants Democratic," Walt Whitman claimed that even high wages contradicted the republican ideal of economic justice: "Neither a servant nor a master am I, / I take no sooner a large price than a small price." As late as 1903, George McNeill suggested, in a poem dedicated to his mentor Ira Steward, that workers would never garner the full fruits of their labor under the wage system. "God speed the day when those that toil / Shall

61

reap the products of the soil, / From 'wages' free!" In this producerist vision, wages, no matter how high, represented the immoral sale of the self, what one critic of the wage system derided in 1898 as the "purchase of manhood as a commodity." As David Montgomery has observed, from the perspective of post–Civil War working-class leaders, the delivery of the worker "into a day's bondage for a day's wages" was "the very essence of the concept of 'wage-slavery.'"[5] Others, as we have seen, compared wage labor to prostitution.

Roy McCardell, however, put forward a radically different vision of economic justice. His "wage slaves" demanded living wages rather than self-employment as a means to achieve just recompense, rejecting the contention that wage labor necessarily implicated workers in a kind of slavery as well as the view that wage earning was incompatible with republican citizenship.[6] This call for living wages, although relatively new, was not unique. Before the Civil War the term would have been viewed as an oxymoron, but after the war it became ubiquitous — and not only in works of fiction like McCardell's.[7] Coined in the early 1870s by workers on both sides of the Atlantic, the phrase quickly became a staple of American labor rhetoric, reflecting a momentous change in attitudes toward wage labor. One of its leading proponents, Samuel Gompers, called the living wage "one of the most important contentions of labor."[8]

The phrase "living wage" is significant for a number of reasons, not least because it suggested the possibility that wage labor might at least theoretically be an integral part of a just social order rather than an obstacle to it, as the discourses of wage slavery and prostitution suggested. "The relation of a workman to his work implies wages — without money paid to the worker for subsistence there can be no labour," noted the British labor radical Hugh Lloyd Jones in the 1874 article in which the term "living wage" probably first appeared in print. Similarly, Justus O. Woods's claim in 1884 that "wages should be gauged by natural rights" implied that there was a positive, indeed necessary, relation between wages and rights, a relation that critics of "wage slavery" would have hotly denied, but one upon which living wage advocates depended. Father John Ryan, for example, argued that a "just price for labor is never less than a living wage."[9]

Having rejected or modified the critiques of wage earning as a form of slavery or prostitution, in the decades after the Civil War the "new wage earning majority," with emotions ranging from enthusiasm to reluctance, turned (or was forced to turn) increasingly to wages to solve the puzzle of how to determine just rewards.[10] Although a vast chasm separated

George Gunton's view that wages are "as elastic as human wants and desires" from Big Bill Haywood's call for the "abolition of the wage system," most workers came to some accommodation with wage labor, winding up much closer on the spectrum to Gunton than to Haywood. John B. Rae, leader of the United Mine Workers, for example, called wages "a natural and necessary part of our industrial system." Having concluded that the "average wage earner has made up his mind that he must remain a wage earner," Rae's successor, John Mitchell, similarly believed that "a vast and widespread amelioration . . . can take place under the present system of wages."[11]

George Gunton may have captured the view of an increasing number of labor leaders in asserting that the "wage system is a permanent system" and that "there is no possibility of abolishing" it, but this acknowledgment of permanence did not make the meaning of wages self-evident, nor did it say anything about what level of wages might be legitimate.[12] Treating wage labor as a human artifact rather than a force of nature, Uriah Stephens, founder of the Knights of Labor, in 1871 called the wage system "an artificial and mancreated condition, not God's arrangement."[13] While for Stephens this artificiality was reason enough to reject the wage system as immoral, for a new generation of workers viewing wages as constructed gave them hope that they could be reconfigured for the better.

One did not have to share Gunton's utopian view of wage labor to endorse living wages. For some advocates of the living wage, the turn toward wage labor was premised not so much on a positive reformulation of the meaning of wage labor as on a pragmatic acknowledgment of its omnipresence. While agreeing that wages were not themselves natural, the Reverend William J. White argued that under a regime of wage labor, the natural law of human need necessitated the payment of living wages. "Men have by nature a strict right not merely to a bare subsistence but to a decent livelihood," he wrote in a review of John A. Ryan's influential 1906 book, *A Living Wage*. "In the present industrial situation this . . . right takes the definite form of the living wage."[14] Whereas this "right" to a decent livelihood had previously been, theoretically at least, met outside the wage system, he suggested that under a regime of wage labor, wage earning was the sole practicable means to that end. Although wages themselves were not "natural" or inherently good, they could in particular circumstances serve useful ends.

Many workers who continued to identify wages with slavery also began to lobby for higher wages, often in the form of living wages, as a necessary step in the emancipation of labor. For example, the International Labor Union of America, formed in the wake of the Great Strike of 1877, noted in its statement of principles that "the wage system is a despotism." Nevertheless, the ILU acknowledged in another part of its platform that "as the wealth of the world is distributed through the wage system, its better distribution must come through higher wages." It called this move toward higher wages "the natural and logical step from wage slavery to free labor."[15] Here finally was a conception of "free labor" which equated freedom with good wages rather than self-employment. What seemed contradictory in 1877 came a generation later to be the conventional wisdom of the labor movement: low wages, not wages per se, were the problem.

Many labor and reform constituencies participated in this postwar reevaluation of wage labor. Among the participants were freedpeople and women entering the paid labor force; they did not view compensated labor as a symbol of their enslavement.[16] If anything, these groups tended to treat wage labor, when it amounted to just recompense, as evidence of their liberation.[17] Hence, Elizabeth Cady Stanton spoke on behalf of women for "recompense in the world of work," and African American household workers in Atlanta demanded living wages.[18] Similarly, young people, subordinate in the workshop and the family, often found the "wage relationship liberating."[19] While not always the dominant voices in the living wage discourse, these groups had a powerful effect in shaping its contours, especially as they came to redefine wages in consumerist terms.

Even the trade unionists associated with the AFL, the leader in constructing the living wage discourse, need to be reevaluated in light of the radical possibilities of wage labor they proposed. For this group, the living wage did not merely reflect quotidian bread-and-butter concerns but also built on a long-standing link, the bulwark of working-class republican ideology, between material and political well-being. Samuel Gompers, usually taken as the exemplar of the "pure and simple" mentality, expressed faith that struggles over wages necessarily had a crucial political component when he declared in 1887: "I believe with the most advanced thinkers as to ultimate ends, including the abolition of the wage system. But I hold it as a self-evident proposition that no successful attempt can be made to reach those ends without first improving present conditions. Continual improvement, by opening new vistas, creates new desires and develops legitimate aspirations. It makes men more dissatisfied with unjust conditions and readier to battle for the right."[20]

For those ambivalent about the wage system, working-class notions of "social economy" provided a reason beyond the ubiquity of wages to endorse living wages. Advocates of the living wage described it in explicitly political terms as a "right" — often they used the phrase, "inalienable right" — the violation of which made republican citizenship impossible. As the ILU claimed, "Political liberty cannot long continue under economic bondage." Since "material advantages" were available to workers only through wage labor in postbellum America, living wages became a necessity, for "to prevent a class from possessing all the material advantages of a progressive civilization is as much an act of tyranny as to prevent them from exercising their rights of self-government."[21]

Living wage advocates merged wage labor with citizenship, abandoning the view that they were incompatible. Workers "have burned the new words of the living wage into the bill of rights," Henry Demarest Lloyd announced in a pamphlet published by the AFL in 1893, connecting the economic realm of wages to the political realm of citizenship. In demanding the living wage, Lloyd claimed, the coal miners had "carried the standard of their rights to a new height." In evocative republican language, he declared that workers, "born equal, with inalienable rights to life, liberty, and pursuit of happiness," made these rights meaningful by claiming living wages, by making needs central to any calculation of fair wages. "The demand for the living wage was a rebellion of the people. . . . It was an insurrection against the decree of business that wages follow prices, and prices know no law but the competition between trades. We and our wives and children, the miners said, are not chips for gamblers."[22] According to Lloyd, inalienable political rights empowered workers to make economic claims.

To link wages with independence, another republican ideal, proponents of the living wage had to negotiate the difficult issue of the relation between wages and the market. With the living wage, the market became a benchmark of freedom, but in a complicated way. While vociferously condemning the market, advocates of the living wage quietly depended on it: they condemned commodification and supply and demand as symptoms of the market, but their preferred language of rights and needs was equally market dependent. In defining the living wage they theorized in original ways about the politics of the market.[23]

Emergence of the Living Wage Discourse

Dating the origins of the term "living wage" with precision is difficult. Most contemporaries believed it to have been invented by British miners in the early 1870s.[24] Hugh Lloyd Jones popularized the term in a series of articles in the *Beehive*, to which those seeking the origins of the term invariably pointed.[25] But at roughly the same time, Ira Steward of Boston used the phrase "living wage" several times in his unpublished manuscript, "The Political Economy of Eight Hours," which was written between 1872 and his death in 1883. After the 1877 national railroad strike, "living wage" became a keyword in American labor rhetoric.[26]

Defining the living wage is no easier than dating it. If enemies and proponents agreed on one thing, it was the vagueness of the term. Even its probable coiners had very different ideas about what it meant. Steward considered a living wage to be a bare subsistence. For Jones, a living wage was far more expansive: it "should . . . secure sufficiency of food and some degree of personal and home comfort to the worker; not a miserable allowance to starve on, but living wages sufficient to shield the recipient from the degradation of the workhouse, or from the horror of hunger in his home." Most advocates followed Jones in sharply contrasting living wages with subsistence wages, but the phrase was never without this tension between subsistence and luxury. In 1898 Gompers, for example, called for "the millennium of labor, when an ample 'living wage' shall be assured." Several years later, the influential reformer Henry Seager, rejected the idea that the living wage could "usher in the millennium" or even that it should be "ample"; he promoted instead "a bare living wage."[27]

Rather than seek a precise definition, it is more helpful to think of the phrase as a kind of lingua franca of the postbellum labor movement. Indeed, advocates tended to make a virtue of the fact that it was what Washington Gladden called an "elastic phrase." To "a large extent this vagueness is inevitable," wrote John Mitchell, since needs—on which wages should be based—varied widely. "It is hard to define just exactly what necessaries, comforts, and small luxuries a whole working population should receive. And yet notwithstanding all the vagueness, there remain in the mind of the workingman certain more or less definite things which make up to him what he calls the American standard of living, and a certain sum which he feels or believes is a living wage."[28] Although proponents differed over the cash value of a living wage, the phrase became in the postwar years what the term "full fruits of labor" was to the antebellum era, namely, shorthand for economic justice.

One of the reasons for the difficulties in defining the living wage was the newness and originality of the concept, which can be hard to discern because of the familiar rhetorical scaffolding used by those who constructed the living wage. Most advocates described it as a new means to traditional goals, but such rhetoric obscured the radical implications behind a veil of comfortable catch phrases. The living wage reflected the strong influence of earlier labor ideology, even as it transformed it; it shared with this tradition a critical stance toward the market and a skeptical view of the so-called natural laws of economics, as well as bold political claims and demands for a well-compensated working-class. Christopher Hill has written that for English workers the acceptance of wages necessitated abandonment of preindustrial languages of radicalism. American living wage advocates, by contrast, continued to draw from languages that have been variously called artisanal republicanism, producerism, and labor radicalism.[29]

The living wage, then, was new but had deep roots in artisanal radicalism, preindustrial moral economies, and religious, especially Catholic, doctrine. The widespread hostility to wage labor notwithstanding, certain positive interpretations began to appear before the Civil War. The long-standing ideal of the "competence," for example, called for sufficient rewards to support relatives and to survive a comfortable old age.[30] A particularly important notion in this transition to living wages was the notion of "fair wages," a significant term in both American and British labor radicalism.[31] Terence Powderly, the Grand Master Workman of the Knights of Labor, in spite of his personal distaste for wage labor as well as his organization's formal dedication to the abolition of the wage system, noted in 1882, "The principle of the trade union of late years has been . . . to try and secure a fair day's wages for a fair day's work."[32] Yet, although pointing the way toward the living wage, the notion of "fair wages" was a fundamentally different concept.

While it rested to some degree on the idea that wages should enable a worker to live in modest comfort, fair wages discourse defined economic justice as a productive equivalence, a direct correspondence between the value of work performed and wages paid. The formula generally called for "fair wages" in exchange for a "fair day's work."[33] Fair wages, in this view, amounted to a fair price, that is, the full productive value of one's labor. That one could live on such wages was an expected by-product but not the essence of fair wages. Living wage advocates, defining economic justice differently, suggested that how one lived should be the criterion by which to judge the fairness of wages. The concept of fair wages shared the prevailing producerist assumptions about receiving the value of the product. By contrast, the living wage was defined in consumerist terms.

Seizing on this difference, critics derided the living wage because it lacked the legitimacy of productive equivalence. A review of John Ryan's book *A Living Wage* stressed the differences between "living" and "fair" wages. The reviewer was a strong supporter of the "fair" wage but an enemy of the "living" wage; legitimate wages were tied to production in his view.

> The ordinary person probably regards it [the living wage] as a measure of equality of exchange — "a fair day's wage for a fair day's work." That is not Prof. Ryan's view [in which there is] no necessary correlation between the wage and the work done. Whether a man works well or ill, skillfully or unskillfully, he must be paid not less than a certain sum irrespective of the value and amount of his work. The only condition is that the amount of work be "reasonable." But who is to be the judge of what is reasonable?[34]

"Fair wages," thus, measured justice as a function of the sale of the products of labor; "living wages" by the sale of labor itself. While advocates of both would have agreed with the labor pamphleteer T. Wharton Collins's view that "he who will work has a right to . . . earn a living," they would have done so for very different reasons.[35]

The living wage marked a critical shift toward a positive view of wage labor, a "Copernican Revolution" in labor ideology, as Ira Steward called it. In defining fair wages, Steward linked them not to productive value but only to the things that such wages could "secure" for the worker. A living wage was a new concept because it was based on a consumerist view, not the just price for the products of labor but remuneration commensurate with the needs of workers and their families.[36] Basing remuneration on needs was a startlingly new idea.

The emphasis on consumption engendered a subtle but important shift in the meaning of the link between wages and production. While placing unprecedented stress on needs and desires as the basis of wages, living wage advocates did not neglect the relation between wages and production, which they acknowledged lay at the root of wealth. Despite the consumerist emphasis of his definition, Samuel Gompers also described the living wage as workers' "fair share of the product of their toil." But advocates invoked "fair share" in a new way. Whereas proponents of "fair" or "honest" or "just" wages described them as a return for individual labor yields, those who favored living wages described them in collective terms, as the worker's rightful "share in the products of common toil."[37]

Challenging the notion that it was possible to measure the full fruits of individual labor, living wage proponents collectivized the value of labor.[38] While proponents still described the living wage as a claim on the products of labor, it was no longer an individual claim. In rejecting the idealized — and in their view no longer valid — economy assumed by the notion of "just wages," advocates of the living wage developed a new conception of value. Max Weber succinctly described how the collectivization of the value of labor initiated a trajectory from producerist to consumerist theories of value, which culminated in the living wage:

> Quite generally, where the return is determined by the sale of the product in a freely competitive market, the content of the right of the individual to the full value of his product loses its meaning. There simply is no longer an individual "labor yield," and if the claim is to make any sense it can be only as the collective claim of all those who find themselves in a common class situation. In practice, this comes down to the demand for a "living wage," i.e., to a special variant of "the right to the standard of living as determined by traditional need."[39]

This collective claim was based on needs — the realm of consumption — as much as production, and thus the new wage equation sanctioned and reinforced, rather than undermined, the new emphasis on consumption.

Living wage advocates refused to separate remuneration from production, although their critics accused them of doing so. The living wage, however expansively construed, was a demand for wealth earned by the sweat of workers' brows, and therefore Samuel Gompers insisted that it should be understood as an "entitlement" rather than "charity."[40] Economic justice depended on this producerist side of the equation; living wages derived from wealth that workers themselves created. As the radical Bob Ingersoll framed it, the living wage was not a claim for unearned wealth but a way to establish economic justice in the classic producerist sense. "Why should labor fill the world with wealth and live in want?" he asked in 1882.[41]

Living wage proponents usually qualified the emphasis on production in a number of ways, however. First, they claimed that the fruits of production had become so vast in America as to constitute an almost infinite pool of wealth from which to draw wages. The "power of consumption has not increased in proportion to the increase in productive power," declared Gompers. The living wage had become feasible only in the "last generation," John Mitchell claimed in 1903; because of the productive power of industrial capitalism, for the first time "it is possible to give the workingman a wage upon which he may live with reasonable comfort and decency, and with which he may obtain the necessaries and some of the pleasures of life, which in the past society was too poor to provide for him." Proponents of the living wage tended to agree with the Reverend John Chadwick's claim that industrial production in America had produced "enough for all." They also argued that workers had been denied their full fruits for so long that the living wage could be justified as redress of past wrongs. As an 1892 article in a labor newspaper declared, "The great question that agitates the civilized world is—how much shall the wage worker receive for his labor and how much shall the capitalist retain for his profit. The wage worker produces all the wealth of the country and has grown tired of providing all and receiving comparatively nothing."[42]

It was one thing to demand that wages reflect the rightful share of the common toil, but what was the rightful share? Labor's faith in the nearly infinite capacities of production made bold claims for high wages commonplace. Although acknowledged in theory as a limiting factor, as a practical matter, production presented no real limits as far as most workers were concerned since, as Samuel Gompers put it, "the workman has created, creates, and will continue to create, in excess of his ability to consume." In addition, higher wages would spur production; the expansion of needs would expand both production and wage levels. Beyond subsistence, B. W. Williams noted, the laborer "should receive as much more as the profits of the business will justly allow," suggesting that wages could exceed basic needs. Gompers insisted that it was impossible for a worker to "demand more than an equivalent for his services" and claimed that "the wealth augmented by the additional result of his labors above his ability to consume" legitimated living wage demands.[43]

Without abandoning the view that wages were determined in part by production, then, many workers came to define them largely in consumerist terms. Rather than as exploitation that inevitably fell short of full compensation, wages came to be defined positively in need-based language.[44] Even relatively modest living wage demands were framed in terms of need. One proponent wrote in 1895 that the living wage "should enable [the wage earner] with economy and sobriety to maintain a comfortable and healthful home, under conditions which make possible the cultivation of virtue." Despite this stress on thrift, the demand is for more than subsistence. Some recognized that producerism was being abandoned. The Massachusetts labor activist Frank Foster declared in 1900, "It is not . . . the value of what is produced which determines the wage rate, but the nature and degree of the wants of the workers."[45]

In promulgating this innovative consumerist theory of wages, proponents fought conventional wisdom on several fronts. Not only did they modify producerist conceptions, they also challenged the increasingly popular view that wages were a product of the operations of the market, in particular the "laws" of supply and demand. A critic of this view explained: "The theory of orthodox political economy . . . is that if laborer and employers are left absolutely free to make whatever contracts they like, the wages of labor will be fixed by the law of supply and demand, and the rate thus determined will be, according to one school, just; according to the other school, absolutely necessary, whether just or not."[46] Proponents of the living wage charged that the wages being paid were neither just nor necessary. Instead of the market-based law of supply and demand, living wage advocates suggested that the proper criterion was what the labor pamphleteer and politician William Howard called the "natural law" of need.[47] In redefining the value of labor, Howard articulated two principles, one negative and one positive, which became central to living wage claims. First, labor could not be properly rewarded on the basis of the market categories of supply and demand. Second, only human needs formed a valid basis for wage determinations. This rejection of market-based wage determinations in favor of a standard of needs had contradictory implications. On one level, needs, based on the political concepts of natural law and inalienable rights, trumped the impersonal and amoral machinations of the market, but in a more fundamental sense, need-based wages were utterly dependent on the market. The living wage discourse reflected an unprecedented working-class engagement with the market, which became understood as a site where needs were satisfied, not blocked. Although claiming to be rejecting the principles of the market, living wage advocates were in fact reinterpreting it. They politicized the market by challenging the notion that it was a "natural" force governed by immutable laws. Instead, the essence of "natural law" as they defined it mandated a very different type of market, one subject to working-class control.

The Living Wage and the Market

The living wage was quite literally born in relation to the market.[48] Most advocates described it as both an alternative to and a rejection of market-based determinations of wages. Hugh Lloyd Jones used the term in an 1874 article titled "Should Wages Be Regulated by Market Prices?"

in which he counterposed (just) living wages with (unjust) market-determined wages. Labeling the living wage "sacred ground to be defended from intrusion" by the market, Jones answered no to the rhetorical question posed by his title: wages governed by impersonal market forces could not be just. For Jones, living wages were the only legitimate form of wage labor precisely because they were determined instead by needs and the worker's "cost of living." Workers had long associated the market with two nefarious tendencies: the commodification of labor and the forces of supply and demand. Both, in their view, degraded working people. "To the employer," William Howard wrote, laying out the problem in a single sentence, "human labor is a marketable commodity subject in its price to the law of supply and demand." He declared in a campaign pamphlet promoting his 1880 candidacy for Congress, "You cannot regulate wages by the law of supply and demand as you would so much merchandise without making slaves of the workmen."[49]

The antimarket aspect of the living wage discourse, like so many other components of it, drew on the legacy of producerist radicalism that had shaped the American labor movement from its inception. Indeed, at first glance, it appears to be a simple extension. Sean Wilentz suggests that the defining component of American working-class consciousness has been the rejection of the idea that "labor is a marketable commodity."[50] In describing the market as a metonym for capitalist hegemony and working-class disempowerment, living wage advocates followed a long tradition of popular protest against the dangers of the free market.[51] Anticommodification rhetoric links the earliest working-class organizations of the 1820s to Samuel Gompers, who called the 1914 Clayton Act "labor's magna carta" because it explicitly stated that labor is not a commodity.

All labor leaders, whatever their ideological orientation, claimed to reject commodification. G. B. De Bernardi wrote in 1897 that workers did not want to be reduced to "marketable instruments," because to be so reduced led directly to commodification and wage slavery. According to Howard, "Human labor is practically the human being; they cannot be separated, to merchandise the one is to merchandise the other." Making the connection between the market, commodification, and slavery explicit, he declared that however much it was "disguised under a fictitious freedom," wage labor amounted to "slavery," and he concluded elsewhere that "strikes, violence and bloodshed will always be imminent . . . so long as wages are regulated by the law of supply and demand, and not by the cost of living."[52]

Notwithstanding the ostensible rejection of the market, the living wage discourse was deeply embedded in the language and economics of the market. Leon Fink has remarked on a broad pattern in American labor ideology, a "sincere ideological ambivalence toward the capitalist marketplace." In claiming that needs as much as production should determine wage allocation advocates acknowledged that the living wage was a market-based concept. As William Howard wrote in 1894, "Remuneration for his labor must be based on his own life necessities and not upon the business necessities of his employer," but both "necessities" were market driven. The issue was who was to control the market, whose needs would predominate, labor's or capital's?[53]

Despite the vociferous rejection of the commodification of labor, proponents of the living wage came reluctantly to accept what Marxists took as a foregone conclusion—that under the capitalist mode of production, like it or not, labor was in some sense precisely a commodity governed by market forces.[54] They might claim to despise what Henry George denounced as the "higgling" of the market, but they also acknowledged the need to shape that market by taking an active role in such higgling. According to George Gunton, "The prior fact of all industrial prosperity is the market," which he defined as "the consuming capacity of the individual units in the community."[55] Even Gunton's ideological enemies agreed that the value of labor could not be determined outside of the market.

Living wage proponents directed their wrath not against the selling of labor but against the unfairness of the sale. George McNeill complained that "the wage worker is forced to sell his labor at such price and such conditions as the employer of labor shall dictate." The converse of this view was that the sale was acceptable if labor could "dictate" the terms. For living wage advocates control of the market marked the crucial distinction between selling their labor legitimately and commodifying, prostituting, or enslaving themselves.[56]

If the laws of supply and demand were not a legitimate way to determine wages, how could workers arrive at the "true" value of labor? Living wage advocates, invoking the political language of rights, entitlements, and citizenship, turned to rights and needs as an alternative to supply and demand. They argued that the impersonal and amoral workings of the market had to be secondary to human need in determining wage rates. A letter writer to a labor newspaper, for example, contrasted "the inalienable right of the wageworker to life, liberty and happiness" to the notion that "labor was a marketable commodity" and found the latter principle wanting because this "law" destroyed citizenship. A group of labor leaders complained that, by regarding labor as a commodity, the capitalist "forgets that the laborer is a man, a citizen, and a Christian, that he raises a family and that families make the state."[57]

Those who accepted need as a basis for wages disagreed among themselves over exactly how to define need. Religious leaders and most reformers who advocated living wages defined needs in terms of subsistence, but labor advocates drew a more generous picture. Commentators had long recognized that "need" could have a variety of meanings. Karl Marx, for example, acknowledged both biological and social dimensions. Building on the work of David Ricardo, Marx distinguished between subsistence wages and "social wages." Culture determined the distinction:

> The value of labor is formed by two elements — the one merely physical, the other historical or social. Its ultimate limit is determined by the physical element: that is to say, to maintain and produce itself, to perpetuate its physical existence, the working class must receive the necessaries absolutely indispensable for living and multiplying. . . . Besides this mere physical element the value of labor is in every country determined by a traditional standard of life.[58]

This distinction between objective and subjective needs pointed to the shifting demarcation of wages. Living wage advocates saw a great difference between mere existence and an active, virtuous life. Like Marx, Father John Ryan devised two categories: an "absolute standard of necessities" and a "conventional standard." Ryan noted, "In order to live becomingly, men must have not only those goods that are objectively necessary, but in some measure those that they think are necessary. Indeed, the latter may become more vital to decent living than certain goods that are objective and primary." In his review of Ryan's book the Reverend William J. White contrasted "bare subsistence" to the "decent livelihood."[59]

Critics of the living wage questioned whether needs were a legitimate basis of wage determination, since this theory of value conflicted not only with traditional producerist conceptions of the labor movement but with the dominant bourgeois view that wages should be regulated only by the laws of the market. Critics deemed the distinction between subsistence and a decent standard of living maddeningly imprecise compared with the scientific accuracy of market forces. In 1872 E. L. Godkin, the liberal editor of the *Nation*, condemned this new attitude toward wages because it seemed to reward workers regardless of the value of work performed.

He noted that "workingmen . . . firmly maintain the belief that the rate of wages ought to be what a workingman needs to make him 'comfortable', let his habits and the size of his family or his views of 'comfort' be what they may." Godkin blamed workers for promulgating the view that "the market rate of wages is a mere invention of the capitalists; that the proper rate of wages is what will provide a man and his family with 'a comfortable subsistence', and that this rate, be it much or be it little, all employers ought to be made to pay . . . that the reward of labor is something wholly regulated by an abstract rule of right, and in no way dependent on the laws of the physical universe." For Godkin this "abstract rule of right" was mere rhetoric, lacking the power of the scientific laws of the market; he named this disturbing movement "communism."[60] Thus he deftly reversed the working-class view of the market as abstract and rights as real. As we will see, this market-based critique of the living wage continued well into the twentieth century.

Invoking a discourse of civilization, living wage advocates tried to allay fears that wants and needs would escalate out of control. One strategy was to argue that wages should maintain but not improve the standard of living to which a worker was accustomed. Adopting this tactic, Samuel Gompers maintained that a living wage should be "commensurate" with a worker's "economic and social surroundings." In 1894 William Cunningham expressed a similar view: "The living wage, in any social grade, is the payment which will enable the ordinary man to maintain the standard of comfort of his class. In the economic conception of a standard of living we have the correlative of the living wage. This standard differs greatly for different social grades." Frank Foster claimed that wages should reflect the wants of the workers, as "embodied in their customary standard of living." The living wage, William White wrote, "should conform in a reasonable degree to the conventional standard of life that prevails in any community or group."[61] The problem with the view that one needed only what one was used to was that it undercut notions of social and economic mobility that were central to many workers' understandings of the living wage.

More common and less problematical was the strategy of ensuring the respectability of need-based wage demands by framing them in the context of family. This domestic rhetoric countered opponents' charges of greed, since in this schema, what was being supplied was not individual hedonism but the good of the family. "Wages," Gompers wrote in 1888, "are simply the provision of daily or weekly wants of the workman and of his family." B. W. Williams described the "natural minimum" for workers

as the sum of family needs: the "workingman must have the prime necessaries of life—food, raiment, and shelter, for himself and family."[62]

No matter how respectably or domestically they were framed, wages
based on needs opened up radical new possibilities. Under a system in
which wages were based upon the products of labor, they necessarily
faced an upper limit: the value of the product. No such limit capped wages
governed by the principles of the living wage. Unlike "full fruits," which,
however difficult to achieve, were finite, needs were potentially infinite.

The Protestant minister Henry Ward thought the living wage should
satisfy "normal desires."[63] But what was the difference between "normal"
and superfluous needs? One Bradford Dubois gave a standard list of
the "primary needs of mankind," naming "food, fuel, raiment and shelter." But Dubois also listed certain cultural necessities, including "luxuries, refinements, amusements and diversions of life." Others made the
same shift from needs to desires. "We must no longer be content with a
living wage which is measured by the iron bound law of supply and demand," proclaimed the journal published by the Union Label League of
Denver, proposing a living wage that would supply "all the good things
that help to make life bright and happy and comfortable." The living wage
should "enable us to educate our families, to participate in art, literature,
music. . . . And the workingman who does not secure this is falling short
of what he deserves."[64]

Rather than place limits on this need-based conception of wages, living
wage advocates argued unapologetically for continual expansion. John
Mitchell claimed that "no limit should be set to the aspirations of the workingmen, nor to the demands for higher wages." Since "the consuming
power of the community" rested on the backs of workers, wrote George
Gunton, it was their duty to "unite and struggle" continually for the "expansion of human desires and necessities." In this rhetoric, needs tended
to grow rather than shrink. By 1913 the AFL treasurer John Lennon announced that "the labor movement has now reached the point where we
insist that every man and woman in the world performing useful labor is
entitled to a living wage." Silent on what counted as useful labor, Lennon
insisted that a living wage was not one "upon which they can merely exist." Rather, it was a combination of retirement plan, workmen's compensation program, and family trust fund.[65]

Fundamental to the concept of the living wage for most proponents
was the belief that needs were ever expanding, that wages should grow
correspondingly, and that the limitless capacity of production made continual growth possible. The living wage had "elevated the standard of

living of the American workman and conferred upon him higher wages and more leisure," declared Mitchell, and it should continue to do so indefinitely. Wages should reflect the expanding consumption habits of the workers. "The American of today," noted George McNeill, "wants something today that yesterday knew nothing of: tomorrow he will have a new want." Stressing the consumerist dimension in his well-publicized 1898 defense of the living wage, Samuel Gompers demanded a wage that would enable workers to maintain the American standard of living; it should, he declared, prevent the breadwinner from becoming what he called a "non-consumer." Gompers refused to be pinned down to a specific definition since, as he put, "a living wage today may be denounced as a starvation wage in a decade." Placed in this context, Gompers's famous demand for "more, more" emerges as part of a long working-class tradition of political economy. The notion of the ever-increasing living wage was an ideal to which all groups of workers aspired.[66]

While opening up new rhetorical avenues for labor, the emphasis on needs and the market also had a drawback. Basing wages on workers' "customary standard of living," had the potential to reinforce and harden social divisions and to produce racial and gender discrimination.[67] The next chapter examines the most divisive aspect of the consumerist social economy, the appeal to an American standard of living.

4

Inventing the American Standard of Living

The American standard of living was central to organized labor's ideology between 1870 and 1925. Yet, as with the living wage, few workers defined the term when they invoked it. Labor historians have not investigated its meaning either. David Montgomery suggests that it was the equivalent of "white man's wages," but he does not pursue this point.[1] In this chapter I develop Montgomery's suggestion, showing how all three terms — white, man, and wages — that is, the corresponding categories of race, gender, and political economy — lay at the core of the idea of an American standard.

The American standard allowed workers to reground the distinction between freedom and slavery in a wage labor economy by making needs, rather than production, the mark of virtuous character. While this regrounding reinvigorated labor ideology by replacing a dying producerism with a vibrant consumer-oriented language, it also had negative effects. In addition to rehabilitating the freeman/slave distinction, the American standard reestablished male/female and American/alien dichotomies. In adjusting to the wage labor economy, organized workers used the idea of the American standard of living not only to reclaim economic and political rights that they feared they were losing in the new economy but also to exclude other groups from its benefits. If it allowed white, male workers to escape "slave" status, it also gave them a way to call others "slaves" and to exclude working-class immigrants, African Americans, and women from participation in the American standard.

The American standard of living discourse, far from eclipsing politics, revitalized and remade working-class consciousness through an emphasis on consumerism. As labor leaders accepted permanent wage labor, they developed many intriguing ideas about the relation between consumerism and working-class ideology. Labor's turn to consumerism should not be understood as inherently depoliticizing. The American standard had a variety of political valences, some quite radical, others downright reactionary.

Consumption and Freedom

As the reigning metaphors in labor's economic language changed from "wage slavery" and "prostitution" to the "living wage" in the late nineteenth century, organized workers continued to invoke a dichotomy between slavery and freedom, but they placed it in a different context. Slavery became a synonym not for wage earning itself but for low or inadequate wages. Living wages made it possible to avoid slavery and achieve republican freedom. Although the distinction between slavery and freedom remained central to the labor movement, workers began to equate well-paid wage work with freedom. The new slavery, in this context, was a low standard of living, and the new republican freedom was the American standard of living.[2]

Like the wage slavery discourse, the language of the American standard promoted economic independence, civic participation, and working-class character development. Like the living wage discourse of which it was a part, the American standard emphasized the role of the wage-earning worker as a consumer and a creature, not a victim, of the marketplace. Under the old ideology, workers staked their claims to political rights on their position as the producers of the nation's wealth. While laborers did not abandon their producerist rhetoric, with the American standard they claimed that, as citizens, they deserved a comfortable existence. Furthermore, they viewed consumption as a more effective agent of social change than production. The discourse deemphasized thrift and stressed the importance of circulating money; it deemphasized production and stressed consumption. George Gunton, for example, contrasted a "stultified social life," which "furnished no market for the multiplied and diversified products," to "diversified consumption which only grows apace with the possibility of new desires."[3] With the American standard, workers adopted new means to traditional republican goals, locating virtue within, rather than outside, the wage labor market.

If labor's measure of the morality of society before the Civil War was the

absence of wage labor and the presence of a broad stratum of independent producers, its new economic view labeled "high wages as a criterion
of civilization." Whereas the Knights of Labor foresaw a cooperative com-
monwealth in which the lack of wage labor symbolized the health of society, high wages came to signify the possibility of social uplift. To "raise
wages . . . would be worth more than all other reforms put together,"
wrote W. E. Hart.[4]

Many workers understood themselves as part of the market, but as we
have seen, they did not accept the conservative tenets of orthodox political economy. According to their "social economy," the sign of a healthy
working class was not frugality but a multiplicity of wants and desires. In
this view, such desires were not frivolous but absolutely necessary because increased demands would lead to increased production and higher
wages. The worker's needs, as much as his or her production, lay at the
basis of economic life.

Although he never used the term "American standard" (he did write of
the "American way of living"), Ira Steward pioneered a style of working-
class consumerist thinking which rejected the middle-class view that
thrift was the best way out of poverty. For Steward, consumption did
not mean adoption of bourgeois values. Rather, he considered productive
consumption, that which translated desire into wealth, a hallmark of
good citizenship and "necessary for human progress."[5]

Underconsumption or the wrong kind of overconsumption were dangerous in Steward's view. The unproductive consumer's desires for the
debilitating trap of unseemly commercial amusements and drink did
not translate into greater working-class wealth or power. The dissipated
worker, who "wears shoddy and rags, and lives in a tenement or a hovel,"
was a poor consumer because his consumption did not stimulate production. Furthermore, such unproductive patterns of consumption signaled
a general weakness of character and were the sign of a worker unlikely to
know how to stand up to his employer. As Steward wrote, "He is frequently distressed by his vices into the slavish necessity of accepting the
only terms possible from the most selfish employers."[6] Slaves, on this
view, were not wage earners but workers who consumed poorly.

Steward's belief in the importance of acting on socially productive desires through consumption and the dangers of not doing so led him to
challenge the popular connotations of the terms "economy" and "extravagance." Indeed, he called one of the central chapters of his magnum opus
"Economy and Extravagance." Middle-class moralists, he charged, defined scrimping as a virtue and spending as a vice, economy as prudent

and extravagance as wasteful. Steward reversed these judgments. He viewed spending as far more socially productive than saving. "Economy is the real extravagance," he noted, because it dissipated the potential stored within all demands.[7]

Steward argued that the negative meaning assigned to spending was nothing more than a linguistic defense of the class interests of the bourgeoisie. "The charge of extravagance is made to sustain the claim that wages ought not to be any higher." When "a more expensive style of living . . . is denounced as 'extravagant,'" he wrote, it "is another way of saying that the laborer must accept less wages." In his view, progress consisted of precisely such increases in the standard of living. Steward insisted that the praise of economy as a social good signified the desire of the rich to prevent workers from enjoying the fruits of their labor.[8]

American standard proponents, following Steward, challenged the belief that workers should restrain their desires. In 1886, for example, a labor reformer criticized the worker "who indulges in unnecessary and niggardly economy" thereby depriving "some brother producer of a proper market for the products of his labor." By attaching the notion of self-indulgence to excessive frugality, the author demonstrated the need to rethink economic categories.[9] There was a point to this linguistic subversion: it emphasized the connection between frugality and slavery on one pole, and consumption and freedom on the other. In a series of articles written in 1887, significantly titled, "Wage Slavery as Seen by a Wage Slave," A. S. Leitch, noting the connection between consumption and production, argued that without increased demand workers were in danger of becoming "wage slaves." These slaves were workers unwilling to circulate money and by their refusal setting off a chain of events which made the American standard unreachable: "The wage workers' extravagance is the wage-workers' salvation. . . . Suppose all workingmen of the United States . . . at a certain time conclude to squander no more of their earnings in the purchase of tobacco — thousands of tobacco workers would soon go hungry. Or beer: the brewers would be ruined. To shut down on 'superfluous luxuries' of books and papers, the printers would get a tough deal." Drawing on Steward's ideas, he concluded with an attack on the critics of working-class "extravagance," insisting, "It is what press and pulpit term the extravagance of workingmen, that keeps money in circulation . . . and gives employment to thousands of our brother wage-slaves by means of which they gain a livelihood."[10]

The same year, the freethinking radical Robert Ingersoll made a similar argument. The capitalist, he said, "tells the workingman that he must be economical — and yet, under the present system economy would only lessen wages. . . . Every saving, frugal, self-denying workingman is unconsciously doing what little he can to reduce the compensation of himself and his fellows. The slave who did not wish to run away helped fasten chains on those who did. So the saving mechanic is a certificate that wages are high enough."[11]

The American standard complemented labor's "consumerist turn" by positing a direct correlation between character and desires. To meet the standard, the worker had to have many wants as well as the means to fulfill them. In this view, wages were the products of worker's desires, not "natural" economic forces, and labor controlled the market rather than being coerced by it. The worker who achieved the American standard could actually help to set the wage rate by consenting only to high-paying jobs. George McNeill called this the "Great Law" of economic life. After Ira Steward first promulgated the theory in the 1870s that high wages resulted from high standards of living, many working-class leaders followed suit. As a Detroit Knight of Labor leader put it in 1885: "The rate of wages does not depend upon the amount the wage-earners produce but the amount they will consent to live upon and raise a family." According to the *Encyclopedia of Social Reform*, the most popular late nineteenth-century theory held that "wages depend upon what the working man considers the lowest level upon which he can live." The labor reformer and onetime Massachusetts gubernatorial candidate Edwin Chamberlin concluded, "The greater the wants, the higher the wages."[12]

Many workers, then, defined the standard of living qualitatively rather than quantitatively. The American standard, in their view, did not refer to a monetary figure but rather to a type of character that would make American workers insist upon a certain level of consumer comfort; it was a mindset rather than a particular wage level. This does not mean, however, that American workers refused to enumerate specific requirements. Discussions of the American standard were laced with demands for various fruits of the incipient consumer society. For example, B. W. Williams spoke plainly in 1887: "The American laborer should not be expected to live like the Irish tenant farmer or the Russian serf. His earning ought to be sufficient to enable him to live as a respectable American citizen. His living therefore must include not only food and raiment for himself and family, but also such other items as taxes, school books, furniture, newspapers, doctors bills, contributions to the cause of religion, etc." Similarly, John Mitchell wrote in 1898 that the American standard should enable the worker to purchase "a comfortable house of at least six rooms," which contained a bathroom, good sanitary plumbing, parlor, dining room, kitchen, sleeping rooms, carpets, pictures, books, and furniture.[13] Other labor leaders incorporated symbols of modern consumerism — recreational opportunities, home ownership — into their definitions.[14] In their minds, this booty was not so much a cause of high standards as a product of them, albeit a welcome one.

As with the living wage, labor leaders resisted quantifying the American standard because they believed that it should be ever increasing. "The American Standard of Living in the year 1903 is a different, a better and higher standard than the American standard of living of the year 1803," wrote John Mitchell. George Gunton suggested that "expanding the social opportunities of the masses" would "crystallize" a higher standard of living which ultimately would lead to higher wages. He wrote that the cultivation of desire "would make a general rise of real wages inevitable."[15]

Labor leaders believed the American standard was one of the most effective ways to reconnect the working class to the body politic. According to the *Voice of Labor*, the standard would protect fragile republican institutions: "In a political sense, the high standard of living is a chief requirement for the preservation of republican institutions. And it is a public duty of the most sacred kind to protect the workingmen of the country . . . to secure a high standard of living. They are American citizens, and the safeguarding of liberty and virtue is entrusted to their charge." In order to maintain a "self-governing Republic," the Anthracite Coal Commission declared several decades later, "all American wage earners have a fundamental economic right to at least a living wage, or an American Standard of living." Once again, the justification was political as much as economic: without it "there could not be an intelligent and sound citizenship." Moreover, "failure to realize this right . . . breeds revolutionary agitation."[16]

The language of the American standard served a function strikingly similar to that of the earlier republican language of virtue. Workers described the standard as both an inherent trait and a quality that could be developed in people, just as antebellum artisans understood virtue. Certain conditions, usually related to economic organization, could promote it, while others would seal its destruction. Possessing the American standard would enable the worker to fight injustice in the form of low wages and long hours, just as virtue enabled the artisan to fight it in other forms, such as the concentration of political power. An unjust economy, however, would prevent perpetuation of the American standard. Like virtue, it was a quality reciprocally linked to economic and political life. Its presence was a symbol of a healthy republic, its absence a telltale sign of danger. As the labor leaders who contributed to the *Voice of Labor* noted: "The wage earners' standard of living, which rests so largely upon the wages received and upon the hours of labor, determines the physical, mental and moral foundations of the masses upon which the structure of American institutions must rest."[17]

Another political aspect of the American standard was the connection it drew between high wages and national identity. Whereas previously, labor leaders had distinguished the United States from other countries by the sovereignty of its large class of small producers, in the late nineteenth century they began to maintain that America's high standards set it apart. According to this new category of "American exceptionalism," it was the need for high wages and the ability to consume which properly distinguished Americans from others. George Gunton, for example, drew a distinction between "stupefied peasants who have no new wants" and American workers with their "multiplication of wants and tastes." The "American mechanic" George McNeill described had "a parlor with a carpet on it, a mantelpiece with ornaments on it, pictures on the wall, books on the tables, kitchens with facilities" — amenities that even the "comfortable" of Europe did not possess. American republican institutions rested on a broad bed of affluence and taste, and those with lower standards of living, claimed Ira Steward, were "eminently un-American."[18] Refusing to submit to low wages (as if there were an element of choice in this submission) became understood as an act of national and cultural self-definition.

The flipside of this nationalism was a fear of those perceived as having "lower" standards. This fear often took on racist, sexist, and nativist overtones. Proponents based national health on the American standard and interpreted lower standards as a grave danger to the country. If the "standard of living is the measure of civilization," Frank Foster wrote in 1900, low standards threatened civilization. "The low standard of living has produced the degradation of labor witnessed among the Orientals," noted the contributors to the *Voice of Labor*, selecting the group most frequently denounced for threatening the standard by replacing the American worker with "brutes." They equated brutishness and despotism with the low standard of living and thus highlighted the danger to the republic. "If this standard is lowered," they concluded, "American citizenship would be debased."[19]

Once the American standard was defined as a quality ingrained in white male wage earners through years of cultural habit, it became easy for these workers to find others lacking in the acculturation and genetic makeup necessary to maintain such standards. The American standard was used not only to separate the United States from other countries but to promote a hierarchy within the country. Organized workers wielded the standard against immigrants, blacks, and women as often as they did against stingy employers.

Race, Gender, and Identity

James Duncan, a leader of the Granite Cutters' National Union and a vice-president of the AFL, revealed a great deal about the nature of the American standard when he defined the living wage as a "rate of wage sufficient to permit the maintenance and progressive improvement of the American Standard of Living in the group to which the worker belongs." By assuming a multiplicity of "American standards," Duncan acknowledged what many trade unionists tried to conceal: that they were willing to accept a variety of standards, reserving the pinnacle of the American standard for white, male, trade unionists. Below were ranged the standards acceptable for women, African Americans, immigrants, and unskilled workers. One 1925 study titled, *Social and Economic Standards of Living* was explicit about this hierarchy. It contained chapters contrasting the American standard of living with the "Immigrant," the "Feminine," and even the "Rural" standard of living.[20]

Understanding of the American standard was somewhat tautological: the only way to achieve it was through high wages, but the only way to gain such wages was to possess high standards. McNeill expressed this ambiguity well: "Those who have the least want the least, those who have more want more; in this fact is the hope of the labor movement." This vision of the labor movement was hardly inclusive, for it refused to admit those judged as having too few wants into the house of labor. In like manner, George Gunton explained the standard of living as a function of national cultures. "The standard of living in any community will be high or low . . . as the number of the daily wants of the people is large or small. It is lower in Asia than in Europe, lower in Europe than in America . . . for the reason that the wants of people in the former places are fewer and simpler than those of the latter." According to his model, only those with high standards could hope to improve their lot. Others would forever be locked into a cycle of low wants and low wages. "An American will starve or strike rather than accept Chinese wages," wrote Gunton, "because the

American standard of living demands higher wages," but the "Chinaman receives low wages because he will live in a low way." Gunton perceived isolation from the market as a mark of primitive society, as in "darkest Africa, in Asia . . . or in the Southern states of America." Conversely, he believed that market relations and high levels of consumption signaled modern civilization.[21]

The American standard provided workers, especially trade unionists, with a discourse about politics and civilization which served their specific interests even as it invoked universal values. According to its logic, those who were civilized became increasingly so through higher wages, but the uncivilized were not equipped for a high standard of living and would either fritter away their wages or hoard them unnecessarily. The quality that made the American standard possible — a mindset disposed to think in terms of consumerism and ever-increasing levels of wealth — had different meanings for different groups. Without character and trade unions, these forces would be improperly assimilated and would not translate into a high standard of living.

In 1897 Henry White connected the consumerist logic with exclusion in his plea for immigration restriction. "Production has increased many fold, but the consuming power of the people . . . is not sufficient to buy what has been made, hence overproduction." Instead of stopping at this standard trade union explanation of the consumerist basis of economic life, White went on to lay out the other half of the equation. Underconsumption, he suggested, could only be stopped by eliminating the underconsuming immigrant. "The struggle of the wage workers for a higher living . . . is rendered more desperate by the constant addition of others . . . who, accustomed to lower standards of living, make possible the sweat-shop and the slum."[22] In this interpretation, the weak character of immigrants, reinforced by the low wages they would inevitably receive, could make the American standard of living unreachable for all. Under these circumstances, the standard became as much a pipedream as the search for virtue in a despotic polity.

In keeping with their new political economy, workers grounded their critique of groups that threatened the American standard in the realm of leisure rather than productive labor. White workers routinely conceded that the Chinese worked hard and competently; it was in the area of leisure that they found them deficient. "While the Chinaman works industriously enough, he consumes very little, either of his own production or of ours," declared Samuel Gompers and a union colleague in a 1906 anti-Chinese pamphlet tellingly titled *Meat vs. Rice: American Manhood against Asiatic Coolieism. Which Shall Survive?* They claimed that "the white laboring man . . . is injured in his comfort, reduced in his scale of life and standard of living, necessarily carrying down with it his moral and physical stamina." The title of one section of the pamphlet, "Asiatic Labor Degrades as Slave Labor Did" suggests that trade unionists treated the subversion of the American standard as the moral equivalent of slavery. Similarly, while granting that the Chinese were "tireless" workers, a San Francisco newspaper criticized them in 1901 for their "mean-living": "They present the American workingman with the alternative of committing suicide or coming down to John Chinaman's standard of wages and living."[23] In this scenario, maintaining the American standard was literally a matter of life or death for white workers.

Labor leaders claimed that workers could not compete with groups that possessed lower standards without threatening the foundation of the republic. They often framed this argument in racial terms. "It is an insult to the respectability and manhood of an American to expect him to compete in the labor market with the heathen of Asia," declared two members of the Knights of Labor. "Such competition is an utter impossibility" since no "American can offer to work for wages so low that the Chinese will not bid lower." The "caucasians," Samuel Gompers bluntly wrote in 1905, "are not going to let their standard of living be destroyed by negroes, Chinamen, Japs, or any others." In 1885 an article in *John Swinton's Paper* declared Chinese standards a threat to American workers: "Does any one class imagine it can compete with men who live like vermin, whose families cost nothing, and whose food and clothing are but nominal in cost?" In contrast, "American" workers defined themselves by their elegant lifestyle and expansive purchasing habits. The article argued that, because of their low standards, the Chinese would never Americanize.[24] The Chinese Exclusion Act of 1882 ensured that they never would.

The American standard enabled white male workers to refashion themselves as wage-earning citizens and gave them a means to declare others unfit for membership in the polity. In an open letter "To the Friends of Labor Everywhere," a San Francisco labor organization castigated the Chinese for defying "white Christian" labor's economic and political understandings. They were, this group insisted, antirepublican, uninterested in freedom, and ignorant of the meaning of citizenship: "They come here more as slaves than anything else . . . robbing their fellow man of his just heritage, — the right to live in a decent manner, and to raise his children to become useful citizens of this republic."[25]

A central component of the Chinese slavishness was the inability to consume properly. It was a portent of a new kind of critique of the labor movement when Thomas Armstrong, a Pennsylvania labor radical, condemned the Chinese in 1876 because they were not "true consumers." Whereas American workers understood the significance of circulating their money, according to the San Francisco workers, the Chinese "take out of circulation daily the sum of seventy-five thousand dollars. . . . They trade and traffic entirely with themselves. They spend none of the money they earn with the white merchants of the city. They import most of the articles they use." The article continued: "It is madness for the white to think of competing with them. . . . They can live on five cents a day; they eat rice and the offal of the slaughter-houses and we are inclined to think they eat something worse in the shape of vermin." A St. Louis labor newspaper declared: the "Chinaman hoards his money; he is of no benefit to the community, morally, socially, or financially."[26] According to this argument, the Chinese worked for less because they were willing to spend less, not vice versa. In other words, Chinese standards were not a result of low wages but rather a cause of them.

Although proponents of the American standard emphasized the importance of cultivating desires, they did not believe that all desires were equal. They praised the practical over the sensual, the respectable over the rough. They distrusted most popular amusements, believing that they would destroy the good character necessary for the preservation of civil society. Ira Steward condemned leisure entrepreneurs who "minister to human follies and vices," especially those who "sell rum, print dime novels, race horses or play base ball for a living." Rather than praise the saloon as the site of a working-class culture of mutualism, like many native-born labor reformers he considered "inebriated or dissipated laborer" a detriment to the labor movement. "The cheap and contemptible amusements of the poor," Steward lamented, sounding like a nineteenth-century member of the Frankfurt School, "are their wretched attempts to forget." Workers seeking such amusements, he complained, "are not sufficiently ambitious to agitate for anything"; they "attend the circus, but never go to labor meetings; and are generally ready to take the strikers vacant places." Truly class-conscious workers, according to Steward, put their wealth to its "highest moral uses."[27]

It was not simply needs in general, then, but "civilized" needs—often defined by a gender-conscious vision of domesticity—that characterized the American standard. Following Steward's example, Gunton argued that the home, not the saloon or the whorehouse, should be the "focal point" of consumption. The manly American worker, in this view, stood for respectable, rather than profligate, consumption through the framework of the patriarchal family. The San Francisco labor leader W. W. Stone, for example, contrasted the breadwinning needs of whites and Asians to show that domestic tastes created an unbridgeable gap between the two groups: "The caucasian must add to his own individual needs the cost of maintaining a wife and family. There is rent to pay, clothing to be provided, books to buy, and, added to all this, the many little wants that arise out of the conditions of a Christian civilization." In contrast, critics charged, the Chinese had few wants and no nuclear family to speak of. Chinese workers, Stone wrote, "content with a fractional interest in the body of a female slave," did not share the "Caucasian family's" faith in domesticity. The American standard was linked to a vision of a well-nourished, respectable family life. Ownership of a whole woman cemented this patriarchal family structure. "The conditions of life in America and Asia are so entirely different that the laboring men of the two continents can never meet on an equal footing," declared two San Francisco workers. "The American has a home and a family to support. . . . The Chinese in San Francisco and California are not hampered by any such social duties and social obligations and social necessities. They have no homes and families."[28] Lacking the personal and familial impetus to consume, the Chinese represented the antithesis of the American standard.

The Chinese were not the only group vilified for violating the logic of the American standard through excessive thrift, cheap taste, and a lack of family values. "The Dago . . . lives far more like a savage or a wild best than the Chinese" and therefore can "underbid the American workingman," declared Eugene Debs in 1891. "In respect to economy and frugality they greatly resemble the Chinese," noted the Democratic Party platform of 1884 in reference to South and Eastern European immigrants. "One of them will walk miles, if necessary, to a butcher's shop and carry off thankfully the offal and refuse given them." The same year, Congressman Martin Foran, the former labor leader, described Italian and Hungarian immigrants as ignorant of American economic logic: "They are brought here precisely in the same manner as the Chinese were brought here. . . . very many of them have no conception of freedom. . . . They do not know to purchase any of the luxuries which tend to elevate and enlighten people. . . . they are . . . willing slaves."[29] The rhetoric is strikingly similar: Ignorance of the newly defined consumerist boundary between freedom and slavery, inability to purchase properly, and lower standards conspired against the possibility for white native-born workers to achieve their birthright, the American standard.

The logic of the American standard propelled the critique of other groups in another direction as well. Whereas the Chinese were faulted for underconsumption, blacks were said to consume mindlessly and limitlessly.[30] The two groups represented two poles of primitivism in a modern economy: excessive self-denial and instant gratification. Either extreme would disrupt the seamless web of economic life as laid out by trade unionists, who defined their own consumption patterns as the American norm: respectable, Christian, and civilized.

A decade after his critique of Chinese underconsumption, Gompers ascribed the St. Louis Race Riots of 1917 to what he called a "clash of standards"—that is, differing patterns of consumerism. "East St. Louis became a sort of convention center for excited, undisciplined negroes who were intoxicated by higher wages than they had ever known." World War I had opened a plethora of high-wage jobs previously off-limits to black workers. The result, according to Gompers, was the natural consequence of paying high wages to workers not yet in possession the American standard: "Low wage workers found unfamiliar opportunities involving responsibilities in living and a social obligation for which they were totally unfitted by experience." However high their wages, blacks were still "low wage" workers, according to Gompers, who invoked the oft-stated belief that character preceded standards of living: "Inevitably [racial] conflict comes through a clash of standards—standards of work which means also standards of life."[31]

Women wage earners were also accused of threatening the American standard, but for reasons relating to working-class constructions of gender roles. Organized workers, experts, and politicians were united in the belief that women had fewer needs than men, and therefore a lower standard applied to them. Frequently an analogy was drawn between women untrained in the art of breadwinning and the culturally unrefined male immigrant. Whereas the immigrant had few needs because of his uncivilized culture, women did not know how to cultivate their desires because men had traditionally fulfilled them. Even though women made most purchases, it was not their job to cultivate desires. "Everywhere the laborer gets what he has learned to consume and no more," as Edwin Chamberlin put it in 1888. "It is the standard of living which determines wages. . . . That is why women get less wages than men, and children less than either. Why the wages of a family where all work is no more than that of the father when he alone labors."[32] By entering the wage labor marketplace, women endangered standards that had become second nature to their brothers, husbands, and fathers.

Yet women's low standards were not interpreted in quite the same sense as those of other groups with "degraded" standards of living. The problem was not that women had low standards but that they possessed no standard of living whatsoever. It was, after all, defined as a male quality. "Their effort to be self-supporting is of so recent an origin that a large proportion of them are satisfied if they can merely add something to the family income," wrote Henry Seager in 1913. "They have no definite, independent standard of living and consequently are contented to accept wages that lighten more of the burdens of their support for their fathers, brothers or husbands, but are pitifully inadequate for that increasing number who do not live at home or whose home conditions are such that they must contribute."[33] The qualitative definition of the American standard of living, then, squeezed women out as it did other groups, making it difficult for any of them to be recognized as even potential bearers of high standards.

With its market orientation and emphasis on consumption, the American standard of living discourse could be understood as exemplifying an apolitical, "pure and simple" American labor movement, but such an interpretation robs the discourse of its complexity. The American standard represented a modern attempt to link economics to morality and politics. Yet it is significant how little the discourse of the American standard referred to work itself. By marking consumption as the site for the development of working-class character, organized labor tried to create a new discourse of virtue, replacing a producerist republicanism with a consumerist one. In so doing, these workers emphasized the centrality of material well-being to class consciousness.

By stressing the subjectivity of standards of living, organized laborers placed themselves at the center of any consideration of the nation's political economy. Yet by promoting the idea that living standards are a function of race and gender, white male workers maintained that others were incapable of expanding their social needs and consuming respectably. By defining "American-ness" and civilization against the "other," the discourse made consumption as much a terrain of exclusion as production had ever been.

PART III

WORKERS OF THE

WORLD, CONSUME

"**T**he Consumer, of course, represents society as a whole." So M. E. J. Kelley matter-of-factly concluded her 1897 article introducing the well-to-do readership of the *North American Review* to the burgeoning working-class strategy of the "union label." Despite her use of the expression "of course," Kelley was not conveying a universally accepted idea. The producerist ideology dominant in the nineteenth-century placed the makers of useful goods at the moral and political heart of the nation. Consumers, by contrast, were generally regarded as either wasteful or extraneous to an ideal economy, since they did not produce anything of value.[1] Yet Kelley was on to something. By the late nineteenth century many workers had begun to question the privileged place of producerism and to emphasize the promise of consumption. The union label, on which Kelley reported, was one of several consumerist ideas to arise in working-class thought in the postbellum decades.

No longer treating production as singularly paramount or discrete, labor leaders began to understand the economy as a dynamic system to which both forces were essential, and they tried to understand how they were related. Some considered production and consumption equally important. George McNeill, for example, argued that the "equilibrium between production and consumption must be adjusted."[2] Increasingly, however, working-class leaders considered consumption the more important aspect of the equation, and they began to see high wages as based on consumption.[3] A statement by a Milwaukee trade union organization in 1900 reflects this consumerist turn. "Inasmuch as the means of sustaining life can only be produced by labor, it follows that labor . . . constitutes the true measure of value," the statement began, adopting a position consistent with the tradition of producerist rhetoric. But in fleshing out the practical meaning of labor value, it drifted far from conventional notions of producerism:

> To make this measure of value . . . requires that the people should be organized in their capacity as consumers. . . . It is the consumer who is the real employer of the producer, and whereas the producers constitute the great masses of the consumers, it does seem, from a business point of view, that they ought to be able to pay themselves at all times and under all circumstances an equitable compensation for all the services they render to society, that is to themselves.[4]

By proposing that workers organize as consumers and that, as consumers, workers could become their own "employers," this organization endorsed a new kind of class consciousness which rooted even the labor theory of value, the quintessential element of producerism, in consumption.

Workers would seem to be unlikely participants in this "consumerist turn." Lacking the financial resources of middle-class shoppers, entrepreneurs, and investors, how could workers claim special status as consumers?[5] American workers had proudly identified themselves as producers and staked political claims upon that identity, which they contrasted to the nonproduction of fops, millionaires, and bankers, who, precisely because they did not produce, had no rightful place in a republic. Prior to the consumerist turn, the celebration of producers usually involved a simultaneous condemnation of consumers. W. J. Rorabaugh writes: "Mechanics almost universally held that all wealth was created by labor . . . while merchants, attorneys, absentee owners, and others were . . . consumers of wealth who had cleverly transferred into their own pockets wealth created by others." William Sylvis, leader of the powerful Iron Moulders Union in the 1860s, contrasted manly producers with "effeminate non producers" and "consumers." Moreover, who could deny that even the hated "speculators" consumed?[6] Was it not a mistake to universalize an act that virtually defined bourgeois social practice, one for which workers could claim no special ability and which, moreover, was off limits to all but the richest workers?

Yet certain advantages accrued to these late nineteenth-century workers who began to identify themselves as consumers. Just as "producer"

could be interpreted broadly to include all but the most outlandish speculators, so too could "consumer" be inclusive while casting the laborer in
a special light. Union label campaigners claimed to be "extending democracy through purchasing power." Similarly, organized labor defended the
eight-hour day as a "right of citizenship, a concrete expression of social
equality." In addition to securing workers the full fruits of their labor, the
goal of the new consumer practices was to assure workers of a satisfying
life when not engaged in toil, and a new means to political power. "The
fact that in the end the toilers must be the great body of the consumers,
has been given little or no consideration at all," declared Samuel Gompers in 1893. "The prosperity of a nation, the success of a people, the
civilizing influence of an era, can always be measured by the comparative
consuming power of a people."[7] Gompers was not alone in developing this
class-conscious consumerist vision.

If the label "consumer" raised difficult questions of working-class identity, another thorny issue for labor was that both the shorter hour and
union label movements were products of a wage labor economy about
which some labor radicals were uneasy. Many anarchists, for example,
opposed the eight-hour movement precisely because the acceptance of
wages implied a separation — which they vehemently rejected — between
labor and capital, wage earner and owner. "To accede the point that capitalists have the right to eight hours of our labor," editorialized the Chicago anarchist newspaper *Alarm* in 1885, "is more than a compromise, it
is a virtual concession that the wage system is right." In this view, reducing the number of hours of wage labor did not make it acceptable.
"Whether a man works eight hours a day or ten hours a day, he is still a
slave" to his "capitalist masters," wrote Samuel Fielden, later notorious
as a Haymarket anarchist. As Alan Trachtenberg has noted, "The label
seemed to signify labor's willingness to accept the wage system in exchange for a secure place within the social order."[8]

As with the living wage discourse, both movements operated within the
market, rather than outside of it. In his pathbreaking interpretation of
the humanitarian sensibility, Thomas Haskell writes of "the power of
market discipline to inculcate altered perceptions of causation in human
affairs." With the rise of market culture, he argues, people became aware
of the "remote consequences of one's acts." Market man, according to
Haskell, has to "devote such close attention to the remote consequences
of the various choices before him that he lives partly in the future." Haskell's analysis provides a useful model for interpreting the union label and
eight-hour movements. Both were situated in the market and spawned

a new type of causal thinking in which consumption had far-reaching consequences.[9]

The following chapters explore these two movements as examples of organized labor's growing fascination with consumerism. Among the first working-class movements to understand the worker as inextricably connected to market culture, both treated consumption as characteristic of modern life and tried to turn it to labor's advantage. The eight-hour movement, rooted in the shorter hours movements of antebellum labor radicalism, gained momentum after the Civil War, reaching its peak as a mass movement in the 1880s and remaining a major reform goal of organized labor until the New Deal. "As the years have gone by," Samuel Gompers noted in 1915, "the eight-hour philosophy which originated in the misery and toil of workers has become an accepted principle of society and industry."[10]

The promotion of union labels by organized labor began in 1874 and quickly became a common trade union practice. By 1897 E. Lewis Evans of the Tobacco Workers Union could reel off a wide array of labeled goods marketed to trade unionists, pointing out that if workers so chose, they could supply virtually all their needs with labeled goods.

> On the garments we buy we request to be shown the tailors' or garment workers' label. We make our purchases from a clerk who carries his card ready to show that he belongs to the union of his calling. Our wives and mothers, when they want a broom, choose one which bears the . . . label. . . . When buying tobaccos, we demand of the dealers that the plug or package . . . shall bear the . . . label. When we desire to indulge in a draught of the amber fluid brewed from malt and hops, we find the brewery workers' label on the barrel or on the bottle in the case.[11]

The two movements quickly gained broad acceptance in working-class culture and transformed the meaning of class consciousness. They share parallel histories that shed light on the strengths, weaknesses, and dilemmas of working-class consumer activism.

5

Merchants of Time

"Men who are compelled to sell their labor, very naturally desire to sell the smallest portion of their time for the largest possible price," wrote George McNeill in his widely quoted 1887 discussion of the eight-hour day, *The Labor Movement: The Problem of To-day*. "They are merchants of their time." The phrase "merchants of time" conveyed McNeill's ambivalence toward wage labor. On the one hand, he was evoking the artisanal ideal of the control of time. Craftsmen frequently demonstrated their independence and "manliness" during periods of industrialization by refusing to work regular shifts. They viewed the capitalist control of time, most evident in routinized shifts and wage labor, as a degrading portent of proletarianization, which they fought by taking periodic "Saint Mondays," spontaneous drinking binges, and other unscheduled breaks. Employing a gendered rhetoric of their own as "freeborn American women," working women also fought the oppressive rhythms of industrial work.[1]

Yet the idea of "selling" time as a merchant sold wares was new, reflecting a shift, endorsed by eight-hour theorists, from the artisanal notion of skill as capital to the wage-earning notion of time as capital. In 1886, the *Knights of Labor* approvingly quoted Karl Marx's comparison of workers to salesmen in language similar to McNeill's: "You [businessmen] are continually preaching to me the gospel of 'saving' and 'abstinence.' Good! I will, like a sensible, saving business man preserve my own faculty, my labor force, and abstain from any foolish expenditure of it. . . . I demand . . . a working day of normal length . . . because I demand the value of my commodity like every other vendor." American workers echoed Marx's view that they could subvert bourgeois values by applying them to their own experience as wage laborers. "The capitalist maintains his rights as purchaser when he tries to make the working day as long as possible," noted Marx, "the laborer maintains his right as seller when he wishes to reduce the workers' day."[2] The principles of capitalism, they thought, could be turned against capitalists. The point of comparison for workers in their campaign for shorter hours was not the artisan but the capitalist, not the producer but the merchant, and not the artisanal moral economy but the market-based social economy.

Wage workers, as McNeill made clear, were "compelled" to sell their labor power; they had become "merchants" by necessity, not choice. The element of compulsion, however, did not necessarily mean that workers had no control over the exchange of time for money. This view of wage labor as entrepreneurship, with the worker acting as a sort of capitalist, was one of the recurring themes of the eight-hour movement. The goal, according to labor leaders, was to exchange labor for as much free time and money as possible. George Gunton titled one section of his eight-hour pamphlet commissioned by the AFL, "Leisure the Basis of Opportunity." Demanding as twin goals "more wages and more time, — more wages to obtain more comforts, and more time wherein to enjoy them," McNeill highlighted the consumerism at the root of the eight-hour movement. Free time and money would enable workers to consume. A successful "merchant of time," was not a "wage slave" but quite the opposite, the proud possessor of an American standard of living. "The reduction of hours of labor reaches the very root of society," declared Samuel Gompers. "It . . . makes of [the worker] what has been too long neglected — a consumer instead of a mere producer."[3]

The eight-hour movement reasserted the importance of time in working-class ideology. Some market-based interpretations of time were consistent with artisanal republican notions of leisure, according to which working citizens needed time for civic participation.[4] Others insisted upon workers' need for time to plot their emancipation. The Eight-Hour Committee of the AFL revealed a romanticized conception of this process in 1891: "The taste for freedom grows from that upon which it feeds, and would-be oppressors of labor well know that if the wage-earner is once given the time and opportunity to learn his own strength, to husband his own resources, to organize his own faculties, and to widen his own horizons, he is thereby furnished with the weapons which shall secure for him industrial emancipation." Some took a more radical view. The eight-hour day, Horatio Winslow wrote in 1911, "will give workers the time they need to think about revolution." Many labor radicals endorsed the shorter day as a first step toward the destruction of the wage system. "It is folly to speak of wiping out the wage system altogether at an early date unless we have a well fed, healthy, intelligent working class and only with short hours and good wages can such a class exist," declared the newspaper of the Cigar Makers in 1876.[5]

But the new linkage between time and politics also differed from the republican view, most crucially in the conception that workers negotiated the control of time through the market rather than outside of it. In addition, eight-hour proponents associated free time with increased consumption and stressed the economic, as well as the political, benefits of shorter hours. McNeill claimed that "leisure acts upon the minds of men and creates new wants." Free time and increased wages would allow the worker to consume, enhancing the circulation of wealth in the economy. "If the mechanic devotes the major portion of his working hours to an unvarying monotonous toil his wants are simple and his wages poor," wrote Edwin Chamberlin in 1888. "Every reduction of the hours of labor has been followed by an increase in production and consumption, that is, by an increase of wages on account of new and greater demands."[6]

The poem, "Blessings of Eight Hours," which appeared in the Garment Workers' newspaper in 1907, also connected shorter hours to material improvements:

> Eight Hours means higher wages,
> More work for willing workers,
> More hours for blissful pleasure,
> Less tramps to sell their manhood,
> Less women combatting drudgery,
> More comforts in each family . . .
> More things produced for more and better people,
> More things consumed, a greater, grander market,
> More wealth, more health, less poverty and sickness,
> A nobler manhood, woman and children glorified.[7]

The poem gives the world of consumption special privilege. With its frequent use of the word "more" (which appears seven times in ten lines), and with references to "blissful pleasure," "comforts," "things consumed," "wealth," and the "greater, grander market," the poem describes a world in which material wealth makes moral health possible.

From the beginning in the 1860s Ira Steward cast a huge shadow over both the practice and the rhetoric of the shorter hours movement. The twelve-hour days Steward logged as an apprentice machinist in the early 1850s converted him to the cause, and as a leader of the Machinists' and Blacksmiths' International Union, he helped found Boston's Eight-Hour League in 1863. Steward spent the last twenty years of his life working for shorter hours as a labor activist, pamphleteer, and lobbyist. So obsessive was his focus that his enemies in the labor movement called him an "eight hour monomaniac." But he gained a devoted following among a wide range of trade unionists and labor reformers, including Wendell Phillips, F. A. Sorge, and Samuel Gompers. George McNeill and George Gunton considered him a mentor despite his prickly personality. McNeill named a son after him and dedicated poetry to him; both men continued to work in the eight-hour movement after Steward's death.[8]

Steward was the first labor leader to abandon the view that only the destruction of the wage system could redeem the republic. He maintained that the core of the republican vision could be realized through shorter workdays and higher wages, and he believed the first step must be a legislatively enforced shortened workday.[9] Although Steward's rhetoric approached the producerist ideal, it did so in the new context of wage labor. Despite claims that the ultimate goal was to eliminate wage labor, shorter hour rhetoric was premised upon the idea of the buying and selling of labor power. Notwithstanding his qualms about the system, Steward believed that wages could be manipulated to the worker's benefit. He commented: "The wages we receive, under the present system, are not a just equivalent for our Labor. . . . From time to time Employers decide that we are making too much money. We have decided that They are making too much money! They cut down our Prices! We Shall cut down their hours!"[10]

In his most important published essay, "A Reduction of Hours an Increase of Wages" (1865), Steward declared, "As the hours are reduced, wages will increase until every producer shall receive the full value of his services."[11] Thus he did not question the moral foundation of producerism, the right of workers to the full value of their product. Nevertheless, he claimed that the dual goals of producer ideology — an equivalence between payment and product in the economic realm and respect for the worker in the social arena — were no longer feasible through artisanal production but could be attained in a wage labor economy. Whereas most labor leaders thought that a wage system would increase inequality between labor and capital, Steward believed that it was not wage labor per se but low wages that led to economic and social inequality.

Steward's pamphlet can be read as one of the first attempts to make the republican moral economy relevant to the grand army of wage earners in postbellum America—a task that became a central preoccupation of the labor movement in the late nineteenth century. Like the living wage idea, Steward's political economy legitimated wages while reinterpreting them as a measure not of production but of the consuming powers of the worker. As he put it, "More leisure will create motives and temptations for the most ordinary laborer to insist upon higher wages." The wage increase in this schema results from increased "motives" and "temptations," not from increased production. Steward invoked a nascent vision of a consumer-driven economy in which higher wages would lead to greater consumption, which in turn would drive production in an endless cycle of economic advancement. Long hours and underconsumption were the major cause of low wages, in his view. Conversely, "tempting workers through their new leisure to unite in buying luxuries now confined to the wealthy" would lead to high wages and a healthier republic.[12]

Production as Exchange

David Montgomery has argued that what made the eight-hour movement radical was its focus on production rather than distribution. Whereas populists, according to Montgomery, "located exploitation in the process of exchange of commodities," eight-hour activists, such as Steward, came closer to the fundamental source of exploitation: "the process of production itself."[13] Eight-hour proponents, however, would have rejected the distinction between exchange and production; although still understood as distinct moments in the cycle of economic life, they were being subsumed into a single circular multivariable equation, in which no one strand could be isolated. The wage earner lived within a web of related identities and activities. He or she was a worker, a producer, a merchant, a consumer, an owner of labor, a self-owner, and a citizen. Workers produced goods and sold labor power. With their free time and wages, they consumed, thereby becoming owners of labor and citizens. In this web, consumption played a singularly important role, linking workers not only to production but to public life.

This joining of production and consumption was related to a new view of economic life. Like Thomas Haskell's humanitarians, eight-hour activists believed that market transactions had a direct effect on faraway events and people. "The world has virtually become one vast community," declared Walter Logan, a proponent of shorter hours, in 1894. In

eight-hour theory, all economic actions catalyzed a chain reaction of responses, including the cultivation of tastes and the creation of wants.
Shorter hours, according to Steward, "stimulated" men "to demand
higher wages." Long hours, by contrast, had a debilitating effect on the
nation's economy and culture, since those who work too many hours refuse "to ask for anything more than will satisfy bodily necessities." Offering the example of a mechanic who labored fourteen hours a day, he
asked: "How many newspapers or books can he read? What time has he
to visit or receive visits? to take baths? to write letters? to cultivate flow-
ers? to walk with his family? Will he not be quite as likely to vote in opposition to his real interests as a favor? . . . What will he most enjoy, works
of art, or rum? Will he go to a meeting on Sunday? . . . His home means
to him his food and his bed." Gompers declared, "The cumulative effect of
improvements is cheaper and increased production, hence lower selling
prices and the benefit of all society." Thus he demonstrated the kind of
causal thinking characteristic of the consumerist turn. No longer was the
producer uncontested king of the market. The new view understood wage
earners as sellers of labor and as consumers whose actions affected the
entire economy. As a result, the lines blurred between various economic
actions.[14]

The Paradox of Shorter Hours
and Higher Wages

In the 1870s Ira Steward's wife, Mary, wrote a couplet that served for the
next several decades as a slogan of the eight-hour movement: "Whether
you work by the piece or by the day / Decreasing the hours increases the
pay." The "fundamental principle of short-time advocates" Lemuel Danryid concurred in his AFL eight-hour pamphlet, is that "wages rise as
hours are shortened."[15] Ira Steward's pamphlet, "A Decrease in Hours an
increase in Wages," articulated, in a characteristically less pithy way, the
same logic as his wife's poem.

For producerists the paradox seemed unresolvable. How could working
less increase wages, when working less meant producing less? It seemed
clear to them that the more one worked the more one earned. Eight-hour
advocates dismissed this view as "a fallacy" because it failed to take into
account the new consumerist social economy of labor, associated with
the living wage and the American standard of living discourse. "It is the
cost of living rather than the long number of hours employed which has

ever determined the standard of remuneration for labor," Danryid argued in his eight-hour pamphlet. Against the grain of producerist thought, eight-hour proponents insisted that by working fewer hours workers actually increased the value of their labor. Yet they did not reject producerism outright so much as extend its logic into the domain of wage labor. In addition to the civic benefits of leisure, fewer hours would mean that capitalists owned less of workers and therefore that workers could recapture more of themselves. George McNeill rejected economic orthodoxy: "The oft-repeated statement, that less hours of labor means less wages, is historically untrue and theoretically unsound, and is based upon a false theory of the law governing wages." Following the logic of the American standard, he invoked international comparisons to demonstrate the fallacies of the mainstream view: "If wages were regulated by the number of hours of work, then among those classes or communities where the day's work was longest, wages would be highest, and where a day's work was shortest wages would be lowest." In fact, he argued, the "reverse is true." "Civilization follows the line of less hours of daily work; and civilization simply means, materially, the highest purchasing power of a day's labor." [16] Eight-hour advocates thus modified producerism to suit a wage labor regime in which workers did not own the means of production but sold their time.

For many labor leaders, the eight-hour movement was the surest way to promote healthy wants and desires as well as the means to fulfill them: high wages. "A reduction in the hours of daily labor gives the workers the opportunity for leisure, rest, and recuperation," wrote Gompers, "and these give the further opportunity for the cultivation of better desires, improved surroundings, and the conception of a higher life; in other words, improvement in their standard of life." Shorter hours would embolden workers to resist any measure that threatened to reduce their level of respectable comfort. Gompers wrote: "The individual who works eight hours or less . . . goes to and from work when well-dressed people are on the streets. . . . He has longer time to stay at home, sees other homes better furnished, and consequently wants a better home for himself. He wants books, pictures, friends, entertainment." [17]

Respectable Desires and the Leisure Ethic

Middle-class commentators feared that working-class leisure would promote less than respectable desires. They did not see shorter hours as a way to improve civic life and the standard of living of workers; rather they feared that an overpaid, underworked proletariat would pursue the unsavory habits of drinking, whoring, and desecrating public spaces. Some upholders of high culture feared that shorter hours would promote debauchery. The New England poet James Russell Lowell, for example, predicted soon after the Civil War that shorter hours would create a "material and unideal world" that he "would not care to live in."[18] Working-class leisure looked to him like a threat to civilization.

Eight-hour advocates responded to these fears by emphasizing that workers would use their newfound freedom constructively. "The charm of the Eight hour system," Ira Steward wrote, "is that it gives time and opportunity for the ragged, the unwashed, the ignorant and ill-mannered to become ashamed of themselves and their standing in society." Given the leisure, he believed, workers would develop "ten thousand schemes for the amelioration of the condition of man." George McNeill similarly predicted "the now-dawning day [which] shall witness a well-built, fully equipped manhood, using the morning hours in the duties and pleasures of the sunlit-home; taking his morning bath before his morning work, reading his morning paper in the well-equipped reading room of the manufactory."[19]

Romantic descriptions of life after eight hours became such a staple of labor rhetoric that they can be considered a genre. Labor spokesmen tended to paint a sentimental picture of the uses of leisure, exaggerating the likelihood that workers would follow respectable pursuits. A "Stone Cutter" provided a classic example of this sentimentalizing impulse, beginning with an accurate catalog of bourgeois fears: "We learn from hundreds of Satanic newspapers that if eight hours were fixed as the length of a day's labor, the working people would not know what to do with their leisure time; they would spend it in loafing and gambling, riotings, debauchery and drunkenness, hanging around the street corners and sitting in bar-rooms drinking liquor and wasting their money." To refute the charge of debauchery, the worker described his own stereotypically respectable week. "Monday," he began nobly, "I went to the meeting at the Union; Tuesday, I was at home with a sick baby; Wednesday, I took my wife to the theatre; Thursday, I took a turn down Third Avenue with her to buy some things for the house; Friday, I called on some friends; to-night I'm in the house before going to the market, and to-morrow I'll spruce up and go to Church."[20] Such use of leisure to attend to community and family responsibilities created an image of domesticity to make Catherine Beecher proud.

Invoking a similar narrative, Terence Powderly denied the romantic view of the artisanal past so often invoked. Old-timers, he wrote, "will remember that workmen" lived slovenly lives of unremitting toil and poverty, regarding "corned beef and cabbage . . . as delicacies." With fewer hours workers "naturally acquired new tastes and habits," all respectable in Powderly's account since they fostered "home consumption and adornment."[21]

George McNeill posited a direct relationship between fewer hours and moral improvement. He declared that workers who remained "occupied in discussing the fighting merits of gamecocks or men" and who spent their "periods of rest in filth and drunkenness" would "be paid to the level that will enable the laborers to enjoy themselves in their own low condition." The goal of the eight-hour movement was to "disturb this class of men from their sottish contentment" and thereby to lift "the level of their manhood."[22]

Eight-hour rhetoric was often connected to the temperance movement and general working-class uplift. "The eight-hour work-day is more than an economic question—it can be termed a great Christian and moral one," wrote Val Fitzpatrick in the railroad workers' newspaper. "Excessive hours of labor not only stunt the intellect and the body and breed disease, but burden and becloud that spiritual, rational and immortal part in man which distinguishes him from brutes—the soul."[23]

The debate about shorter hours and respectability reflected the fear prevalent in the late nineteenth century that working-class libido threatened civilization. Both workers and reformers agreed on the need to channel dangerous desires. Whereas some middle-class Americans believed that increased leisure and wages would spur such urges, organized labor argued that they were caused by overwork and underconsumption. The eight-hour movement sought to take the (male) worker out of the factory and put him in the home, the church, and the store, where he would contribute to the nation's economy, civil society, and moral life. Union labels provided another means to channel consumption toward respectability and class consciousness.

6

Producers as Consumers

With the eight-hour movement, trade unionists began to think about the market as a tool workers could use to strengthen themselves rather than an enemy bent on stripping their power away. The union label movement took this rethinking a step farther. As Edgar Perkins, the president of the Indiana State Federation of Labor declared in 1897, the union label "makes it possible for us to use our power as consumers, a force that can be wielded to incalculable benefit." Capitalizing on their newfound appreciation of the market, union labelists organized their collective consuming power. With the union label, wrote John Mitchell, "the power of the workingman as a consumer was enlisted in support of his demands as a producer."[1]

The union label movement did not share the noble origins of the living wage and eight-hour movements. Its roots lie closer to those of that more morally ambiguous working-class consumerist notion, the American standard of living. The union label began in 1874 as part of the anti-Chinese movement when white cigar makers in California used it to distinguish their product from that of "Coolie labor." As in the American standard of living discourse, the focus of the union label was consumption rather than production. White workers rarely criticized the quality of the product produced by Chinese workers; instead, they blamed the "coolies" for accepting "starvation wages" and for "hoarding money" through underconsumption. The union label represented a "question of race," noted John Graham Brooks, since "all a priori theories of liberty and brotherhood yield quickly before the actual competition of different standards of living in a common market." Union labelists summed up these complaints in the claim that their Chinese competitors did not, and could not, possess such an "American" worldview.[2]

The white cigar makers encouraged all white San Franciscans, especially trade unionists, to aid them by purchasing only white-labeled cigars. The reward for such consumption would be the maintenance of living wages for white workers and the unemployment, and ultimate exodus, of their Chinese competitors. Cigar makers should not have to "live like coolies," declared William Wolz, the leader of the San Francisco union, in 1878, noting that working-class consumers had great power to "redeem" the cigar makers' trade by "creating demand" and compelling manufacturers to employ white labor. In an essay that took second place in a contest sponsored by the AFL in 1904, P. H. Shevlin wrote that the label would help the "purchaser discriminate between a union cigar, manufactured under sanitary conditions, and the rat-shop, coolie-made, filthy product."[3]

Born as a trade union strategy, the union label also served an important ideological function: it reconstructed artisanal values for a modern wage economy. The union label provided a way to ensure through consumption the qualities that "producers" demanded: self-ownership, ethical exchange, decent working conditions, and good remuneration. Artisans generally fought for these at the point of production; the union label was aimed at the point of consumption. Within a few decades, the act of purchasing union label products took on the significance previously granted only to shop-floor actions.

Yet there was an inherent conflict in working-class consumerist tactics, which John Mitchell inadvertently expressed when he noted that workers "are interested as producers in obtaining as high wages as possible; as consumers in being charged reasonable prices."[4] How could workers reconcile their desire to buy the cheapest products possible with their recognition that proper consumption was an act of working-class solidarity? Working-class women, charged with the dual tasks of managing the household budget economically and supporting trade unionists through the purchase of labeled products, bore the brunt of this dilemma. Market-based solidarity, however powerful a weapon, bore the seeds of its own destruction.

Purchasing as Employing

If the eight-hour movement showed that producers understood themselves to be consumers as well, the union label movement demonstrated that consuming workers thought of themselves as producers, owners, and employers of labor, even though they did not own the means of production. Walter Macarthur, a member of the Coast Seamen's Union and the winner of the AFL's union label essay contest, declared that the label "constitut[es] the purchaser [as] the real employer." M. E. J. Kelley concurred: "The consumer is the real maker of goods."[5] The market had transformed the meaning of ownership for union label advocates. No longer did it connote simply owning the tools and "fruits" of production. Through consumption, they believed, self-employment, and thus self-ownership, once again became possible.

The new conception of collective self-employment treated consumer demand, not producer prerogative, as the first cause of production. Through demand, the working-class consumer—described by a Milwaukee labor organization as a "power possessing shopper"—"hired" the help to satisfy the wants. Label proponents likened this employment in familiar terms to that of an artisan hiring a journeyman to make a product, even though the "employment" was indirect, mediated by the market. In a 1907 letter about the union label, a garment worker named Bowler declared that he would refuse to purchase nonlabeled products, for to do otherwise amounted to "hir[ing] unfair help." Bowler equated purchasing a product with hiring the labor that produced it.[6]

Markedly departing from previous labor ideology, union labelists believed that consumption initiated the process through which workers became employers and, ultimately, owners of their own labor. The purchaser, whom the labor reformer Herbert Morley called the "ultimate employer," acted as owner by "creating a market for the product of the worker" through the act of buying goods. Treating the purchasing power of workers as an untapped resource, Charles Blaine, general secretary-treasurer of the Boot and Shoe Workers' Union, claimed that "every dollar spent for union label products is a dollar spent to support and increase the power of organized labor." The "wage-earners are, in a large sense, their own employers," as the *Shoe Workers' Journal* noted in 1916. "The workmen in a shoe factory, in a narrow sense, do not employ themselves, but with a proper organization of the purchasing power of all the wage earners of all trades and callings, the shoe workers, acting in concert with all their fellow-workers in other trades, would become their own employers, in a collective sense, of the shoe manufacturer for whom these particular shoe workers were working."[7] The path to "self employment" prescribed by the union label markedly differed from older understandings of the concept. The "narrow sense" of employment described by the shoe workers' newspaper would have seemed simply common sense to an earlier generation. The very basis of the wage slavery discourse had been that the wage laborer did not employ himself or herself but lived under the thumb of an employer.

According to the market-based logic of the union label, employment could no longer be limited to the workplace. The new conception of self-ownership operated not on the shopfloor but in the storefront. As the *Union Label Advocate* adjured, "You as the consumer are the employer of labor and if you have to work for wages see to it that your hard earned money is not expended to support employers who do not recognize any organization of the men they employ."[8] The union label movement enabled workers to employ their employers as well as their fellow workers. Without working-class patronage, construed as a form of self-ownership, the "real" employers were doomed. Shopping had become a class-conscious activity.

A corollary to the concept of purchasing as "hiring" was the belief that the failure to purchase labeled products resulted in the "firing" of fellow trade unionists. "Every time a union man buys an article that does not bear the union label he is throwing union men out of work," declared Earl Hoage, secretary of the Denver Union Label League. Furthermore, labelists claimed, poor purchasing habits resulted not only in the dismissal of comrades but in the hiring of enemies. As Charles Blaine wrote, "Whenever any wage earner spends a dollar of his wages for the product of non-union labor, he is employing non-unionists just as effectively as if he started an independent business of his own and actually employed people working under his personal direction." Others used blunter language. Breaking a picket line was not the only way to support "scabs"; the careless worker could inadvertently "hire" them through purchasing. Thus, the inaugural issue of the newspaper of the Union Label League of New York City declared in 1918: "When a union man buys goods without the union label he is doing just what he condemns employers for doing — employing non-union labor." Buying the right products was, by contrast, an act of solidarity. "When all the money earned by trade unionists is spent strictly for union-made products," Morley wrote, "think of the great force for good that will be thereby exerted. With the consequent greatly increased demand for such products, how much easier it would be to secure further improved conditions in all crafts . . . to what extent such a condition would tend to clarify the labor question and bring labor truly into its own."[9]

Union labels provided a way for labor to come "into its own" through consumption. If "all wage earners could be persuaded to concentrate their purchasing power on behalf of union label products," a labor newspaper claimed in 1916, "the cause of organized labor would be very materially advanced." The enormous aggregate "purchasing power" of working-class Americans made organized consumption especially important since "the wages of labor . . . constitute the great volume of the market in which the goods and wares of merchants and manufacturers are sold." The welfare of all classes depended on working-class consumption, since workers were what the Knights of Labor newspaper called the nation's "chief consumers." They were the most important, noted Gunton, "not because wage earners are better than anybody else" but because they are more numerous. Nearly three decades later John L. Lewis declared that "the purchasing power of the American masses is the pivot upon which our whole economic system turns."[10]

Positing that collective action through consumption was more effective than direct action at the point of production, union labelists encouraged and reinforced new understandings of the market and consumption. The *Shoe Workers' Journal* maintained that collective consumption through union labels could equalize power relations between employer and employee in a way no longer feasible in the productive arena.

> If the combined wage earners thought that that particular shoe manufacturer was fit to be employed by them, and if they were satisfied with his goods, they could continue to give him employment, but if they did not like his goods and were not satisfied with his general conditions they could discharge that shoe manufacturer just as easily, by withholding their patronage from his goods, as the shoe manufacturer could discharge the humblest workman in his employ.[11]

If the economy consisted, as many workers imagined, of a seamless web of buying and selling, production and consumption, the union label movement acted concretely upon this belief by claiming to turn working-class consumers (and others) into owners and employers of labor. Through the activity of shopping, the notion of proprietorship, central to antebellum labor ideology, reemerged in modern consumerist form. Fashioning a new kind of class consciousness, labelists linked purchasing to ownership and tied solidarity and independence to consumption.

Consumerist Working-Class Consciousness

"The union label . . . appears to be the only means of helping workers in the factories to help themselves," wrote John Graham Brooks in an 1898 article for the journal of the Department of Labor. Brooks's comment, written barely two decades after the birth of the label, revealed the extent to which consumerist thinking had affected working-class consciousness. For factory workers to "help themselves," said Mitchell, it was necessary for them to organize "as consumers just as they have already organized as producers." Ida Van Etten told the AFL convention in 1890, "It is one of the most imperative duties of the working people that they awake to a sense of their responsibilities as consumers."[12] Buying union label goods was the foremost of these consumer responsibilities.

The conception of purchasing as collective self-ownership promoted by label proponents provoked a more general rethinking of the meaning of class consciousness. Consumerist approaches came to supplement, if not replace, point-of-production strategies. Robert Hunter argued in 1916 that traditional working-class values could best be promoted through consumption. "Workers must stand by each other, believe in each other, work with each other and love each other in the shop," he began, repeating the classic expressions of producerist culture. Yet the rest of the sentence added a new twist to the meaning of solidarity: "But there must also be unity where they go to the grocer or the clothier."[13] This was a unity based in all corners of the web of market relations.

Hunter was hardly unique in his view that to disregard aggregate power at the cash register was to negate the power of shopfloor solidarity. Union labelists viewed shopping as a new and powerful form of class expression. According to Hunter, labor needed a philosophy of spending to complement its philosophy of production, a consumerism to work in tandem with producerism, since "union men of this country as a body spend no less than $1,500,000,000 a year to purchase the necessities of life." Workers who proudly paid union dues but unthinkingly shopped at non-union stores more than negated their dues: "Today union men often spend $40 a month to destroy unionism where they give $1 a month to build up unionism." With each penny spent, workers either aided themselves or abetted the enemy. Spending, for these union labelists, was a zero-sum game; as Morley put it, "Every cent spent by a union man is . . . spent in the employment of some kind of labor." Workers, wrote Hunter, must support the right kind: "Every dollar of that immense sum that is spent for non-union goods is spent to break down the unions." He juxtaposed the new pole of working-class activism to the old: "If the union men bought right, they would not have to strike so much."[14]

The union label promoted an altered conception of working-class duty. In the process, what David Montgomery has called "mutualism" — namely, traditional codes of honor governing workers' relations with one another—began to be applied to consumption. The union label, wrote Matthew Woll, was a "constant reminder of common interest and common duty," not solipsistic but communal.[15]

The kinds of coercion long used to enforce solidarity in the workplace began to be applied at the cash register as well. Evoking older codes of masculine honor before a Senate committee in 1901, Samuel Gompers called the purchasing of union label goods an "unwritten law." In 1918 Peter J. Brady, president of the New York State Allied Printing Trades Council, applied standards of mutualism to shopping and decried improper spending as traitorous. Edward Spedden, in a study of the union label, concurred that a large part of the movement's success rested on traditional forms of trade union coercion applied to new contexts. He described coercion among union members that seemed no different from the more familiar images of, say, forcing an open union vote or intimidating a fellow worker into joining the picket line. Socially oriented consumption had become central to the "creed of trade unionism."[16]

The union label represented a socially oriented approach to the market. As a turn-of-the-century union label organization in Philadelphia put it, "You are your brother's keeper to the extent of your purchasing power. Every cent you spend for bread, for instance, can become a potential demand for better conditions for one of the most oppressed class of workers—the bakers." Solidarity could not be abandoned in the "hardcash fight of the open market." Label proponents repeatedly reminded workers of the need to be "consistent," that is, to act class consciously when consuming.[17]

Nowhere was the producerist meaning of class consciousness challenged more cogently than in the newspaper published by the New York City Union Label League. Each issue of the *Union Label Advocate* contained a cartoon that drove home the same point: old-fashioned producerist class consciousness, if practiced in isolation from the newly discovered consumerism, was not only irrelevant but downright harmful to the cause of labor. Class consciousness must be consistent on the shop floor and at the cash register. One cartoon, for example, depicts a union meeting of seemingly class-conscious workers (fig. 3). A sign bearing the old aphorism "United We Stand, Divided We Fall" hangs on the wall. The second panel contains a hint of change; a sign in the background reads, "In Union There is Strength—Demand the Union Label." Otherwise, the scene evokes class-conscious producerism. Yet when the workers are forced as an act of class solidarity to discard all their non-union-label clothing, nearly every one at the meeting winds up covered only with a

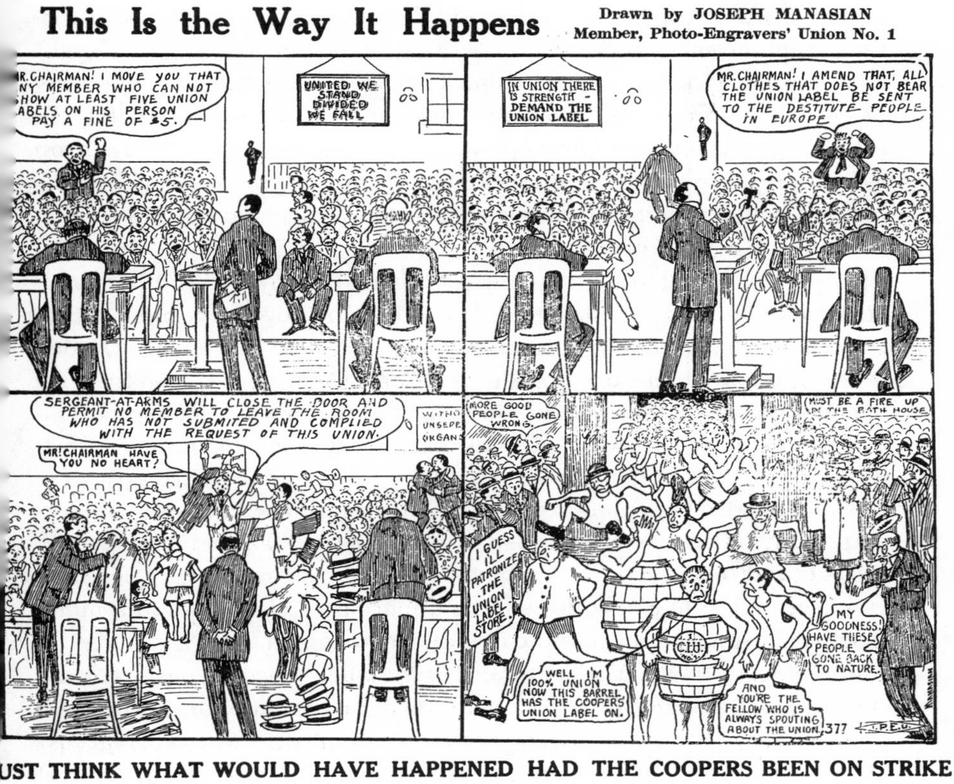

Figure 3. Joseph Manasian of the Photo-Engravers' Union No. 1, "This Is the Way It Happens," *Union Label Advocate* (March 1920), 8. Courtesy Tamiment Institute Library, New York University

barrel. Workers are literally stripped bare before the power of consumption. Another cartoon demonstrates that buying goods made in "scab" factories would negate even unanimous strike votes, whereas patronizing union label stores might altogether obviate the need for strikes (fig. 4). Another points out that fair employers cannot continue to employ union workers if no one buys their goods (fig. 5). Once again, solidarity at the point of production meant nothing unless it was accompanied by consistency at the point of consumption.

Proponents frequently compared the label to the boycott, another popular form of consumer radicalism.[18] Whereas the boycott punished merchants who refused to abide by union principles, the label rewarded those who sold union-made products. If the boycott represented the stick of consumer ostracism, the union label was the carrot of consumer patronage. Both rested on a conception of the market as an arena in which workers could reward or punish, and proponents treated the two strategies as flipsides of the same coin. "When a man, whether he be a workman or any other consumer, insists upon a label," John Mitchell wrote, "he is boycotting every article which does not bear that label." The union label seemed to many workers to be a more positive option, and many labor spokesmen hoped it would make boycotts unnecessary. In his prize-winning essay, Walter Macarthur called the label "powerful because it accomplishes by peaceful means, with absolute certainty and little cost, that which the strike and boycott seek to accomplish, always at great cost and sacrifice and often without apparent results." "Since the union label has come so generally into use," E. Lewis Evans noted, "the boycott, while necessary at times in urgent cases in conjunction with the label, is becoming obsolete."[19] This was the difference between rewarding your friends and punishing your enemies.

Despite its emphasis on consumerism, the union label did not completely sunder the essential working-class connection to production. The movement did not promote consumption for its own sake but tied necessary consumption to working-class interests. Union label proponents argued that solidarity had to be maintained on all fronts if it was to be meaningful.

Gender and Working-Class Agency

At the turn of the century, workers were not the only group to organize as consumers. Middle-class consumer organizations such as the National

This Is the Way It Happens

Drawn by JOSEPH MANASIAN
Member, Photo-Engravers' Union No. 1

Demand the Union Label and Patronize Union Stores, Thereby Keeping Union Factories Running Full Blast and Making Strikes Unnecessary

Figure 4. Joseph Manasian of the Photo-Engravers' Union No. 1, "This Is the Way It Happens," *Union Label Advocate* (January 1920), 8. Courtesy Tamiment Institute Library, New York University

Figure 5. Joseph Manasian of the Photo-Engravers' Union No. 1, "This Is the Way It Happens," *Union Label Advocate* (September 1920), 8. Courtesy Tamiment Institute Library, New York University

Consumers League also flourished.[20] Noting the support that middle-class Americans had often provided workers in the nineteenth century, John Mitchell advocated strategic alliances with sympathetic consumers.[21] Writing in the *American Federationist*, Frances Williamson also counseled coalition building. We "must enlist the buyers," that is, the general public, to "turn on the current of purchasing power." Williamson assumed that the bulk of these buyers would be women.[22]

The union label muddied the waters of traditional working-class rhetoric, making it hard to distinguish fundamental acts of class consciousness from those which were merely ancillary. In July 1920, for example, the *Union Label Advocate* admonished, "Demand the Union Label—Do Your Duty as a Union Man." It was a new conception of duty—not striking or fighting for control of the means of production but proving one's manhood through class-conscious shopping. This reconceptualization of agency and power in working-class life had gendered ramifications, since women were seen in the social division of labor as consumers and men as producers.[23] A headline in the *Union Label Advocate* in March 1920—"To the Consuming Public, All Organized Labor and All Fair Minded Housewives"—encapsulated one of the problematic aspects of consumerist class consciousness. By sandwiching "organized labor" between two other constituencies, consumers and housewives, the headline implied that male wage earners could not go it alone. They must have the support of consumers, housewives, and others outside the domain of male shopfloor culture.

If consumption was the defining activity of the workers, did women not have a major role to play in labor success? Invoking a traditional dichotomy, one cartoon in the *Union Label Advocate* expressed this problem by showing how women's consumption was as important to the labor movement as men's production (fig. 6). The cartoon offers a critique of the hypocritical union man who continues to buy nonunion products, while his wife dutifully shops at the union store. Its critique of male incompetence at the point of consumption lauded women's ability to consume in a class-conscious manner and at the same time revealed anxiety that "feminine" traits might become more central to the labor movement than "masculine" ones. Union labelists often noted that women controlled the purse strings of labor's vast aggregate wealth and therefore had a crucial role to play in promoting the new class consciousness.[24] Union men, concerned about the prospect of increasing female power in the labor movement, developed two conflicting images of working-class women: as dependent on men and as controllers of men. "Union men's wives, mothers,

This Is the Way It Happens

Drawn by JOSEPH MANASIAN
Member, Photo-Engravers' Union No. 1

CONSISTENCY THOU ART A JEWEL

Figure 6. Joseph Manasian of the Photo-Engravers' Union No. 1, "This Is the Way It Happens," *Union Label Advocate* (February 1920), 8. Courtesy Tamiment Institute Library, New York University

and daughters above all others must know that they are the direct beneficiaries of the [union label]," noted Gus Burquist in 1917. "They cannot
help but know that if it were not for the unions the breadwinners of the
nation would not be receiving one-half of the wages which they are now
paid."[25] Although dependent on the male breadwinners' earnings, they
also, through consumption, determined the size of the pay packet.

One strategy to overcome gender anxiety was belittlement. A cartoon
in the *Union Label Advocate* inadvertently revealed the anxiety of male
workers toward those outside of their sex and class (fig. 7). A woman reformer, dressed in frumpy do-gooder attire, complete with horn-rimmed
glasses, unfashionable hat, and drab coat, is put in her place by a union
man. The mild ridicule of a middle-class woman, a type usually seen as a
representative of mainstream consumption, forms a pointed contrast to
the portrayal of the men's self-assurance about consumption. By describing male working-class tastes as superior to female middle-class tastes,
moreover, the cartoon undermined the idea that consumption was a
realm outside the purview of the typical male worker.

But more often ambivalence rather than belittlement reigned. An article in the *Union Label Advocate* of March 1920, reflecting this confusion,
valorized male workers as the chief agents of working-class activism. The
action it advised them to take, however, was far from traditional: "Fellow
workers have your wives, mothers and sisters give a square deal and receive a square deal by demanding the union show card of the butchers."
The article implied that working-class men could aid the cause by insisting that their female relatives shop properly.

Labelists struggled to find ways to make label activism reinforce rather
than subvert gender roles. But in so doing, they reflected the gender ten-
sions inherent in this new class consciousness. Walter Macarthur commented, for example, "The instincts of woman and the interests of labor
are conjoined in the union label." Women, Macarthur suggested, are
natural born consumers, who could initiate male unionists in the mysteries of consumption. "Who have the largest per cent of [purchasing]
power in hand?" asked Frances Williamson. "Those who buy the children's clothes, the family groceries, and other supplies. Who else, then,
but the wives, daughters and sisters of labor union men should lead in
establishing this reform?" According to Williamson, a woman's job was
"simply to ask for and purchase none other than goods bearing the workers' guarantee that the right to sanitary condition and living wages were
respected in the making." The success of the union label, in this view,
depended upon the purchasing choices of women. Although they hoped

This Is the Way It Happens

Drawn by JOSEPH MANASIAN
Member, Photo-Engravers' Union No. 1

WE POSITIVELY AGREE WITH THE LAST SPEAKER

Figure 7. Joseph Manasian of the Photo-Engravers' Union No. 1, "This Is the Way It Happens," *Union Label Advocate* (April 1920), 8. Courtesy Tamiment Institute Library, New York University

to reinforce traditional gender roles, label advocates of necessity stressed the centrality of women to the success of the movement. As one proponent claimed: "We want [women] to be union purchasers and large purchasers, that is to say, we want to earn the highest wages."[26] However reluctantly, labelists ceded a central element of activism to working-class women.

If the main task of the labor movement was to "create demand" and to consume wisely in addition to acting at the point of production, how could the sexual division of working-class agency stand? "Housekeepers have it in their power to make or unmake the bakers, broom-makers, and a host of other trade unions," declared M. E. J. Kelley, assigning to women the power to support or destroy organized labor. She urged women to use their power wisely "to help create a demand for union labels by refusing to wear shoes, hats, collars, cuffs or coats or trousers which do not carry on them the union workman's guarantee of fair making." Treating consumption as the motor of economic life and the key to trade union success brought women's activities to the fore.[27]

Despite this rhetoric, trade unionists generally relegated women's purchasing to a secondary category. Even as labelists acknowledged the significance of women's consumption, they stressed the power of men to force women under their control to purchase properly. The label, declared P. H. Shevlin, "seeks to enlist woman as the chief auxiliary."[28] Similarly, the *Shoe Workers' Journal* noted in 1916 that "we must support all forms of auxiliary movements that are calculated to assist in strengthening the union cause," and it singled out for special mention the Women's Trade Union League.[29]

If purchasing was a form of employment and women did the bulk of the shopping, then it was women who most directly faced the problem of making consumption the bulwark of the labor movement. Which behavior brought more financial reward: stretching a husband's paycheck as far as possible or loyally purchasing labeled goods? Union label organizations, fully aware of the importance of managing the family budget, urged union women to eschew cheap, unlabeled products. "'Bargains' are usually the product of the sweatshop," warned a Duluth labelist. "Don't imagine that your tastes are so refined that you cannot satisfy them with labeled articles," chastised another labor newspaper. Although acknowledgments of women's importance were a standard part of the union label rhetoric, a good deal of attention was focused on women's failure to meet their responsibility. Laurel Koster, an organizer for the Woman's Label League, noted that workers tended to blame "scabs" when the root of many problems at the workplace should also be assigned to "the woman who is either too careless or indifferent to demand the label on all the food and clothing she purchases for her family." Women were seen as potential agents of subversion. Is it any wonder that, as Dana Frank has shown, working-class women never fully embraced the union label strategy?[30]

Ethical versus Free Consumption

Advocates saw the label as a way to reconnect ethics and economics by providing consumers with a tool to improve the working conditions of those who made the goods they bought. In his 1898 report on the union label, John Graham Brooks viewed the ethical possibilities with enthusiasm. The label, he wrote, "promises a quiet adjustment, through business methods, of these ethical difficulties which are now troubling the minds of consumers." In a modern industrial economy, John Mitchell agreed, "the label makes the consumer for the first time a responsible agent capable of passing judgement and knowing good from evil." Conversely, declared the Reverend William White, the consumer "is morally answerable for insufficient wages in proportion to his power to make reasonable effort towards bettering them." It was incumbent on working-class consumers to be good "employers," thereby assuring living wages to their "employees." M. E. J. Kelley believed that conscientious consumption would lead to concrete changes in the workplace. Ultimately, she expected "the ethical sense of the community" to become "so highly developed" that "the sweatshop will disappear." Although consumers no longer bought goods directly from craftsmen, the productive process did not have to remain hidden. The union label would enable consumers "to meet a desire for some guarantee that the articles are what they are represented to be." The label, she predicted, would "bring an ethical element into economic transactions."[31]

In an age in which producers and consumers rarely experienced face-to-face contact, advocates expected the label to reinstate this connection. "In the simpler economic relations of the middle ages when the consumer usually dealt directly with the market of the goods he bought, the obligation to pay a price that would cover fair wages was easily perceived and acknowledged, but the complicated mechanism of modern industry obscures this obligation and divides responsibility," noted William White. Ethics did not have to be sacrificed at the altar of the market, however, wrote Walter Macarthur, since the label would allow "every good citizen" to practice morality and honesty through consumption.[32]

George Gunton was of an entirely different mind. He disliked precisely what many union label proponents praised: that the label put "ethical considerations prominently into their bargain-making." Gunton feared the ramifications of injecting morality into economic transactions. "The union label asks us individually to go around inquisitorially into the shops and do two things at once, buy our goods and inquire into the economic conditions under which they were produced," he wrote in 1899. "That is taking away the freedom of the purchaser."[33]

These competing views reflected a dispute about the role of the consumer in market society. For supporters, the union label evoked an earlier era of face-to-face economic transactions and restored the transparency that characterized the artisanal economy. Others thought the mysteries of the market redounded to the benefit of working-class consumers. Through his support of eight hours and high wages, Gunton promoted policies that would enable workers to purchase more. He remained unalterably opposed to the idea that workers should tamper with the gears of consumer capitalism, criticizing the "obnoxious inquisitorial function [of] demanding the history of every article [one] buys." Gunton believed it to be "almost impossible to make the consumer in his capacity as a consumer, to be a reformer, a trade unionist, and a legislator." Rejecting the consumer surveillance promoted by many union labelists, he proposed a vision of separate economic spheres in which workers acted as producers when working and consumers when shopping. What would help consumers most, he believed, were abundant cheap goods and the money and time to enjoy them. Gunton disliked the coercive aspect of the label because he believed that it interfered with the workings of the market. The duties of the worker were rigidly circumscribed: "to fight for his wages . . . [and] to see that all industries are organized." Consumers, in his view, had an equally important countervailing agenda. It is "the consumer's interest," he argued, "whether he is a member of a labor union or not, to buy everything where he can to the best advantage."[34]

Workers deserved every opportunity to participate in the game of consumption, Gunton believed, but they had no right to change the rules. If the rules were not set by the market, "uneconomic conditions" in which "freedom does not and cannot exist" would prevail. Consumption must operate freely within a large population of consumers looking for the best price. Gunton was not blind to workplace abuses and believed that the populace should promote good conditions and unions; he went so far as to call it the "duty of the consumer, as a citizen" to do so — but only as a citizen, not as a consumer. The "real way to improve the laborer's wage is not to go and wrangle at the counter. . . . It is too late then; we must help the laborer before his product gets to the counter."[35]

Others agreed that the union label movement was misguided. From a middle-class perspective, Starr Hoyt Nichols concurred with Gunton's assessment of its likely success. "Not one consumer in a thousand," Nichols maintained, "would ever buy an article" on the basis of how the workers who made it were treated. "The consumer buys because he wants the thing he purchases, and because he is satisfied with its quality and price." Ethical considerations were irrelevant to the shopper, who "no more thinks of asking how its maker lives than he thinks of asking about the living of the farmer of whom he buys his wheat, or the condition of the men who grew his sugar or tea." Even if shoppers wanted to base purchases on such considerations, the modern market made it virtually impossible to do so: "Such inquiries reach too far beyond the possible circle of business activities to be prescribed to any great extent. One has too much to do to keep one's own conditions satisfactory to oneself to ask about the concerns of people who make his soap and shoes and hats. . . . nor could any society or union . . . make sure . . . that all kinds of goods were produced under conditions the best for their producers." The "circle" of economic life had become so unwieldy that the attempt to understand all aspects of it was as impractical as it was unwise. It was unrealistic to expect consumers to make sure that producers were well paid, especially since "high prices have never been a public craving, and never will be." Furthermore, consumerist do-gooders were "not heeding the needs of workmen who cannot be employed at such rates because they are not worth them."[36]

Maud Nathan of the National Consumers' League proposed a general "consumer's label" attesting that the producer was paid a living wage regardless of union affiliation. Nathan, too, thought it would be difficult to get consumers to pay attention to working conditions since "the mass of shoppers are selfish . . . eager only to obtain the greatest bargains at the least cost to themselves." Unlike Gunton and Nichols, however, she thought that consumers had an obligation to concern themselves with this issue. "Of what use is it to 'build up commerce' if the standard of living and the welfare of the wage earners are not to be built up too?" Too many workers received not living wages but "dying wages" because of irresponsible consumption. Nathan endorsed the idea of purchasing as owning in order to encourage consumers to concern themselves with working conditions. "It is a well-established economic fact that purchasers create what they purchase. Their desires create economic demands."[37]

James Boyle investigated the union label in Milwaukee and concluded that workers and proprietors rejected it for reasons similar to those outlined by its critics. Several years later Edward Spedden would note that "the consumer not affiliated in some way with the trade union movement does not show great enthusiasm for a label which stands simply for union versus non-union conditions." But Boyle found that even those in the trade union movement had problems with the label. "The label is a mistake; it is contrary to human nature," one trade union leader told him. "It puts unnecessary burdens on the union man who is expected to purchase the label goods." A union label storekeeper bitterly concurred. "Across the street there is a union man now, going into a cheap, shoddy store, where he can buy a few cents cheaper," he complained. "So it is with union men. They rant and bellow and then sneak around to some scab shop to find sweat-shop clothes made by little children. They want to receive union wages, but don't want to pay union prices." Another merchant claimed: "I have no demand whatever for label goods. A department store must stand for bargains. We cannot afford to pay union prices for goods. We have a big union trade on our non-union stock, because we buy cheap and sell cheap." Yet another told Boyle: "Union men like to use trust-made goods. They smoke Duke's mixture, chew Battle Axe plug, and smoke Henry George Cigars — all trust-made (and under the boycott of the AFL)."[38] While the market opened up the possibility of working-class solidarity, it also gave workers strong incentives to act in their own best interests.

Both the eight-hour and union label movements extended the domain of the worker into previously uncharted economic and political territory. As with the living wage discourse, the consumerist emphasis of both movements did not signify an abandonment of working-class identity; rather, it was an attempt to adapt to new circumstances. By emphasizing consumption as essential for the health of the worker and the republic, the eight-hour movement shifted the focus of labor ideology away from production. Union labelists tried to reestablish control over the means of production through the collective organization of purchasing power. Both movements, regrounding the meaning of working-class solidarity in ways that, like the living wage discourse, made leisure and consumption central to labor's notions of freedom, independence, and democratic citizenship. Yet the label brought with it a new vision of class consciousness which threatened masculine and consumerist prerogatives and was never fully accepted, even by male trade unionists. Clearly, many consumers (including those in the working class) could not be bothered to investigate the conditions under which their purchases were made, and some critics maintained that such tactics actually defeated the goals of the consumerist turn.

In spite of the successes of these movements between the Civil War and World War I, by the 1930s neither was central to labor activism.[39] The reasons for this transformation have as much to do with the broad currency many of these ideas gained within the wider culture — particularly among business and policy elites — as with the failures of consumerism as a strategy within the labor movement. Both movements introduced models of economic and political thinking that deeply affected twentieth-century reformers, politicians, and business leaders. In the first half of the twentieth century, consumerism as activism was replaced by consumerism as public policy, shifting from a labor strategy to a strategy promoted by government and business.

PART IV

THE LIVING WAGE IN

THE TWENTIETH CENTURY

From the coining of the term in the early 1870s, middle-class commentators addressed the living wage with varying degrees of applause, bewilderment, and criticism. They perceived this discourse as firmly rooted in working-class culture. For "fifteen years this idea of a 'Living Wage' simmered in the minds of Trade Unionists" before reformers discovered it, observed the British reformer Sidney Webb in 1899. In 1907 the *New York Times* called the living wage "Mr. Gompers' Slogan," indicating the degree to which outsiders associated the idea with the labor movement.[1]

Late in the Progressive Era, however, reformers appropriated the living wage as an idea of their own. Although their interest clearly followed — indeed, directly resulted from — labor's agitation for the living wage, progressive commentators often claimed that they had invented the idea *ex nihilo* or that nonworkers had coined the term, and even that the idea was relatively new. In 1916, for example, Edwin O'Hara, the chairman of the Industrial Welfare Commission of Oregon, suggested that Pope Leo XIII had coined the term in his 1891 papal encyclical *Rerum Novarum*. Secretary of Labor James Davis claimed in 1922 that the recent "war first gave us the living wage to think about."[2] Its new advocates failed to recognize that several generations of workers had struggled for the living wage — their demands well publicized in the popular press — by the time of the Great War.

Yet in a sense middle-class advocates were right to claim that they had invented the term, for the living wage they promoted differed markedly from the working-class version.[3] Most reformers expressed little enthusiasm for arguments that tied living wages to workers' wants and desires or for workers' advocacy of the benefits of mass consumption. James Young, for example, took up the "new issue," by defining the living wage in a way that would have shocked Samuel Gompers, as "the least a man can live on."[4] Young was one of many who used the terms living wage and minimum wage interchangeably. As reformers came to conceive of themselves as definers, not refiners, the living wage became synonymous with subsistence.

Although the middle-class definition of the living wage was only a faint echo of the working-class version, middle-class debates about its meaning recapitulated many of labor's themes, notably the critique of wages based on supply and demand and the idea of need-based wages (though they set the level of need quite low). Even subsistence wages faced criticism. The arguments against them, which reached their climax with the Supreme Court decision in *Adkins v. Children's Hospital* (1923), paralleled the main argument against the older version of living wages — namely, that to ground wages in needs was to violate "natural" economic laws.

As middle-class commentators began to shade the meaning of the living wage toward subsistence, the "living wage era" appeared to draw to a close. Organized labor gradually lost interest in the term as it came to be identified with the bare minimum. Labor leaders sometimes endorsed minimum wages for poorly paid women workers but not for union members, for these wages were defined at a level well below the consumerist version they demanded.

Although the living wage discourse seemed to lose its force, fading (among workers) or being redefined downward (by middle-class advocates), there is another side to this story. The consumerist turn that developed with the living wage discourse continued to gain popularity and flourished in the 1930s as never before. During this decade, labor's high wage, high consumption arguments gained currency as economists, politicians, and commentators came to see the twin problems of low wages and underconsumption — issues that living wage advocates had singled out as the most pressing dangers in a republic of wage earners — as crucial to ending the Great Depression.[5] The term "living wage" may have temporarily lost its place in labor rhetoric; yet the ideas and practices it represented and promoted became central to the discourse of the revived labor movement in the Depression decade. Indeed, as I argue in Chapter 8, the legacy of the living wage was central in the construction of the New Deal consumerist political economy.

7

Subsistence or Consumption?

The living wage had become a uniquely potent issue in American political culture, reported the popular business journalist Samuel Crowther in an examination of the concept that appeared in *Collier's* in late 1922 and early 1923. The "country is due for a season of political agitation over a purely economic issue that may involve every one of us," he wrote. The living wage would prove even more important than the economic issues that had deeply engaged an earlier generation of ordinary Americans:

> The phrase "living wage" . . . is going to go much deeper to the root of things than did "Free Silver" and "Sixteen to One" twenty-odd years ago, but with this difference. . . . The phrase "free silver" was not compelling. It did not mean anything until it was explained. The phrase "living wage" is compelling. It means something very direct and personal to every one of us. And it does what free silver never did. It brings up in review nearly the whole state of existence. . . . The question is being asked: "What is the use of wages, and therefore what is the use of working unless thereby one gets enough to live?"

The living wage, Crowther predicted, would gain unprecedented power as a cultural symbol and social force. Crowther was not the only one to make bold claims for the term. James Young expected that it would "assume a national and economic importance overshadowing almost any problem of industry." Secretary of Labor James Davis spent a good part of the year barnstorming the country, advocating what he called a "living and saving wage."[1]

These predictions were borne out several months later when the Supreme Court set off a storm of protest by overturning the minimum wage law of Washington, D.C., in *Adkins v. Children's Hospital*.[2] The living wage and its increasingly popular companion term, the minimum wage, had become the foremost economic issue in public consciousness.

The practical question, no more self-evident to Americans in the early twentieth century than it was in the nineteenth century, remained: was it feasible or desirable to guarantee a rate of wages based on needs? By the turn of the century America's astonishing productivity was widely noted, but could the country ensure subsistence to every working citizen and his or her family? If so, could the minimum wage exceed subsistence and ensure an American standard of living for all? Progressives began to answer these questions in the affirmative, though there was significant ambiguity about what this affirmation meant — expansive living wages or bare subsistence. Samuel Crowther believed that "for the first time in the history of the world" it was possible to pay workers "enough to satisfy all of their necessities and many of their desires." In 1945, Aaron Abell reached a similar conclusion: "In view of the country's ample productive resources, a living wage for all was morally imperative and ultimately attainable."[3]

A transformation in the ideas of professional economists provided a key impetus in the development of a national debate about living wages. In the late nineteenth century the profession came to reject the reigning orthodoxy, the "wage fund" theory, which held that wages came out of a fixed sum of capital and that therefore raising wages for one group would necessarily lower the pay of other workers. American economists, led by Francis A. Walker of MIT, argued that wages could rise as far as the country's productive capacity could take them. Even if economists did not see the living wage as wise, by the turn of the century most believed it to be theoretically possible. Many even endorsed it. "For the benefit of those who think the minimum wage proposition fantastic and contrary to what is conceived of as 'economic law,'" wrote one advocate, Elizabeth Glendower Evans, "our Massachusetts bill was endorsed by pretty much the whole economic department of Harvard College."[4]

Religious reformers were the first group outside of the labor movement to call for a living wage, beginning with Pope Leo XIII's encyclical of 1891, which catalyzed Catholic demands for a guaranteed living wage. The pope echoed the meaning if not the tone of organized labor's language: "There is a dictate of nature more imperious and more ancient than any bargain between man and man, that the remuneration must be enough to support the wage earners in reasonable and frugal comfort." John Ryan, a Catholic priest and social activist, placed the living wage on the Progressive agenda for social reform in 1906 with *A Living Wage*, in which he urged lawmakers to reign in the free market by recognizing ethically grounded natural laws. As a theologian wrote in 1922, the church understood wages in the context of a "larger conception of economic and social well-being."[5]

Between 1910 and 1923 almost half the states in the union, responding especially to the vigorous lobbying of female reformers and social workers, adopted minimum wage laws for women workers.[6] Nebraska proposed the first state minimum wage law in 1909 (enacted in 1913) designed to protect "the American standard of living." Massachusetts passed the first minimum wage law in 1912, and more than a dozen states quickly followed. The minimum wage stayed in the public eye through the initiatives of political parties as well. In 1912 the minimum wage appeared on the platforms of the Progressives and the Socialists. In 1916 it was on the Democratic platform and by 1920, spurred by the exigencies of World War I when the National War Labor Board pursued a policy of living wages, even the Republican Party called for a minimum wage to "preserv[e] standards of living."[7] Presidents Theodore Roosevelt, Wilson, and Harding all claimed to support living wages.[8] Nevertheless, there was significant opposition to a legal minimum. It was not until 1938 with the Fair Labor Standards Act that a national minimum wage law was enacted.[9]

Contesting the Living Wage

Despite the new interest, there was no new unanimity. The meaning of the term "living wage" was contested as it had been from the start. "A majority of men and women find it necessary or expedient to work for wages," wrote William Giles, a sociologist, in 1903, "and the question of a fair compensation for labor and of a fair and equitable division of the products of toil is a most important one," but the real question as expressed by Michael O'Kane, a Catholic priest, in 1899, was "how are we to determine the value of labor?" This question, which had been vigorously debated by workers since the 1870s, became, as Crowther and many others noted, a national obsession. Americans, William Allen White said in 1922, were in search of a "philosophy of the living wage."[10]

The terms of the twentieth-century debate about wages were uncannily continuous with those of the earlier era. Middle-class reformers, whether for or against minimum wages, used a vocabulary reminiscent of nineteenth-century producerism. Opponents invoked producerist beliefs to assert the need to maintain a productive equivalence between work produced and wages paid and to critique wants and desires as ill-defined, capricious, and likely to lead to working-class debauchery. In addition, some critics also invoked the new concept of "freedom of contract" against even subsistence wage proposals.

Although both workers and reformers used the terms inconsistently and ambiguously, it is clear that the views of workers differed radically from those of reformers, even those who supported minimum wage laws. Thus, although the terminology sometimes confused matters, a major political struggle took place in the early twentieth century, centering on the question of how society should value labor. Labor argued strongly for the need to modify (but not eliminate) market forces and to reward workers on the basis of their capacity to consume. By contrast, most middle-class minimum wage advocates and opponents believed that wages should be based upon productive value, which was best measured, they claimed, by the market. Workers rejected the distinction between living wages and minimum wages in order to preclude the possibility that minimum wages might become a national standard for wages; for them, all wages should represent some kind of living wage. Their middle-class opponents also rejected the distinction, but for precisely the opposite reason. They wanted to define the living wage at the low level of a subsistence minimum wage.

Working-Class Definitions

In connecting high wages and consumption to moral and political health, most labor leaders favored the term "living wage," but they also used other terms to describe this commitment. They invoked the "American standard of living" or the "natural value of labor," and they denigrated earnings that did not measure up to this level with gendered and racialized slurs: "girls' wages" or "slave wages." They drew a clear distinction between acceptable and unacceptable wages, but they did not consistently distinguish between living wages and minimum wages. In an 1898 debate at the Nineteenth Century Club in New York, Samuel Gompers titled his lecture, "A Minimum Living Wage," leaving ambiguous which adjective was the more important modifier. In 1902, he reflected labor's conflation of the terms: "Organized labor stands for a minimum wage, that minimum being a living wage." On this circular definition, a living wage was a minimum wage and *vice versa*. To further confuse matters, in defining the living wage a few years later, he replaced the word "living" with the word "minimum," otherwise quoting the exact same definition that he had promoted in his 1898 debate.[11] As late as 1912 an article in his *American Federationist* treated the two terms as synonyms.[12]

For organized labor, the minimum wage represented the low end on the spectrum of conceivable living wages. Labor's living wage advocates rarely defined the living wage in minimal terms. "A living wage does not mean simply a bare subsistence wage," noted the economist Edwin Seligman in 1898, summarizing organized labor's view. "It does not mean simply enough bread and enough drink barely to keep body and soul together." In determining the living wage, the labor journalist James Boyle wrote in 1913, workers should ask, "What is the American Standard of Living? — and what is the minimum wage sufficient to maintain that standard?" Organized labor generally distrusted legal minimum wages, which were far below their conception of living wages. The AFL "is not in favor of the legal minimum wage, although of course it is strenuously trying to secure a living wage for all its members," noted Boyle, pointing to the crucial distinction for organized labor between minimum and living wages.[13]

The distinction helps explain Gompers's otherwise puzzling lecture title, "A Minimum Living Wage." Gompers conceived of a spectrum of living wages which would compensate a worker in accordance with his needs. To speak of a minimum living wage was to imply the existence of more desirable living wages that far exceeded the minimum. As we have seen, Gompers himself elucidated a consumerist vision of a living wage. Most other labor leaders followed suit. For those within the house of labor a wage affording mere existence did not qualify as a living wage.

Although trade unions generally supported minimum wages for their less fortunate peers, they distinguished them from the living wages appropriate for their members. "The question of a living wage does not appeal directly to those workmen whose remuneration is high," noted Henry Macrosty in 1898. E. E. Clark, leader of the Order of Railway Conductors of America, made a similarly telling remark in a 1903 round table of labor leaders, who were asked their views on minimum wages defined in narrow terms as subsistence wages for indigent workers. Although Clark considered the issue "a very important one," he maintained that it did not "apply to the classes of employment in which the members of Our Order are engaged."[14] Conductors wanted living, not minimum, wages.

Fearing an emphasis on subsistence at the expense of consumption, organized workers opposed the attempt to make minimum wages the centerpiece of Progressive labor reform. Within the labor movement opinions varied about whether minimum wage laws should be supported at all. "In asking for a living wage," wrote William Cunningham in 1894, "we do not demand a maximum wage that shall never be exceeded." Gompers, actively opposed to any such legislation, repeatedly expressed the fear that the "minimum would become the maximum."[15]

Middle-Class Definitions

In struggling to define the living wage, middle-class advocates, like workers, frequently commented on the terminological confusion. These definitional debates reflected not airy linguistic exercises but a struggle to determine the proper value of labor. Some saw the differences as academic. "Economists recognize a difference between a 'minimum' wage and a 'living' wage," James Boyle wrote in 1913, "but generally the terms are used synonymously; and for practical purposes, in America they may be considered the same thing." Samuel Crowther, too, believed that the "phrase 'living wage' has a very definite and very plain meaning," but he conceded that for most Americans "it is all but impossible to define the phrase in words." Well into the next decade, other commentators continued to decry the ambiguity and vagueness of the various terms used to connote living wages. B. C. Forbes wrote: "We have been hearing and reading a great deal lately about the 'living wage,' the 'saving wage,' the 'minimum wage,' and other kinds of wages." He did not mention the "family wage," which was just then coming into vogue. "Nowadays very few persons object to the principle of the living wage," the Bureau of Municipal Research of Philadelphia confidently declared in 1919, but then it conceded the difficulty of defining the unobjectionable term.

> Too often we have been disposed to confuse a living wage with the minimum for which a worker can be hired. . . . When we speak of a living wage, we must have in mind a certain standard of living that such a wage is to make possible. In the popular mind, however, this standard has been at best a very vague concept. Even the so-called American Standard of Living, which has been so much bandied about by political orators, is extremely indefinite.[16]

Notwithstanding these clarion calls for clarity, no clear definition emerged. "Perhaps the main obstacle to the application of the minimum wage," the Philadelphia group continued, "has been our lack of definite understanding of what constitutes a living wage." Alongside the issue of what to call the living wage was the question of what standard of living should attach to this "wholly relative phrase." An article in *Literary Digest*, noting the wide variety of possible living wages, claimed that workers had no "right to a living wage. So long as the 'living wage' was only an abstraction, nobody quarreled with it. It was economically nebulous and innocuous. But when people tried to apply it concretely, its illusory character became manifest. . . . A dollar has a different value for nearly every earner and user. . . . In the same surroundings a 'living wage' for one workman might mean either affluence or indigence for another."[17]

Many reformers solved the definitional problem by sharply distinguishing between living wages and minimum wages. Thus, Emily Green Balch, an economist at Wellesley College, explained that living wages were those that permitted workers to raise "the standard as far as progress might enable them to do," and minimum wages provided only for basic subsistence.[18] Several generations of reformers echoed William Cunningham's 1894 claim that it was "necessary . . . to distinguish the living wage from a starvation or minimum wage." In describing the minimum wage as the linchpin of the Progressive program for social reform in 1913, Henry Seager, a sociologist and president of the American Association for Labor Legislation, argued that minimum wages should mark "off from the rest of the industrial army the individuals and classes who cannot earn living wages."[19]

Even those advocates who defined the minimum wage narrowly distinguished between subsistence and higher wages. Catholic reformers, especially, saw a difference between reasonable needs and unlimited consumption as a basis for wages. The inherent worth of human beings, they believed, should not be taken as license for hedonistic consumption.[20] Father John Ryan, like other reformers, believed that the living wage corresponded to high standards of living and the minimum wage provided subsistence. Calling the minimum wage "merely the minimum measure of just remuneration," he conceded that "it is not in every case complete wage justice." Ryan promoted a narrow living wage as a way to prevent the most egregious problems of poverty. Admitting that such a standard was low, Ryan wrote that the minimum wage "does not necessarily include any of the intellectual, aesthetic, moral, or social necessities; it is a purely physical standard." Confirming Ryan's view, E. C. Fortey in 1912 listed five groups of workers, ranging from the unskilled at the bottom of the social pyramid to "the class consisting of professional and business men" at the top. "The problem of the living wage concerns the first group alone," he wrote.[21] Even this limited conception of the living wage, however, faced strong criticism.

The Minimum Wage Critique

The belief, voiced frequently in our own time, that the minimum wage violates economic and moral law by overvaluing some forms of labor has deep historical roots. The fundamental flaw of the minimum wage, a business lobby noted in 1915, was that it based wages on needs, when the true measure of wages should be "the quality or kind of service rendered or work done."[22] That same year Rome Brown, a corporate attorney and minimum wage foe, decried the "socialist spirit of compulsory division, of disregard for economic law," which had "pervaded the advocacy of the minimum wage." It was unacceptable to base "the absolute right to a minimum wage upon the mere fact of the existence of the wage earner, regardless of his efficiency."[23] Opponents rejected minimum wages as economically invalid, impossibly vague, socialistic, and infringing freedom of contract.

These condemnations of living wages co-opted and subverted the language of labor republicanism. They evoked the producing classes' traditional object of wrath, freeloaders, those who gained their "unearned increment" by robbing from others. The idea that poor workers somehow extracted surplus value from the rich turned the logic of producerism on its head. In the nineteenth century working people had routinely deplored capitalists as undeserving "parasites." Now the same epithet was being turned on workers — and the poorest ones at that. In 1913 Joseph Lee succinctly summarized this view when he wrote that minimum wages would hand to workers an unwarranted "bonus in excess of wages (in the usual, and competitive sense)." The *Washington Evening Star* said that "one group of people can not get more than its proportionate share of production without robbing others of their just proportion," but in this analysis, it was workers, not capitalists, who were taking more than their share. The Supreme Court gave this view judicial sanction in 1923 when, in the *Adkins* case, it condemned minimum wages that exceeded "fair value of services rendered" as an illegal form of "compulsory extraction."

If workers understood themselves as the producers and rightful owners of the excess wealth enjoyed by their employers, the court viewed workers as robbers. "Requirement of a minimum wage, without corresponding requirement of amount or efficiency of service in return, is the taking of property without just compensation."[24]

The view that the living wage, whether understood as subsistence wages or more, circumvented fundamental principles of economics was central to the rhetoric of opponents. Rome Brown counterposed the artificial machinations of the minimum wage with the "inevitable workings of the natural law of economics." Wages properly corresponded to productive value, not needs. Any violation of this truth, wrote Brown, "has inevitably the tendency . . . to disturb the natural conditions governed by the law of supply and demand, by the law of competition and by other economic laws." A representative of the New York Retail Dry Goods Association condemned as "wrong" any "principle of wage payment which requires wages to be paid on any other theory than value returned."[25]

The only acceptable basis for wages, according to this view, was earned equivalence. Opponents of the living wage viewed the concept of need as constructed and the concept of worth as natural. It seemed to them that any determination of compensation apart from work performed was inherently unjust because it guaranteed what it should be possible to gain only through honest toil. Opponents juxtaposed the "fictional" value of minimum wages to the "real" value of wages paid according to market principles. The "value of labor," wrote Rebekah G. Henshaw in 1915, could not be "fixed by legislation, any more than the value of money." According to Crowther, the fact that "words somehow imply a right to live regardless of" the work performed "stands in the way of the living wage." He rejected the view that wages were a kind of gift: "Something cannot be had for nothing. One of these days we shall have to have a standard of work. It is a necessary precedent to a standard of living. . . . We cannot expect the American Standard of Living to be any higher than an American standard of work—but I have yet to hear anyone talk eloquently on preserving the American standard who so much as mentioned work."[26] These opponents argued in nineteenth-century producerist language that fair wages resulted from hard work, not legislative guarantees.

Confident in the need/worth dichotomy, critics of the living wage contrasted its seductive appeal with the harsh realities of the market. "If contentions were that the Board should establish a 'living wage' the majority would readily accede to the proposition," declared the Railroad Labor Board in 1922. "But the abstract elusive thing called 'the living wage' confessedly based upon a makeshift and a guess [is] a bit of mellifluous phraseology, well calculated to deceive the unthinking." The deception, critics claimed, was rooted in the vague and dangerous need-based core of the living wage demand, which implied, according to one critic, "no necessary correlation between the wage and the work done." In 1919 a speaker condemned the "labor theory that every worker who does a full day's work is entitled 'of right' to a living wage for it."[27] Once again, opponents deployed producerist rhetoric to challenge and delegitimate labor's living wage demand.

Even narrowly construed minimum wages, opponents claimed, could potentially reward workers beyond their just deserts, thereby robbing others of their rightful property. Minimum wage opponents did not always agree on the nature of this robbery — some believed workers to be its chief victims, others saw employers as the robbed — but they agreed that all compulsory wages were inherently dangerous.[28] "The use of the word 'wages' implies an equivalent," declared Edward Atkinson, an economist and businessman, in an 1898 debate with Gompers. "If the work done is not worth the equivalent in money or goods, no individual or corporation can possibly pay the 'living wage.'" Basing wage levels on need violated economic law, no matter how minimally the need might be defined. "In the past, labor . . . had been paid on the basis of supply and demand," James Young wrote in 1922; "labor now demands compensation fixed to its needs." This "new theory of distribution" was invalid, he concluded, because "no wage can be paid in any industry . . . which is higher than the wage earned." Opponents contrasted the living wage to the "earned wage." Victor Morowetz decried the blithe assumption "that every worker is entitled to a living wage" as a violation of economic common sense. "It is not possible to make the theoretical family wage universal because it would exceed total production."[29]

Freedom of contract was another bulwark in the argument against the minimum wage. This idea, valorized in the late nineteenth century by conservative jurists, held that freedom to make contracts was the basis of liberal democracy, and any interference in this process would undermine free government. Central to this argument was the fiction that individual workers and capitalists came to uncoerced agreements. Wage agreements were seen as voluntary, the product of free will; the result of such agreements was the natural, market-determined wage. The doctrine made market values the touchstone of freedom and rejected any government or union interference as a sign of the failure of liberal society. Some judges went to striking lengths to uphold this concept. In *Bunting v. Oregon* (1916), for example, the Court overturned the state minimum wage law because it violated the individuals' right to choose his or her standards of living. "If the amount of money received as a wage is not sufficient to support a laborer . . . is society to demand of the employer an arbitrary increase in wages?" asked the Court. "We have jacked up the standard of living of the ordinary laborer to such a point that any man who is propertyless is so only by choice or misfortune," declared Samuel Crowther, echoing nineteenth-century "free labor" rhetoric that held all workers earning less than a living wage personally at fault.[30]

Some opponents even denounced the minimum wage as "socialistic," amounting to state-sponsored redistribution of wealth. Rome Brown condemned the unfair distribution of property in Oregon's minimum wage law as "a new expression of the paternalistic and socialistic tendencies of the day." "The minimum wage as a rate for industrial payment is a catching slogan, and the dreary-eyed socialist and excited emotionalist gladly declare the minimum wage the utopia for industrial ills," said John Kirkby in a 1913 speech. Crowther complained that the living wage "says in effect that the workers are a class." The Railroad Labor Board in 1922 carried this fear to bombastic heights: "The theory of 'the living wage' if carried to its legitimate conclusion would wreck every railroad in the United States, and, if extended to other industries, would carry them into communistic ruin."[31]

The absolute measure of production seemed preferable to a relative scale of needs, which were notoriously difficult to measure and often misguided or inappropriate. William Giles noted that proponents of need-based wages "do not say what is meant by wants. Men's wants or desires vary greatly: and if such a formula were acted upon, some people's needs would increase enormously, and their efficiency would decrease in proportion." The Railroad Labor Board also insisted that no "arbitrary standard of living" would be appropriate. "That the desires and requirements of all men are equal and alike is not correct, and that any committee of experts would set up an average living standard upon which a wage scale could practically be based has not been demonstrated anywhere."[32] The variety of wage earners' needs must preclude the possibility of allocating wages according to a standard of living.

The critics of minimum wages saw no necessary reason why wages had to approximate needs. Samuel Crowther speculated that avaricious human nature dictated that wants would always exceed wages. Agreeing with labor's consumerist prophets that needs had no clear limit, opponents believed that without very definite limitation of productivity the entire wage system would crumble. J. Laurence Laughlin in 1913 identified as "unjustifiable" the new notion "that wages shall be paid on the basis of what it costs the recipient to live." As the title of his article "Wages and Producing Power" indicated, Laughlin believed the only moral and economically feasible basis for wages was production, not needs — "producing power," not "purchasing power."[33]

Minimum wage advocates and opponents shared the belief that work and value had been torn asunder, but they came to very different conclusions. Opponents viewed this situation as a crisis; supporters saw it as an opportunity to redefine the meaning of labor value. Samuel Crowther commented on what he saw as the excesses of the living wage movement: "Our individual requirements are such that what one man would think ample another would find wholly insufficient. One man's living wage is another's dying wage." Edwin Seligman used strikingly similar language to demonstrate what was good about the movement: "What is a living wage for one man is not a living wage for another. What is a living wage for one class is not a living wage for another. What is a living wage for one country is not a living wage for another."[34] Each used the language of variable desires to support different causes.

Living wage advocates argued that the separation between wages and value would foster a more just political economy. Opponents argued that the nebulousness of the living wage made it dangerous and that it would force capitalists to pay workers well, even if they would not work hard or could not distinguish true needs from luxuries. "Toys and movies, thanks to human cravings, are often bought in place of bread," editorialized the *Nation* in 1922.[35] The problem was not necessarily the wage level but the skewed priorities of some workers, who preferred entertainment to nourishment.

J. N. Darling's cartoon "The Living Wage Puzzle" visually demonstrated reformers' perceptions of the tension between living wages and work values (fig. 8). The ideal wage relation seemed so simple. The problem came when the parties refused to hold up their end of the exchange, either by working below requirements or by profit gouging. Nevertheless, the cartoon reflected concessions to minimum wage critics on the question of value, endorsing the idea of a "fair days' wages for a fair days' work." Admittedly, the concession was partial, for labor drew a distinction between living wages and "fair wages" of this sort.

This partial acceptance notwithstanding, the *Adkins* decision of 1923 revealed a lingering suspicion of the living wage. The Supreme Court reverted to the traditional argument against the minimum wage in its

Figure 8. J. N. Darling, "The Living Wage Puzzle." *Collier's,* December 9. 1922. 17. Courtesy Collier's Publishing

rejection of the District of Columbia law. It decried the violation of freedom of contract and the undue burden on employers to reward workers according to their needs. "In principle, there can be no difference between the case of selling labor and the case of selling goods," the Court concluded, firmly rejecting the core of the living wage ideology, the belief that market forces must be modified for human ends if social justice was to prevail in an industrial society.[36]

8

The Living Wage Incorporated

Denounced as communist by businessmen, condemned as a violation of free contract by judges, and redefined in minimal terms by reformers, the working-class living wage appeared moribund by the mid-1920s. As living wages became equated in the popular mind with minimum wages, organized labor abandoned the phrase. For many American workers living wages came to represent a bare subsistence, not a goal but something to escape. The liberating vision of the living wage, it seemed, had passed into history.

Yet even as the term appeared to be dying, the ideas underlying it continued to gain cultural legitimacy. (As early as 1895, a commentator had noticed the "silent but powerful influence" of the living wage.)[1] The consumerist complex of ideas which flourished and became central to New Deal political economy did not emerge out of thin air as many historians have assumed. During the previous half century of debate about the living wage, the seeds of the New Deal order were steadily being planted.[2]

During the Progressive Era, the middle classes had made the living wage central to their ideology by defining it down from the expansive working-class version of the late nineteenth century to the minimum subsistence wage. The working-class and middle-class visions of the living wage occasionally found common ground in the 1920s, when prominent business leaders and politicians supported the living wage and policy makers began to promote the benefits of working-class consumption. In the next decade a marriage was sealed. In the consolidation of the New Deal, the rival versions of the living wage ideology converged in public policy and political economy to become accepted as economic common

147

sense. In language recalling that of labor's consumerist turn, Franklin Roosevelt declared in a Fireside Chat of 1938, "We suffer primarily from a failure of consumer demand because of a lack of buying power."[3] The living wage had become so integral to the American social contract that some commentators, viewed the matter as settled by the post–New Deal political economy. In the late 1950s Arthur Schlesinger Jr. urged liberals to shift their goals from a concern with "establishing the economic conditions which make individual dignity conceivable — a job, a square meal, a living wage, a shirt on one's back, a roof over one's head," to a focus on quality-of-life issues, such as moral decay and mass culture.[4]

Despite the judiciary's attack on minimum wages, which put a stop to minimum wage laws until the Fair Labor Standards Act of 1938, optimistic claims about the living wage abounded after World War I, as business leaders and reformers trumpeted the rising American standard of living as good for business and for the stability of the republic.[5] While the promoters of welfare capitalism resisted wage increases, they also opened the door to a non-market-based conception of economic fairness, which (theoretically, at least) took workers' needs into account.[6] Even industrial engineers adopted a model of high wages and ever-expanding needs.[7]

This new living wage was not without cost to working people. Reformers had reconceived it as a top-down notion. Secretary of Labor James J. Davis declared, for example, that "the living wage, in its original meaning is something obsolete." Davis identified a "wider conception of what constitutes a truly living wage" and declared that it was now "entertained not alone by the workman himself, but the American people as a whole have willingly conceded it to him." By defining the living wage as something that the American people had "conceded" to workers, Davis robbed the term of its original force. The *Nation* agreed that the living wage was a middle-class gift, an "appealing slogan" offered to workers.[8]

The middle-class adoption and adaptation of the term, however, was more than co-optation. The core of the working-class living wage ideology seeped into the rhetoric of reformers and politicians. Davis, for example, praised the living wage for helping to produce a respectable working class, whose "tastes have been heightened" by "enjoyment of books, of pictures, music, the theatre, a chance at higher education." An "increased standard of living," he predicted, would continue to improve the lot of the worker. "A wage that not only met the reasonable expenses of living but provided a fair margin of saving [would] correspondingly increase the prosperity of all up to the point of full saturation to the limit of human wants, a point not yet even in sight." Neither Ira Steward nor

Samuel Gompers would have said it any differently; reformers and business leaders alike now posited the centrality of working-class consumption to the health of the economy and the polity. It was now taken for granted that as Davis noted, "workers are the great buying public," and widely distributed consumption would provide economic benefits: "If each of the 7,097,283 women clerks and wage earners in the United States and the wives and daughters of the 23,346,373 men clerks and wage earners in the United States would buy another cotton dress, another woolen dress, another silk dress, the question of unemployment in the textile industries would be solved." The president of the National Association of Manufacturers told a Senate committee: "Whatever will increase the earning capacity of our people will make it possible for them to be greater purchasers and increase the value of our market." "The buying power of this country rests with the masses," declared Thomas J. Watson, founder of IBM, before the National Industrial Conference Board. "It doesn't make so very much difference whether we buy anything more this year or not, but the whole thing depends upon whether the masses, the working people of this country are going to buy."[9]

The middle-class version of the living wage may have been built upon its working-class antecedent, then, but it was also shaped by reformers who defended the minimum wage. These defenders transformed midcentury understandings of political economy in critical ways. Continuing to define the living wage differently from workers, minimum wage advocates nonetheless promoted several positions that overlapped with labor's living wage definition: a view of wages as constructed rather than natural; an understanding of the economic benefits of mass consumption; a recognition of the close relationship between the health of American democracy and the freedom, independence, and active citizenship of its workers; and the desirability of a political order that would recognize this state of affairs. More than half a century after organized labor had first proposed the living wage, the continuing emphasis on recasting value and modifying the market showed the struggle was ongoing. The ideas of the living wage discourse remained central to the economic vision of the American Century.

The Redefinition of Value

Some minimum wage advocates, recapitulating the logic of critics, tempered their demands with the proviso that wages not rise above work value. They accepted so-called natural laws of wages dictated by abstract market forces. J. H. Richardson, for example, wrote in 1927 of the need to "prevent the payment of wages lower than the economic value of the work done." Despite Richardson's belief in the "elastic character of living wage," he accepted the notion that it was possible to overvalue wages. After declaring that there was "a minimum wage below which [a worker] cannot go," Michael O'Kane conceded that the "employer is not bound to give wages in excess of the certain or probable profits which the labourer's work is likely to realize." An article in the *American Catholic Quarterly Review* declared of the minimum wage: "Its fundamental intention is summed up in the phrase, 'a fair day's wages for a fair day's work.' It does not aim at robbing employers of even a single dollar of property which they have individually acquired." With a significant shift from earlier working-class rhetoric, these supporters took seriously the possibility that the minimum wage could overvalue labor. They supported as a compromise what Aaron Abell called a level of "comfort," understood as "a standard midway between the extremes of luxury and subsistence."[10] Such a standard, they assumed, would incorporate both need and value.

Other minimum wage advocates set aside the value question and pointed to the specter of a discontented working class. They suggested that the minimum wage would avert more radical working-class political action. James Boyle called it "the only alternative to Socialism." "Any effort to force American workmen below the recognized standards of living will inevitably result in industrial strife," wrote Edward Filene, a progressive business leader, in the wake of the *Adkins* decision. J. A. Norton declared in 1919 that a legal minimum wage would result in the "natural death of the Bolsheviki." In 1921 the Anthracite Coal Commission endorsed the living wage as a bulwark against revolution: "All American wage earners have a fundamental economic right to at least a living wage, or an American Standard of Living. . . . Failure to realize this right . . . breeds revolutionary agitation, and prevents our self-governing Republic from being what it should be."[11]

Echoing labor's arguments that a high-wage economy was a healthy economy, others endorsed the minimum wage for its macroeconomic benefits. For example, the economist John Hobson argued that the minimum wage would increase "the general purchasing power of the worker," and the resulting increased consumption would "enlarge the volume and regularize the character of employment." Filene debunked the concept of overvalued labor and claimed that high wages abetted commerce while low wages made business "dull."[12]

Many minimum wage advocates, however, asserted an alternative theory of value. Understanding wages as a social construction, they maintained that society, not abstract forces, should properly determine the value of work. These arguments converged in the consensus that the market's allocation of wages had to be modified to ensure a just society. Echoing working-class defenses of social economy, Henry Rogers Seager, for example, denounced "the dreary science of political economy." Seager, like other minimum wage proponents, believed that workers must be protected from the dangers of an unregulated free market. "We are passing from the era in which the subsistence of any class of our working population can be left to the uncontrolled fluctuations of supply and demand and the higgling of the market," declared one minimum wage advocate, Sidney Brooks, in 1912.[13] This claim echoed Henry George's nineteenth-century warning about the dangers of overreliance on market "higgling" to determine social value.

Religious arguments contributed to the shift away from the determination of wages solely by abstract, unproblematic application of the concept of value. Rather than treat wages as unchanging and sacrosanct, theologians argued that no eternal principles of justice could be said to inhere in the wage relation, which was, they pointed out, "a comparatively new thing." Treating wage levels as contingent rather than natural, just as labor's living wage advocates had done, opened them up for political struggle. Wages "are but a means toward the achievement of a higher human existence," wrote Father Cuthbert in 1922: "The first consequence of admitting this principle is that wages should properly be based not upon the market value of a man's work, but upon the necessity of his well-being as a man. Market value enters into the question not as a primary determining factor, but as a secondary consideration for the securing of the worker of a wage which will enable him to attain to a proper human existence." For Cuthbert, as for working-class living wage advocates, wages were properly a function of needs, not markets.[14]

Even before *Adkins*, a group of living wage defenders lashed out against those who accepted the logic of the opposition. "Most people's notion of a minimum wage is based upon the slave-owner's idea, enough to keep the worker alive and fit for work," Alice Henry wrote in 1913. "The minimum wage we are hearing most about today can only mean the least remuneration that the poorest paid employe can be compelled to accept." In her view minimum wages that were not tied to decent standards of living were precisely the kind that workers had traditionally dubbed "slave wages." Two years later Walter Lippmann criticized the narrow version of the liv-

ing wage which offered "just enough to secure existence amid drudgery."
He called instead for wages that would "make life a rich and welcome experience."[15] With minimum wage and living wage increasingly used interchangeably, Henry and Lippmann used different terms to make similar
critiques of subsistence minimum wages.

The *Adkins* decision spurred a vigorous middle-class defense of the living wage. Despite the optimistic predictions of James Davis and others,
Elizabeth Brandeis feared that the "oppressive wage" would replace the
"living wage." Supporters of the living wage, the voluntarist Gompers included, denounced the decision. The *New Republic* condemned it by re-
covering the epithets of the earliest living wage advocates, wage slavery
and prostitution. Noting the incompatibility of "democracy and wage-
slavery," the magazine insisted that the "choice between slow starvation
and moral degradation" was no choice at all and concluded that it was
"time for organized labor to formulate a national conception of the minimum below which no class of labor should be permitted to fall."[16]

Even the avowedly antisocialist John Ryan, a reformer rather than a
radical, condemned objections to minimum wages as based upon a mis-
understanding of the nature of wage labor. Mindful that the living wage
had begun as a critique of the market's allocations of wages, Ryan believed
that an unfettered free market would inevitably produce low wages.
Wages, he perceived, were less a product of "natural laws" than of power
relations, and the "worth" of labor was a function of what capitalists were
willing to pay and workers able to demand, rather than an objective measure of work value. In a 1923 letter to the labor reformer Florence Kelley,
Ryan questioned "the wisdom of trying to embody in a law a requirement
that the wages should not exceed the value of the services." He proposed
instead a different understanding, that the "value of the worker's services
is always equal, in the only intelligible sense of the phrase possible, to the
legal minimum wage."[17] For Ryan, as for labor's living wage advocates,
human needs trumped market forces as the proper measure of wage
justice.

Like the pioneering working-class living wage theorists, reformers abandoned the notion that labor value could be measured at the point of production alone. The act of laboring itself should be the only requirement
for living wages. "Having performed his part of the general task of production," wrote Ryan in his earliest articulation of the living wage in 1902,
"the laborer's right to live from the common product becomes actual and
unquestioned."[18] Implicit in this formulation, as in the working-class discourse, was the idea that "the common product" was large enough to sup-

port all workers in reasonable comfort. Since individual contributions to the product were immeasurable, Ryan and other living wage supporters believed that pay should accord with needs. Although these advocates claimed that production and wages should roughly correspond, they based their claims on collective, not individual, productivity.

Minimum wage advocates also rejected the idea that only production measured the "true" value of labor. They believed the only adequate measure was needs.[19] "The living wage is based, not on the value of a man's work, but on his requirements as a man in civilized society," one advocate declared.[20] This replacement of market value with human value became a key element of the minimum wage argument, as it had been of the living wage discourse. Rejecting the dogma that "wages must be proportionate to the value of services rendered," J. W. Sullivan argued that it was impossible to separate value from questions of power: "Every one knows that there is little connection between value of services and wages paid; the employer pays no more than he must." The Massachusetts Minimum Wage Board said much the same in 1912:

> There is a common and widespread erroneous view that [minimum wage] legislation is an attempt to provide by government that low-paid workers shall receive more than they earn; that it runs counter to an economic law which, by some mysterious but certain process, correlates earnings and wages. There is no such law; in fact in many industries the wages paid bear little or no relation to the value or even to the selling price of the workers' output.

The board concluded that minimum wage critics were using the idea of natural law to mask raw power with the patina of principle. The typical worker, according to Father Cuthbert, "did not usually obtain the price his labor was worth in the market, simply because there was no real freedom in the barter on the worker's part." Since the market reflected the dominance of capital over labor, it was wrong to take its determinations as the final word on economic justice, as Father Cuthbert noted: "The taking of market value as the ultimate basis of the worker's wage was wrong ethically, in that it limited the responsibility of the employer to paying a reasonable price for the mere product of Labor apart from wider considerations of the workers' welfare."[21]

The appeal to natural law, minimum wage advocates charged, was not a turn to transcendent truth but an attempt to obfuscate the power disparity between labor and capital. The "objection to a legal minimum wage which is most persistent in people's minds," Walter Lippmann wrote, concerned the question of value. "They say to themselves, 'How can you force an employer to pay a girl more than she is worth?' Isn't that against all business, common sense and the laws of economics? . . . Isn't it absolutely wrong to force any woman to receive more wages than she earns?" Lippmann responded by charging that opponents did not have a better or more just system of value than proponents. Indeed, he claimed, there was no way of "telling how much she is worth," since "no one has the least idea whether their income has anything to do with their productivity or their efficiency." Wages, then, were more a function of the employer's power than of any objective measure of productive value: "That is why . . . talking about wages depending upon 'wage-worth,' is using a catchy phrase and a neat theory which in practice means literally nothing at all. The kind of women's work to which the minimum wage would apply has no standard by which wages are fixed." [22]

Turning critics' views on their head, these middle-class advocates of higher wages promoted their own rival versions of economic justice. "Under the present social system," wrote Scott Nearing in 1915, "there is no relation between the social needs of a man and the wage which he receives." It seemed clear that "the term worth should be abandoned" until users of the term recognized its fundamental connection to needs. For Nearing, a living wage providing "a return in proportion to social needs" marked "the barest beginnings of a policy of economic justice applied to wages." [23]

Proponents of living wages challenged the ideal of free contract, the bulwark of opponents' conception of work value. They stressed the unequal nature of the wage bargain and pointed, once again, to the constructed nature of wages. Workers argued that power imbalances made the ideal of the free contract unreachable for most workers. As the *Independent* caustically observed in 1912, "An appalling mass of human wreckage has been produced by the assumption that legal freedom of contract" could exist "when the parties to the bargain were respectively Might and Helplessness." Edwin O'Hara saw the invocation of freedom of contract for low-wage workers as "the height of irony." A wide variety of politicians and labor leaders condemned freedom of contract as a masked justification for low wages. If the state had power to act for the welfare of the people by regulating hours and working conditions, concluded a 1911 editorial in the *American Federationist*, "it would seem to follow that it is equally with the power of the State to fix a minimum wage." The state, it concluded, "has both the right and the duty to protect its citizens in their right to a decent livelihood." [24]

The 1930s and After

Although reformers advocated the living wage throughout the 1910s and 1920s, it was not until the Depression decade that consumerist ideas became conventional wisdom and economic policy, as they remained for the half-century reign of the New Deal order. What was new in these years was the recognition of their significance by political elites. Although New Dealers and their descendants played a critical role in shaping and implementing this vision, they no more created it than had the generation of Progressives that preceded them. Nor did the new generation of labor leaders invent the language of the living wage; instead, they adapted and modified the inheritance of late nineteenth-century American workers.

As it became increasingly consonant with mainstream views, labor's consumerist language in the 1930s and 1940s was more widely publicized than ever before. In these years, labor's demands for high wages, purchasing power, and an American standard of living won public acceptance. New Dealers, as Lizabeth Cohen notes, endorsed labor's concept of "moral capitalism," including its demands for a "need-centered pay system."[25] Political and business leaders doubtless had their own agenda in promoting consumption, but they did not so much invent this complex of ideas as implement it in public policy and business practice. In this crucial way, to borrow Cohen's phrase, workers "made the New Deal." In theorizing about the relationship between consumption and industrial democracy, living wage advocates had laid the ideological groundwork of New Deal economic thinking.

Historians have generally depicted labor's consumerist posture of the 1930s and 1940s as new, imposed from above, and conservative: new, because consumerism marked a sharp departure from traditional labor ideology; imposed, because the consumerist ideas were rooted in middle-class culture and foisted on workers; and conservative, because this constellation of ideas led labor to abandon opposition for incorporation. These depictions are interrelated. Nelson Lichtenstein, for example, writes that in the postwar years, "the labor movement began to substitute the language of technical Keynsianism—'purchasing power,' 'aggregate demand,' 'wage-price stability'—for much of the prewar lexicon of power, justice and industrial democracy." Michael Kazin argues that working-class consumerism of the 1930s "marked a change in labor's language from the nineteenth century when consumer was a synonym for parasite." Steve Fraser suggests that the consumer focus of the postwar era drained the labor question of "its moral preeminence, its political threat, and its elemental social significance."[26] The gains of the labor movement in the 1930s were undermined, on these views, by its willingness to adopt a new consumerist vision not of its own making.

In the context of the long history of the living wage, however, labor discourse in the Depression decade is a story of continuity.[27] The important shift in labor language from producerism to consumerism occurred not in the 1930s but after the Civil War, when the discourse of wage slavery gave way to the language of the living wage, unleashing a powerful working-class vision that has continued to shape politics, economics, and culture from the New Deal to the present. Far from being new or imposed, the terms "purchasing power," "consumption," and "aggregate demand" were born, along with the living wage, in working-class political economy. The living wage was the prolegomenon of New Deal labor discourse.[28]

This is not merely an antiquarian debate about timing. The continuity in labor discourse calls into question the sharp divide that the post-1930s period is said to represent in the political standpoint of organized labor. Historians have often depicted the consumerist turn as an abandonment of labor's oppositional tradition.[29] Living wage advocates, however, did not see a contradiction between a republican language of politics and an emphasis on high wages and consumption; from the inception of the living wage idea they stressed the compatibility, indeed the symbiosis, of these ideas. They would not have recognized the sharp division drawn by the political theorist Michael Sandel, for example, between the "political economy of citizenship" and the "political economy of growth."[30] For living wage advocates, high wages and organized consumption were the very basis of citizenship in the republic of wage earners.

"I believe we are at the threshold of a fundamental change in our popular economic thought, that in the future we are going to think less about the producer and more about the consumer," declared the presidential candidate Franklin D. Roosevelt in May 1932.[31] Roosevelt was able to envision this future largely because of the previous half century of American working-class activity. As living wage advocates had maintained for more than fifty years, producers and consumers were one and the same.

Coda: Interpreting the Living Wage and Consumption

In his 1939 play *Abe Lincoln in Illinois*, Robert Sherwood recreates one of the famous 1858 debates between senatorial candidates Stephen Douglas and Lincoln. The scene reaches a climax when Douglas scores points with the large crowd by supporting the demand of the white workers of Illinois for a "living wage." Despite its dramatic success, the line is in historical error. Aside from the fact that the term "living wage" would not be coined for another decade and a half, such a demand would not likely have drawn cheers from the workers in Douglas's audience, who in 1858 did not even wish to view themselves as wage earners. To be sure, the racially charged version of "wage slavery" so vividly depicted by Sherwood's Douglas, in which the distinction between white "free" labor and black slave labor was becoming ever more minute, would have resonated among white workers.[1] But for these workers, freedom consisted of independent artisanship, not wage labor, however well paid. Most antebellum workers placed wage labor with slavery along a continuum of bondage. Sherwood, an enthusiastic New Dealer basking in the glow of the 1938 passage of the first national minimum wage legislation, the Fair Labor Standards Act, anachronistically projected into the past the sensibility of his own era, which accepted the legitimacy of wage labor.

Sherwood was far from unique in his ahistorical and imprecise use of the term "living wage." Its origins and history have been left to surmise and half truth, like those of many concepts deemed "traditional."[2] Part of the vagueness associated with its origins is due to the wide variety of Americans who invoked and challenged the term in the late nineteenth and early twentieth centuries without any firm definition. In the absence of consensus, various groups were able to invest the living wage with very

157

different meanings. From its coining in the 1870s, advocates of living wages debated whether they should provide workers with a bare subsistence or a more luxurious lifestyle. In addition, proponents wondered whether everyone, regardless of race, sex, ethnicity, and skill level, should be entitled to the same kind of living wage, or whether distinctions should be encouraged.

Scholars have added to the chronological and definitional confusion. While the living wage has been addressed frequently, its formative years have been largely unresearched.[3] One result of the inattention to its late nineteenth-century origins and development is that many historians use the term "family wage" instead of living wage, substituting a phrase that nineteenth-century workers never used for the one favored by workers, middle-class proponents, and even enemies of the concept.[4] The term "family wage" was rarely, if ever, invoked by workers in the period I study in this book. With the exception of brief mentions of the phrase "family living wage" by the economist William Smart and Father John A. Ryan, neither of whom was a worker and both of whom routinely used the term "living wage," I have found no uses of the term "family wage" before the Progressive Era. Although "family wage" is favored in the historiography and by many contemporary commentators, "living wage" is the proper historical term.[5]

To suggest that the family wage is a category constructed by historians is not to deny that "family wage" scholarship has shed light on a number of critical issues, including the origins of the welfare state and the persistence of patriarchal family structures. It has spawned a fruitful debate concerning gender, breadwinning, and class consciousness. The point is to note the important difference, too frequently ignored by scholars of the family wage, between historically created categories and expressions used by historical actors themselves. Failing to note this distinction has led historians to ignore or misinterpret the meaning of the "living wage." For contemporaries, the phrase "living wage" represented a set of issues not adequately addressed by the historiographical label of the family wage.

The term "family wage," developed by Progressive Era reformers (although not widely used until the 1920s), described a wage, often sanctioned by the state, which would enable male breadwinners to support their families.[6] While some advocates of the living wage proposed similar measures, the family wage had a considerably narrower focus than did most demands for the living wage, inasmuch as it stressed poor families and subsistence rather than organized male workers and consumption. Workers found a term introduced by reformers less appealing than the one that, as Gompers put it in 1894, "the working people establish for themselves." Even as politicians and reformers joined the debate, they continued to use the term "living wage." From its earliest uses in England and America in the 1870s, to the 1898 "living wage debate" at New York City's Nineteenth Century Club, to John Ryan's influential 1906 book, to Secretary of Labor James J. Davis's well-publicized endorsement in 1922 of "A living and saving wage," proponents and opponents spoke of the living wage.[7]

Even more significant than this mislabeling is that lack of research into its origins has also led historians to take the living wage for a kind of working-class *Ur*-demand, always and forever a part of the rhetoric of the labor movement. In her excellent study of women workers during World War II, Ruth Milkman quite rightly refers to it (although she uses the term "family wage") as a "long cherished" and "longstanding" idea that shaped workers' attitudes and practices, but she provides no information as to how far back this "working-class cultural ideal" can be traced.[8] Those who have speculated on the origins of the living wage have inaccurately placed its genesis well before its actual appearance in the post–Civil War world.[9] The existence of the "family wage" in antebellum America has been more often asserted than documented.

Of course, some components of the living wage have antebellum roots. It would be foolish to claim that the notion, which bears an obvious relation to many ideas promoted by antebellum workers, emerged out of whole cloth in the 1870s.[10] The development of the male breadwinner norm, the defining element of the "family wage ideology" as understood by modern historiography, can be traced to the early years of the industrial revolution.[11] Other contributing concepts, including "just price" and "fair wages," antedate the nineteenth century.[12] Indeed, the living wage discourse is incomprehensible without understanding the legacy of antebellum radicalism and the century-old struggle against wage labor; it is best viewed as a crystallization, a culmination of several trends, rather than as an invention.

Despite these continuities with earlier labor demands, there are important grounds for dating the origins of the living wage in the postbellum period. The most important reason is that workers coined the term not in the prewar years but in the early 1870s. In the context of the powerful working-class antagonism to wage labor, the coining and acceptance of the term "living wage" is itself significant, providing a sharp contrast with the pervasive view of wage labor as degrading. Given what Eric Foner calls their "widespread hostility to wage labor," it would be hard to imagine antebellum workers invoking any expression that legitimated permanent wage labor.[13]

Although well aware of the genealogy of earlier labor ideology, most advocates of the living wage described it as something new, part of an innovative political economy in which traditions of artisanal radicalism mixed with novel understandings of both wage labor and consumption. Regardless of whether the term was used prior to the early 1870s (and I have found no such evidence), founding narratives of the living wage firmly labeled both the term and the idea a new and transformative phase in the labor movement. With the living wage, workers developed a positive understanding of wage labor and constructed a new consumerist identity.

The "new labor history" has challenged the powerful legacy of the John R. Commons school of labor history, which depicted, as Amy Bridges writes, "an adamantly nonpolitical working class resolutely focused on earnings."[14] Commons's colleague, Selig Perlman, argued that American workers were, unlike their peers in other industrial countries, "wage conscious" rather than class conscious.[15] Although they have rejected the Commons school in every other way, the new labor historians have tended to view wage struggles as evidence that workers became, in John Bodnar's words, "considerably narrower in their objectives."[16] Instead, labor historians have highlighted political party formation, community conflicts, and shop-floor behavior as signs of an authentic class consciousness, both more important than and distinct from wage demands.[17] Positive attitudes among workers toward wage labor remain either neglected or are offered as evidence of conservatism.

Complicating the Commons school vision of an apolitical working class, the new labor history eschews an "exceptionalist" model that devalues the American working-class experience for not conforming to European patterns in favor of a conception of class consciousness based on workers' actual behavior. Yet for all its revisionism, opposition to wage labor still remains the sine qua non of class consciousness, the sole "essential" aspect of a model that eschews "essentialism."[18] Sean Wilentz, for example, understands class consciousness "not as any particular set of ideas, doctrines, or political strategies but far more broadly as the articulated resistance of wage workers . . . to capitalist wage relations."[19] The living wage demand, though framed within the wage system, was part of a political struggle over the very meaning of wage labor. Indeed, living wage advocates promoted a conception of need-based wages which closely paralleled the Marxist vision of "to each according to his needs."[20] As

Michael Merrill has suggestively written: "The proletarianization of the work force and the spread of the wage system has generally been a demand, not a defeat, of the working-class movement. Most people prefer a wage guaranteed by law to a nebulous right of customary appropriation—witness the continuing demands for wages jobs by women and other members of the unpaid labor force." He continues: "Most workers . . . have preferred . . . to keep the [wage] system and organize within it to secure a larger and larger share of the social product. Continually demanding higher wages. . . may be the only authentic, fully proletarian socialism we have had or ever will have—a socialism in which workers themselves have the greatest power and freedom."[21]

If I propose in this book a new conception of wage labor, it is equally dependent upon a rethinking of the politics of working-class consumption. Like wage labor, this is a subject historians, until recently, have treated with little sympathy.[22] Since Werner Sombart's *Why Is There No Socialism in the United States?* analysts have attributed the absence of radical working-class politics in America to its high standard of living. As Sombart concluded in 1906: "The American worker lives in comfortable circumstances. . . . He is well fed. . . . He dresses like a gentleman and she like a lady, and so he does not even outwardly become aware of the gap that separates him from the ruling class. It is no wonder if, in such a situation, any dissatisfaction with the 'existing social order' finds difficulty in establishing itself in the mind of the worker. . . . All Socialist utopias come to nothing on roast beef and apple pie."[23] For Sombart, the ability to live comfortably obviated the need for class politics. While the new labor history has challenged Sombart's view that American workers lacked class consciousness, it has rarely questioned Sombart's assumption that consumerism eclipses working-class consciousness. What Walter Benn Michaels has written about literary criticism could also be applied to the new labor history: it "has customarily understood itself and the objects of its admiration as being opposed to consumer culture—and with few exceptions continues to do so."[24]

The historiography of consumerism in America, long marginalized, has rapidly moved toward the center. Previously treated—when deemed worthy of discussion at all—as a bourgeois arena in which middle-class Americans fashioned themselves as a distinctive group or, alternatively, as a phenomenon that began with mass production in the 1920s (this is still the standard view of the survey textbooks), consumerism is now recognized as a broad, complex, and long-term development closely connected with fundamental historical transformations.[25]

An unlikely aspect of the reevaluation of consumption has been perhaps the most fruitful: a focus on the participation of workers in the making of modern consumer society.[26] It is now widely noted that the United States began to shift from a producer society to a consumer society in the late nineteenth century.[27] Working-class Americans played an important role in this shift. In the 1980s and 1990s historians have demonstrated the significance of workers' participation in the emerging mass culture of turn-of-the-century America. Kathy Peiss has shown how laboring girls and young women, children of immigrants, made trips to dance halls, amusement parks, and theaters part of their daily lives despite tight economic circumstances. Susan Porter Benson has demonstrated that working-class women shaped the culture of the department store. Roy Rosenzweig has pointed out that workers took an active part in debates about public parks and saloons. Francis Couvares has argued that Pittsburgh workers helped create the mass culture of that city. In studies of Chicago and Los Angeles, Lizabeth Cohen and George Sanchez have uncovered strong links between ethnic workers and mass culture.[28] These scholars treat commercial culture not simply as a site of elite social control or hegemony but as a contested terrain significantly shaped by workers' tastes and participation.[29] No longer would most scholars of consumer society agree with the assertion of Richard Fox and Jackson Lears that "the search for consumer culture should begin by concentrating on the activities of urban elites."[30]

My examination of the living wage contributes to this growing literature by revealing a central, yet unstudied aspect of working-class participation in the development of consumer society, namely, its significant ideological input. Heretofore most studies of labor and consumption have focused on workers' participation in mass culture, not on their more explicitly political engagement with consumption. In reconstructing the relationship between the living wage and an ideology of consumerism, I hope to challenge assumptions about the origins of consumer society and its political valence. The living wage discourse highlights labor's early engagement with nascent consumer society. It uncovers a strand of political thought, still prevalent in a variety of forms such as "green consumerism," closely tied to consumer activism. A more complete history of the development of consumer society should encompass consumer activism as well as popular culture. It should include the development of a consumerist conventional wisdom in state and business policy as well as the rise of advertising. It should treat working-class as well as middle-class identity. In this book I offer the beginning of such a history.

Abbreviations Used in the Notes

AF	*American Federationist*
C and L	*Report of the Industrial Commission on the Relations and Conditions of Capital and Labor Employed in Manufacturing and General Business*, vol. 7 (Washington, D.C.: Government Printing Office, 1901)
GIB	*Gunton Institute Bulletin*
ILWCH	*International Labor and Working-Class History*
JAH	*Journal of American History*
JSH	*Journal of Social History*
JSP	*John Swinton's Paper*
JUL	*Journal of United Labor*
LH	*Labor History*
LM	George E. McNeill, ed., *The Labor Movement: The Problem of To-day* (Boston: A. M. Bridgeman, 1887).
NAM	National Association of Manufacturers Educational Pamphlet
NAR	*North American Review*
NYT	*New York Times*
PAH	Henry Barnard, ed., *Pamphlets in American History* (Sanford, N.C.: Microfilming Corp. of America, 1979)
PEEH	Ira Steward, "The Political Economy of Eight Hours." Unpublished manuscript, State Historical Society of Wisconsin, Madison
RHR	*Radical History Review*
SGP	*The Papers of Samuel Gompers* (4 volumes): Volume 1: *The Making of a Union Leader, 1850–1886*. Ed. Stuart B.

Kaufman et al. (Urbana: University of Illinois Press, 1986)

Volume 2: *The Early Years of the American Federation of Labor, 1887–1890.* Ed. Stuart B. Kaufman et al. (Urbana: University of Illinois Press, 1987)

Volume 3: *Unrest and Depression, 1891–1894.* Ed. Stuart B. Kaufman et al. (Urbana: University of Illinois Press, 1989)

Volume 4: *A National Labor Movement Takes Shape, 1895–1898.* Ed. Stuart B. Kaufman et al. (Urbana: University of Illinois Press, 1991)

WULLJ   *Woman's Union Label League Journal*

Notes

Preface

1. Jacqueline Jones, "Up from the Streets," *Tikkun* 9 (July–August 1994), 69; Neal Peirce, "America Wakes up to a Living Wage," *Charlotte Observer*, May 28, 1996; Leah Samuel, "Fighting for a 'Living Wage,'" *Labor Notes* (March 1996), 1, 10; Lawrence Glickman, "Bring Back a 'Living Wage' for American Workers Again," *State*, May 1, 1996, A11; "The President's Address: We Must Expand that Middle Class," *NYT*, January 26, 1995, A11; Jesse Jackson quoted in *NYT*, August 28, 1996, A17.

2. G. Pascal Zachary, "Minimum-Wage Issue Heads to Ballot Box," *Wall Street Journal*, February 23, 1996; Holly Sklar, "Link the Minimum Wage to Congressional Pay," *Z* (March 1996), 41–44; "A Living Wage for All: Solution to the Nation's Economic Ills," *Commentator* (December 1995), 1, 8; Manning Marable, "Fighting for a Decent Wage," *Witness* (September 1996), 8–9; Louis Uchitelle, "Some Cities Flexing Fiscal Muscle to Make Employers Raise Wages," *NYT*, April 9, 1996, A1, B7. See the following articles from *Bismarck Tribune*: John Risch, "Time for State to Raise Minimum Wage," October 4, 1993, 4A; idem, "Workers Should Benefit as Well," September 26, 1992, 4A. A 1993 attempt to repeal this provision failed. See Fredric Smith, "Lawmaker Wants to End 'Living Wage' Requirement," January 28, 1993. Kim Keller and Jonathan Lange, "Community Group Joins with Union to Fight Inner-City Poverty in Baltimore: AFSCME BUILD Coalition Wins 'Living Wage' for Contract Workers," *Labor Notes* (June 1995), 3–4; Bob Herbert, "City Job, Minimum Wage," *NYT*, July 27, 1995, A27; *Labor Notes* (April 1995), 4; Sal Albanese, "A 'Living Wage' Law Would Benefit New York," *NYT*, January 20, 1996, 22. A group called Portland Jobs with Justice proposing a nationwide "Living Wage Agenda," promised "a slew of living wage ballot initiatives." Leslie Kochan, "Portland: Jobs with Justice Offers an Alternate Economic Vision," *Labor Notes* (June 1995), 16. Steve Perry, "St. Paul Payday," *Nation*, November 13, 1995, 561–62; Scott C. Murray, "Houston's Living Wage Campaign Gets on the Ballot," *Labor Notes* (January 1997), 11; *Platform of the New Mexico Green Party* (Santa Fe, 1994), 45; "It Ain't a Living," *Nation*, June 10, 1996, 7; Jane Slaughter, "Overflow Crowd Expected for Labor Party's Founding Convention," *Labor Notes* (June 1996), 16; David Bacon, "Will the Labor Party Work?" *Nation*, July 8, 1996, 22–24. For the viewpoint of an economist,

see, for example, Richard C. Haas, "The Living Wage Makes Good Business Sense," *U. S. Catholic* (December 1994), 14–20.

3. Barbara Crossette, "Despite the Risks, the U.N. Plans a World Conference on Poverty," *NYT*, January 23, 1995, A7.

4. *NewsHour with Jim Lehrer*, April 28, 1996. On the implications of the living wage for the American family, see Jean Bethke Elshtain, "Feminism, Family, and Community," *Dissent* (Fall 1982), 442–49, and responses (with Elshtain's replies), Barbara Ehrenreich, "On Feminism, Family, and Community" (Winter 1983), 103–9; Marshall Berman, "Feminism, Community, Freedom" (Spring 1983), 247–55.

5. Ira Berkow, "Spring Training in New York City," *NYT*, March 20, 1992, B16; Paul Taylor, "Recipients Critique Welfare's Crunch," *Los Angeles Times*, May 9, 1992, A1.

6. Carey Goldberg, "The Battle of Strawberry Fields," *NYT*, July 3, 1996, A14; "Racial Unrest and Immigration," *Los Angeles Times*, May 12, 1992, B6. Another journalist connected the riots to another central aspect of the living wage ideology, which also relates to consumption: "Ultimately, the cost [of the L.A. riots] is going to come out of the American Standard of Living." Judy Mann, "The Willie Horton Riot," *Washington Post*, May 6, 1992, C29.

7. Heather MacDonald claims that New York City's proposed living wage law would "repeal the law of supply and demand." "'Living Wages,' Fewer Jobs," *NYT*, January 12, 1996, A13. In rejecting the same law, Deputy Mayor Rudy Washington declared, "We might as well dust off the Communist Manifesto." Vivian S. Toy, "Council Backs Higher Minimum Wages," *NYT*, June 7, 1996, B3. "The unintended effect of the minimum wage law has been devastating unemployment among poor teenagers, particularly among black teenagers," wrote John Silber, university president and erstwhile politician, in 1990. "The law sets a minimum price for their labor that exceeds its value . . . [and] there is no economic incentive to hire artificially overpriced labor." *Z* (September 1990), 39. See also Don Terry, "Minnesotans Split on Bill Requiring 'Living Wage': Attacked as Socialist, Defended as Fair Play," *NYT*, March 22, 1996, A12; Daniel B. Wood, "Debate Escalates over 'Living Wage' as Antipoverty Tool," *Christian Science Monitor*, October 17, 1996; and Matthew Miller, "Behind the Living Wage Hype," *New Republic*, February 10, 1997, 12, 14.

8. Walter Lippmann, "Campaign against Sweating," *New Republic*, March 27, 1915, in *Selected Articles on Minimum Wage*, ed. Mary K. Reely (New York: H. W. Wilson, 1917), 55.

Introduction: Rethinking Wage Labor

1. Susan Willis, *A Primer for Daily Life* (London: Routledge, 1991), 89.

2. Christopher Hill, "Pottage for Freeborn Englishmen: Attitudes toward Wage-Labour," in *Change and Continuity in Seventeenth-Century England* (Cambridge: Harvard University Press, 1975), 221.

3. Daniel T. Rodgers, *The Work Ethic in Industrial America, 1850–1920* (Chicago: University of Chicago Press, 1978), 30.

4. Victoria C. Hattam, *Labor Visions and State Power: The Origins of Business Unionism in the United States* (Princeton: Princeton University Press, 1993), 70, 113, 204–5; David Montgomery, "Labor and the Republic in Industrial America: 1860–1920," *Mouvement Social* 111 (April–June 1980), 201–15. Sean Wilentz contends that the "shared vision" of artisanal culture "virtually collapsed" by 1850. *Chants Democratic: New York City and the Rise of the American Working Class, 1788–1850* (New York: Oxford University Press, 1984), 15.

5. For an overview of nineteenth-century "initial proletarianization," see David M. Gordon, Richard Edwards, and Michael Reich, *Segmented Work, Divided Workers: The Historical Transformation of Labor in the United States* (Cambridge: Cambridge University Press, 1982), 48–94.

6. Victoria Hattam writes that workers accepted "their lot as wage earners," but the process was more active than this phrase implies; they attempted to redefine what it meant to be a wage-earning worker. *Labor Visions and State Power*, 205. See also Nancy Fraser and Linda Gordon, "A Genealogy of Dependency: Tracing a Keyword of the U.S. Welfare State," *Signs* 19 (Winter 1994), 309–36, esp. 315–16.

7. Ira Steward, *Meaning of the Eight Hour Movement* (Boston: the author, 1868), 13. In an era characterized by contentious debate over the meaning of wages, workers were not alone in the view that the "wage system has . . . become the question of our age." "The Wage Question," *American Catholic Quarterly Review* 11 (April 1886), 323. Economists ranging from the conservative Edward Atkinson to the liberal John Bates Clark noted the crisis in meaning; Atkinson remarked in 1885 that the "simple and apparently minor question" of the meaning of wages was the "major issue" of "modern society," and Clark commented in 1895 that "the law of wages" was "the subject of desperate controversy." Atkinson, "What Makes the Rate of Wages?" in *The Distribution of Products, or The Mechanism and the Metaphysics of Exchange* (New York: G. P. Putnam's Sons, 1885), 11–13, 19; Clark quoted in James Livingston, *Pragmatism and the Political Economy of Cultural Revolution, 1850–1940* (Chapel Hill: University of North Carolina Press, 1994), 55.

8. George Gunton, *The Economic and Social Importance of the Eight-Hour Movement*, AFL Eight-Hour Series, no. 2 (Washington, D.C.: AFL, 1889), 8.

9. Samuel Gompers, "A Minimum Living Wage," *AF* (April 1898), 25, 29.

10. William Smart, *Studies in Economics* (London: Macmillan, 1895), 33. Gunton wrote that "all discussion of the wage problem" has "to look to the living wage." "Hours of Labor," *GIB*, March 19, 1898, 242.

11. Croly quoted in Christopher Lasch, *The True and Only Heaven: Progress and Its Critics* (New York: Norton, 1991), 207. See also Herbert Croly, *The Promise of American Life* (Boston: Northeastern University Press, 1989), 206.

12. Richard J. Oestreicher, "Labor: The Jacksonian Era through Reconstruction," in *Encyclopedia of American Social History*, ed. Mary Kupiec Cayton, Eliot J. Gorn, and Peter W. Williams (New York: Scribner's, 1993), 2:1449. E. P. Thompson notes: "There is no such thing as economic growth which is not, at the same time, growth or change of a culture." "Time, Work-Discipline, and Industrial Capitalism," in *Customs in Common: Studies in Traditional Popular Culture* (New York: New Press, 1993), 403.

13. See, for example, Alan Trachtenberg, *The Incorporation of America: Culture and Society in the Gilded Age* (New York: Hill and Wang, 1982), 87, 92.

14. John Bodnar, "Immigration, Kinship, and the Rise of Working-Class Realism in Industrial America," *JSH* 14 (September 1980), 45–46.

15. To be sure, one aspect of this question was political in a narrow sense. As a Catholic journal noted in 1886: "Convince the voter in the United States that the placing of any political party in power would add twenty-five cents per day to his wages without any increase of time or of work which he is required to do, and the popular vote would immediately turn in favor of the party." "The Wage Question," 322.

16. Lizabeth Cohen, *Making a New Deal: Industrial Workers in Chicago, 1919–1939* (Cambridge: Cambridge University Press, 1990), 286; Samuel Gompers, *The Workers and the Eight-Hour Workday* (Washington, D.C.: AFL, 1919), 30–31; Ira Steward, "Unemployment," 32, and "Economy and Extravagance," 5, in PEEH; see also idem, "The Power of the Cheaper over the Dearer," in *A Documentary History of American Industrial*

Society, ed. John R. Commons et al., vol. 9: *Labor Movement, 1860–1880, Part 1* (New York: Russell and Russell, 1958), 325; "Unionism vs. Anti-Unionism," *Railroad Trainman* (December 1916), 1040–42.

17.   Gompers quoted in "George's Greatest Rally," *New York World,* October 27, 1886; David Montgomery, *The Fall of the House of Labor: The Workplace, the State, and American Labor Activism, 1865–1925* (Cambridge: Cambridge University Press, 1987), 1; John Francis Bray, "A New Declaration of Independence" (February 1876), in *We, the Other People: Alternative Declarations of Independence by Labor Groups, Farmers, Woman's Rights Advocates, Socialists, and Blacks, 1829–1975,* ed. Philip S. Foner (Urbana: University of Illinois Press, 1976), 97; "The Executive Council of the AFL to the Trade and Labor Unions of San Francisco," June 13, 1888, SGP 2:121–22. The platform of the Central Labor Union of New York proclaimed, "The combined wages-working class represents the great majority of the people. In their hands rests the future of our free institutions." *Labor: Its Rights and Wrongs* (Washington, D.C.: Labor Publishing, 1886), 165. Gilbert Slater, "Trade Unionism and the Living Wage," in *The Industrial Unrest and the Living Wage,* ed. William Temple (London: Collegium, 1913), 107.

18.   Michael Kazin, "The Workers' Party?" *NYT,* October 19, 1995, A25.

19.   By the 1970s, writes Jackson Lears, "hopes for a progressive consumer culture had foundered on the shoals of mobile capital's search for low labor costs and high productivity." *Fables of Abundance: A Cultural History of Advertising in America* (New York: Basic Books, 1994), 236. Yet the issues of stagnant wages and overwork have led commentators to look anew at the need for consumerist solutions to social problems. See, for example, Juliet B. Schor, *The Overworked American: The Unexpected Decline of Leisure* (New York: Basic Books, 1991).

20.   Christopher Lasch, *The Culture of Narcissism: American Life in an Age of Diminishing Expectations* (New York: Norton, 1978). For the genealogy of a long line of American thought that condemns consumerism as an illness, see Daniel Horowitz, *The Morality of Spending: Attitudes toward the Consumer Society in America, 1875–1940* (Baltimore: Johns Hopkins University Press, 1985), xvii–xxxi; Michael Schudson, "Delectable Materialism: Were the Critics of Consumer Culture Wrong All Along?" *American Prospect* 5 (Spring 1991), 26–35.

21.   Susman went so far as to suggest that this was the "proper socialist view." *Culture as History: The Transformation of American Society in the Twentieth Century* (New York: Pantheon, 1984), xxx.

22.   "A Sketch of Political Economy, Chapter VIII. Consumption," *JUL,* December 25, 1884, 865.

23.   Gompers quoted in *Chicago Inter Ocean,* April 23, 1890, *SGP* 2:302. See also "Higher Wages — the Fundamental Issue in Social Betterment," *AF* (July 1913), 526.

24.   George E. McNeill, *Argument on the Hours of Labor: Delivered before the Labor Committee of the Massachusetts Legislature* (New York: Labor Standard, [187?]), 7. Samuel Gompers agreed: "The aim of capital has been to make the worker a constantly greater producer. Whereas the aim of the labor movement is to make him a greater consumer also." *Leader,* July 25, 1887, *SGP* 2:47–48.

25.   One could use the phrase "modern moral economy" as a synonym for social economy; the consumerist concerns of living wage advocates paralleled — in the context of a wage labor economy — those of eighteenth-century English workers. E. P. Thompson commented: "Economic class-conflict in nineteenth-century England found its characteristic expression in the matter of wages; in eighteenth-century England the working people were most quickly inflamed to action by rising prices." "The Moral Economy of the English Crowd in the Eighteenth Century," in *Customs in Common,* 189.

Part I Introduction

1. Quoted in Sean Wilentz, "Against Exceptionalism: Class Consciousness and the American Labor Movement, 1790–1920," *ILWCH* 26 (Fall 1984), 13. On "free labor," see Eric Foner, "The Idea of Free Labor in Nineteenth-Century America," in *Free Soil, Free Labor, Free Men: The Ideology of the Republican Party before the Civil War* (New York: Oxford University Press, 1995). On "artisanal republicanism," see Wilentz, *Chants Democratic: New York City and the Rise of the American Working Class, 1788–1850* (New York: Oxford University Press, 1984), esp. 14–15. For a helpful, if skeptical, overview, see Daniel T. Rodgers, "Republicanism: The Career of a Concept," *JAH* 79 (June 1992), 11–38.

2. Wilentz, *Chants Democratic*, 164–67; Byllesby, quoted in Eric Foner, "The Meaning of Freedom in the Age of Emancipation," *JAH* 81 (September 1994), 447.

3. Samuel Eliot quoted in Michael Kimmel, *Manhood in America: A Cultural History* (New York: Free Press, 1996), 84.

4. Jeanne Boydston, *Home and Work: Housework, Wages, and the Ideology of Labor in the Early Republic* (New York: Oxford University Press, 1990); Susan Strasser, *Never Done: A History of American Housework* (New York: Pantheon, 1982).

5. Victoria C. Hattam, *Labor Visions and State Power: The Origins of Business Unionism in the United States* (Princeton: Princeton University Press, 1993), 76–111; William E. Forbath, "The Ambiguities of Free Labor: Labor and the Law in the Gilded Age," *Wisconsin Law Review* (1985), 767–817; Sean Wilentz, "The Rise of the American Working Class, 1776–1877: A Survey," in *Perspectives on American Labor History: The Problems of Synthesis*, ed. J. Carroll Moody and Alice Kessler-Harris (Dekalb: Northern Illinois University Press, 1989), 83–152, esp. 115.

6. *LM*, 454–55.

7. Ibid., 455, 459. This powerful statement has become a favorite of labor historians as well. See, for example, Leon Fink, *In Search of the Working Class: Essays in American Labor History and Political Culture* (Urbana: University of Illinois Press, 1994), 90, 121, 147, 179; Paul Krause, *The Battle for Homestead, 1880–1892: Politics, Culture, and Steel* (Pittsburgh: University of Pittsburgh Press, 1992), 83; Richard J. Oestreicher, "Urban Working-Class Political Behavior and Theories of American Electoral Politics, 1870–1940," *JAH* 74 (March 1988), 1257–86, esp. 1259; Alan Dawley, *Struggles for Justice: Social Responsibility and the Liberal State* (Cambridge: Harvard University Press, 1991), 35–36; Forbath, "Ambiguities of Free Labor," 768–69; Robert R. Montgomery, "'To Fight This Thing Till I Die': The Career of George Edwin McNeill," in *Culture, Gender, Race, and U.S. Labor History*, ed. Ronald C. Kent et al. (Westport, Conn.: Greenwood Press, 1993), 3–23.

8. Lincoln quoted in Foner, *Free Soil, Free Labor, Free Men*, 30; Conference of Labor Reformers, *Live to help live, an address from Friends of the Workingman, To the Pulpit, the Platform, and the Press in the United States of America* (Boston, 1872), 3, *PAH*, L22; Jesse Jones, *Equity* 2 (May 1876), quoted in Irwin Yellowitz, *The Position of the Worker in American Society, 1865–1896* (Englewood Cliffs, N.J.: Prentice-Hall, 1969), 103–4. As late as 1913 the British reformer Gilbert Slater distinguished between acceptable "apprenticeship wagedom" and unacceptable "permanent wagedom." "Trade Unionism and the Living Wage," in *The Industrial Unrest and the Living Wage*, ed. William Temple (London: Collegium, 1913), 107.

9. "The Fatality of the Wage System," *JSP*, May 25, 1884, 706. Horace Greeley quoted in Foner, *Free Soil, Free Labor, Free Men*, 16, 23–24; Forbath, "Ambiguities of Free Labor," 784; Wilentz, *Chants Democratic*, 302; Lincoln quoted in David Montgom-

ery, *Beyond Equality: Labor and the Radical Republicans, 1862–1872* (Urbana: University of Illinois Press, 1981), 31; Edwin L. Godkin, "The Labor Crisis," *NAR* 105 (July 1867), 213; Beecher quoted in Alan Trachtenberg, *The Incorporation of America: Culture and Society in the Gilded Age* (New York: Hill and Wang, 1982), 149. Yet Beecher and his ilk frequently denounced as communists those workers who demanded living wages to afford these symbols of Victorian consumption. As we shall see, living wage advocates castigated the thrifty, not the spending worker.

10. America's "rough laborers," for example, did not experience a "descent into wage labor." Peter Way, *Common Labour: Workers and the Digging of North American Canals, 1780–1860* (Cambridge: Cambridge University Press, 1993), 5–6.

11. By 1775 approximately one-fifth of the work force labored for wages. Wilentz, "Rise of the Working Class," 83–87; Marcus Rediker, *Between the Devil and the Deep Blue Sea: Merchant Seamen, Pirates, and the Anglo-American Maritime World, 1700–1750* (Cambridge: Cambridge University Press, 1987), 296; Gary Nash, *The Urban Crucible: The Northern Seaports and the Origins of the American Revolution* (Cambridge: Harvard University Press, 1986), 163.

12. Bruce Laurie, *Artisans into Workers: Labor in Nineteenth-Century America* (New York: Noonday, 1989), 15.

13. Wilentz, *Chants Democratic*, 18 n. 29; Alan Kulikoff, "The Transition to Capitalism in Rural America," *William and Mary Quarterly*, 3d ser., 46 (January 1989), 120–44; John Ashworth, *Slavery, Capitalism, and Politics in the Antebellum Republic*, vol. 1: *Commerce and Compromise, 1820–1850* (Cambridge: Cambridge University Press, 1995), 307.

14. Joseph Tuckerman, *An Essay on the Wages Paid to Females for Their Labour* (Philadelphia: Griggs and Dickinson, 1830), 8.

15. Quotation is from Wilentz, "Against Exceptionalism," 9; W. J. Rorabaugh, *The Craft Apprentice: From Franklin to the Machine Age in America* (New York: Oxford University Press, 1986), 69; William L. Barney, *The Passage of the Republic: An Interdisciplinary History of Nineteenth-Century America* (Lexington, Mass.: D. C. Heath, 1987), 35–42.

16. Bruce Laurie, *Working People of Philadelphia, 1800–1850* (Philadelphia: Temple University Press, 1980), 85–106; Daniel T. Rodgers, *The Work Ethic in Industrial America, 1850–1920* (Chicago: University of Chicago Press, 1978), 30–64; Sean Wilentz, "Artisan Republican Festivals and the Rise of Class Conflict in New York City, 1788–1837," in *Working-Class America: Essays on Labor, Community, and American Society*, ed. Michael H. Frisch and Daniel J. Walkowitz (Urbana: University of Illinois Press, 1983), 37–77.

17. Lincoln was speaking about the North. But even in the South, he claimed, "a majority of the whole people of all colors are neither slaves nor masters." Abraham Lincoln, "Annual Message to Congress," December 3, 1861, in *The Collected Works of Abraham Lincoln*, ed. Roy B. Besler, (New Brunswick, N.J.: Rutgers University Press, 1953), 5:52. David Montgomery, *Citizen Worker: The Experience of Workers in the United States with Democracy and the Free Market during the Nineteenth Century* (Cambridge: Cambridge University Press, 1993), 14; Foner, "Idea of Free Labor," xvi.

18. Rorabaugh, *Craft Apprentice*, 208–9; David R. Roediger, *The Wages of Whiteness: Race and the Making of the American Working Class* (London: Verso, 1991), 47. We should not, however, overstate the role of the war in this process. The changes that led to a drastic increase in the percentage of American wage earners are best seen as "long nurtured descendants of antebellum developments." Howard Horwitz, *By the Law of Nature: Form and Value in Nineteenth-Century America* (New York: Oxford University Press, 1991), 149.

19. Women (most of them domestic servants) represented one-quarter of all wage earners and one-tenth of industrial workers in the immediate postwar years. David Montgomery, *Beyond Equality*, 30; idem, "William H. Sylvis and the Search for Working-Class Citizenship," in *Labor Leaders in America*, ed. Melvyn Dubofsky and Warren Van Tine (Urbana: University of Illinois Press, 1987), 3–29; Wilentz, "Rise of the Working Class," 131; Stanley Lebergott, *Manpower in Economic Growth: The American Record since 1800* (New York: McGraw-Hill, 1964); Thomas Dublin, *Transforming Women's Work: New England Lives in the Industrial Revolution* (Ithaca: Cornell University Press, 1994), 23.

20. "Wages," in Massachusetts Bureau of Statistics of Labor, *Fourth Annual Report* (Boston: Wright and Potter, 1873), 440; Alexander Keyssar, *Out of Work: The First Century of Unemployment in Massachusetts* (Cambridge: Cambridge University Press, 1986), 16. See also Trachtenberg, *Incorporation of America*, 78; James Livingston, *Pragmatism and the Political Economy of Cultural Revolution, 1850–1940* (Chapel Hill: University of North Carolina Press, 1994), 65; Robert Wiebe, *Self-Rule: A Cultural History of American Democracy* (Chicago: University of Chicago Press, 1995), 95.

21. David Montgomery, *Beyond Equality*, 30. For similar formulations of this dilemma, see Foner, "Idea of Free Labor," xvii; Scott G. McNall, *The Road to Rebellion: Class Formation and Kansas Populism, 1865–1900* (Chicago: University of Chicago Press, 1988), 37; Michael J. Sandel, *Democracy's Discontent: America in Search of a Public Philosophy* (Cambridge: Harvard University Press, 1996), 168. The number of people engaged in manufacturing rose from 2.6 million in 1870 to 7.2 million in 1900, during what John B. Jentz calls the "classic period of American industrialization." "Labor: The Gilded Age through the 1920s," in *Encyclopedia of American Social History*, ed. Mary Kupiec Cayton, Eliot J. Gorn, and Peter W. Williams (New York: Scribner's, 1993), 2:1459–73. A parallel transformation was occuring in middle-class life: between 1870 and 1910 the proportion of self-employed, middle-class men dropped precipitously. Whereas workers became wage earners, many in the middle-class moved into salaried jobs. Gail Bederman, *Manliness and Civilization: A Cultural History of Gender and Race in the United States, 1880–1917* (Chicago: University of Chicago Press, 1995), 12.

22. "Chief Arthur and Mr. George," *Nation*, October 28, 1886; William Sylvis quoted in David Montgomery, *Beyond Equality*, 228–29; Justus O. Woods, "Mutualism," *JUL* (December 1883).

1. That Curse of Modern Civilization

1. David R. Roediger, *The Wages of Whiteness: Race and the Making of the American Working Class* (London: Verso, 1991), 67; Judith N. Shklar, *American Citizenship: The Quest for Inclusion* (Cambridge: Harvard University Press, 1991), 79–80; Mary H. Blewett, *Men, Women, and Work: Class, Gender, and Protest in the New England Shoe Industry, 1780–1910* (Urbana: University of Illinois Press, 1988), cover drawing, 120. See also David A. Zonderman, *Aspirations and Anxieties: New England Workers and the Mechanized Factory System, 1815–1850* (New York: Oxford University Press, 1992), 190, 202, 277; Eric Foner, "The Idea of Free Labor in Nineteenth-Century America," in *Free Soil, Free Labor, Free Men: The Ideology of the Republican Party before the Civil War* (New York: Oxford University Press, 1995), xvii.

On early and non-U.S. uses of "wage slavery," see Christopher Hill, "Pottage for Freeborn Englishmen: Attitudes toward Wage-Labour," in *Change and Continuity in Seventeenth-Century England* (Cambridge: Harvard University Press, 1975), 219–38; C. B. Macpherson, *The Political Theory of Possessive Individualism: Hobbes to Locke* (New

York: Oxford University Press, 1962), 272, 282; Sean Wilentz, "Against Exceptionalism: Class Consciousness and the American Labor Movement, 1790–1920," *ILWCH* 26 (Fall 1984), 1–24, esp. 9; John Ashworth, *Slavery, Capitalism, and Politics in the Antebellum Republic*, vol. 1: *Commerce and Compromise, 1820–1850* (Cambridge: Cambridge University Press, 1995), 114; Robert Wiebe, *Self-Rule: A Cultural History of American Democracy* (Chicago: University of Chicago Press, 1995), 88. Karl Marx observed that "the wage system is a system of slavery." "Critique of the Gotha Program," in *The Marx-Engels Reader*, ed. Robert C. Tucker (New York: Norton, 1978), 535.

For examinations of the "wage slavery" metaphor in revolutionary and antebellum America, see Marcus Cunliffe, *Chattel Slavery and Wage Slavery: The Anglo-American Context* (Athens: University of Georgia Press, 1979); Rex Burns, *Success in America: The Yeoman Dream and the Industrial Revolution* (Amherst: University of Massachusetts Press, 1976), 91–127; Jonathan A. Glickstein, *Concepts of Free Labor in Antebellum America* (New Haven: Yale University Press, 1991); F. Nwabueze Okoye, "Chattel Slavery as the Nightmare of the American Revolutionaries," *William and Mary Quarterly*, 3d ser., 37 (January 1980), 3–28; Eric Lott, *Love and Theft: Blackface Minstrelsy and the American Working Class* (New York: Oxford University Press, 1993); Christopher Lasch, *The True and Only Heaven: Progress and Its Critics* (New York: Norton, 1991), 64, 180, 203–5; Howard Dickman, *Industrial Democracy in America: Ideological Origins of National Labor Relations Policy* (LaSalle, Ill.: Open Court, 1987), 82–87.

2. McDonnell quoted in Herbert G. Gutman, "A Brief Postscript: Class, Status, and the Gilded Age Radical: A Reconsideration," in *Work, Culture, and Society in Industrializing America: Essays in American Working-Class and Social History* (New York: Pantheon, 1976), 268. *Mechanic's Free Press* quoted in Bernard Mandel, *Labor: Free and Slave* (New York: Associated Authors, 1955), 79. See also Eric Foner, "Abolitionism and the Labor Movement in Antebellum America," in *Politics and Ideology in the Age of the Civil War* (New York: Oxford University Press, 1980), 57–76, esp. 59; Sean Wilentz, *Chants Democratic: New York City and the Rise of the American Working Class, 1788–1850* (New York: Oxford University Press, 1984), 332.

3. Melvyn Dubofsky, *The State and Labor in Modern America* (Chapel Hill: University of North Carolina Press, 1994), xii; Lincoln quoted in Foner, *Free Soil, Free Labor, Free Men*, 30; Wilentz, *Chants Democratic*, 388; Amy Bridges, "Becoming American: The Working Classes in the United States before the Civil War," in *Working-Class Formation: Nineteenth-Century Patterns in Western Europe and the United States*, ed. Ira Katznelson and Aristide R. Zolberg (Princeton: Princeton University Press, 1986), 175.

4. Walter Benn Michaels, "The Phenomenology of Contract," in *The Gold Standard and the Logic of Naturalism* (Berkeley: University of California Press, 1987), 124. See also John R. Wikse, *About Possession: The Self as Private Property* (University Park: Pennsylvania State University Press, 1977); Wiebe, *Self-Rule*, 13, 90–91. The worker's "freedom and independence," said Steward, "is qualified or is compromised by the fact that he must make a bargain with somebody." "Notes on Freedom," 1, 3, in PEEH. Steward also wrote, "There is a closer relation between poverty and slavery than the average abolitionist ever recognized." Quoted in Dr. E. E. Spencer, "Ira Steward: A Lecture before the Prospect Union," November 13, 1895, State Historical Society of Wisconsin Library, Madison.

5. Foner, "Idea of Free Labor," xviii; Sean Wilentz, "The Rise of the American Working Class, 1776–1877: A Survey," in *Perspectives on American Labor History: The Problems of Synthesis*, ed. J. Carroll Moody and Alice Kessler-Harris (Dekalb: Northern Illinois University Press, 1989), 83–152, esp. 99–100. David Brion Davis has argued the abolitionists came closest to supporting wage labor, since they took the uncompensated

nature of slave labor to be its defining characteristic. See Thomas Bender, ed., *The Antislavery Debate: Capitalism and Abolitionism as a Problem in Historical Interpretation* (Berkeley: University of California Press, 1992).

6. The motto of the National Labor Union is quoted in Lasch, *True and Only Heaven*, 214; "The Fatality of the Wage System," *JSP*, May 25, 1884, 706; Powderly quoted in *LM*, 411. See also Richard Oestreicher, "Terence Powderly, The Knights of Labor, and Artisanal Republicanism," in *Labor Leaders in America*, ed. Melvyn Dubofsky and Warren Van Tine (Urbana: University of Illinois Press, 1987), 42. On the popularity of the "abolition of the wage system," see David Montgomery, "Labor and the Republic in Industrial America: 1860–1920," *Mouvement Social* 111 (April–June 1980), 201–15, esp. 205. On the language of wage slavery in post–Civil War America, see Paul Krause, *The Battle for Homestead, 1880–1892: Politics, Culture, and Steel* (Pittsburgh: University of Pittsburgh Press, 1992); Barry Herbert Goldberg, "Beyond Free Labor: Labor, Socialism, and the Idea of Wage Slavery, 1890–1920" (Ph.D. diss., Columbia University, 1979); idem, "Slavery, Race, and the Languages of Class: 'Wage Slaves' and White 'Niggers,'" *New Politics* (Summer 1991), 64–83; E. Springs Steele, "Henry George on Chattel and Wage Slavery," *American Journal of Economics and Sociology* (July 1987), 369–78.

7. An official of the Knights of Labor remarked in 1891, "We do not believe that the emancipation of labor will come with increased wages and a reduction in the hours of labor; we must go deeper than that, and this matter will not be settled until the wage system is abolished." Gerald Grob, "The Knights of Labor and the Trade Unions, 1878–1886," *Journal of Economic History* 18 (June 1958), 176.

8. Henry George to James P. Archibald, August 26, 1886, Henry George Papers, Mss. and Archive Div., New York Public Library. See also George, *Progress and Poverty* (1879; New York: Robert Schalkenbach Foundation, 1979), 388. Mary E. Marcy, "Beginners' Course in Socialism and the Economics of Karl Marx: Lesson VIII. — Shorter Hours of Labor," *International Socialist Review* 12 (July 1911), 38; Steve Johnson, "*Simpsons* Conspiracy Theory," *Boston Globe*, August 18, 1995, 62; Barbara Ehrenreich, "Honor to the Working Stiffs," *Time*, September 9, 1991, 72. Secretary of Labor Robert Reich labeled sweatshop workers "wage slaves." Fred Kaplan, "The Fruit of Their Labor Is Misery," *Boston Globe*, July 12, 1996, 1, 12. The contemporary usage that applies the term to well-paid but unhappy corporate workers aching to strike out on their own, bears a strong resemblance to the earlier discourse, in which wage workers defined freedom as self-employment. Bill Hendrick, discusses "making the jump from the pseudo-secure wage-slavery of corporate life to the independence of owning one's business" in "Going to Bat for Yourself," *Atlanta Constitution*, September 14, 1992, 1; Lisa Gubernick, "I Didn't Want to Be a 'Wage Slave,'" *Forbes*, September 28, 1992, 27. The fanzine titled *Temp Slave* provides further evidence of the continuing salience of the comparison.

9. On this point, see Oestreicher, "Terence Powderly," 48.

10. Charlotte Perkins Gilman, *Women and Economics* (New York: Harper Torchbooks, 1966). On the gendered use of this language, see Mary H. Blewett, "We Are Freeborn American Women: The Persistent Politics of Native-Born New England Women as Nineteenth-Century Industrial Workers," in *Labor in Massachusetts: Selected Essays*, ed. Kenneth Fones-Wolf and Martin Kaufman (Westfield: Institute for Massachusetts Studies, 1990), 124–37.

11. In 1893 the Cigarmakers International Union proposed a political party to solve the problem of "wage slavery." *SGP* 3 : 403.

12. David Montgomery, "William H. Sylvis and the Search for Working-Class Citizenship," in *Labor Leaders in America*, ed. Dubofsky and Van Tine, 12.

13. Huggins quoted in Lawrence W. Levine, *The Opening of the American Mind* (Bos-

ton: Beacon Press, 1996), 168; Edmund S. Morgan, *American Slavery/American Freedom: The Ordeal of Colonial Virginia* (New York: Norton, 1975); Orlando Patterson, *Slavery and Social Death: A Comparative Study* (Cambridge: Harvard University Press, 1982); Eric Foner, "The Meaning of Freedom in the Age of Emancipation," *JAH* 81 (September 1994), 435–60. See also James Oakes, *Slavery and Freedom: An Interpretation of the Old South* (New York: Knopf, 1990).

14. John Mitchell, *Organized Labor: Its Problems, Purposes, and Ideals and the Present and Future of American Wage Earners* (Philadelphia: American Book and Bible House, 1903), 57. On the goals and reception of this book, written with the economist Walter Weyl, see Craig Phelan, *Divided Loyalties: The Public and Private Life of Labor Leader John Mitchell* (Albany: State University of New York Press, 1994), 205, 208, 211.

15. Roediger, *Wages of Whiteness*, 66.

16. As recent work in legal, labor, and intellectual history demonstrates, "free labor" in the nineteenth century could be severely restricting for workers. David Montgomery, *Beyond Equality: Labor and the Radical Republicans, 1862–1872* (Urbana: University of Illinois Press, 1981), 231; idem, *Citizen Worker: The Experience of Workers in the United States with Democracy and the Free Market during the Nineteenth Century* (Cambridge: Cambridge University Press, 1993); Robert J. Steinfeld, *The Invention of Free Labor: The Employment Relation in English and American Law and Culture, 1350–1870* (Chapel Hill: University of North Carolina Press, 1991); Karen Orren, *Belated Feudalism: Labor, the Law, and Liberal Development in the United States* (Cambridge: Cambridge University Press, 1991).

17. As the editors of the Freedmen and Southern Society Project note: "Free labor emerged in the Union-occupied South as freedom was being defined in the North." Ira Berlin et al., eds., *Freedom: A Documentary History of Emancipation*, ser. 1, vol. 3: *The Wartime Genesis of Free Labor: The Lower South* (Cambridge: Cambridge University Press, 1990), 2.

18. Ibid., 3. William E. Forbath notes that "individual ownership—of one's capacity to labor in the worker's case"—became "the essence of personal right and freedom." "The Ambiguities of Free Labor: Labor and the Law in the Gilded Age," *Wisconsin Law Review* (1985), 799; Julie Saville, *The Work of Reconstruction: From Slave to Wage Laborer in South Carolina, 1860–1870* (Cambridge: Cambridge University Press, 1994), 26–28. Under capitalism, according to Karl Marx, "wage labour is defined as free labour." *Wage-Labour and Capital* (London: Lawrence and Wishart, 1933), 19.

19. Sumner quoted in John Ashworth, "Free Labor, Wage Labor, and the Slave Power: Republicanism and the Republican Party in the 1850s," in *The Market Revolution in America: Social, Political, and Religious Expressions, 1800–1880*, ed. Melvyn Stokes and Stephen Conway (Charlottesville: University Press of Virginia, 1996), 138; Garrison quoted in Foner, "Idea of Free Labor," xxiii; George, *Progress and Poverty*, 348; G. B. De Bernardi, "Forms of Bondage," *Labor Exchange* (April 1897), 8. See also Forbath, "Ambiguities of Free Labor," 782–86. Comparisons between the northern worker and the southern slave had been both a favorite of southern defenders of slavery and a "standard component of labor rhetoric" among northern workers during the antebellum era. Foner, "Abolitionism and the Labor Movement," 59.

20. "Hard Words of Nobody," *JSP*, February 15, 1885, 2. Antebellum workers used this argument as well. "The only difference between the free-labor and the slave systems," according to Mike Walsh, was that in the South "the Negro had a master without asking for one, while in the North the wage earner had to beg for the privilege of becoming a slave." Wilentz, *Chants Democratic*, 333.

21. At the founding meeting of the IWW in 1905, Big Bill Haywood claimed that

"rather than be one of the residents of the ghetto down here . . . I would rather be a big buck nigger on a plantation in the South before the days when chattel slavery was wiped out." Michael Kazin, *The Populist Persuasion: An American History* (New York: Basic Books, 1995), 303 n. 30.

22. George E. McNeill, "The Philosophy of the Labor Movement, A Paper Read before the International Labor Congress," Chicago, September 1893, 2. The labor pamphleteer William Howard concurred in 1894: "It is immaterial whether chattel law enables a man to sell his fellowmen, or whether business laws . . . oblige men to sell themselves to the highest bidder, the result—slavery, is the same." "A National Unit of Value for Labor," *AF* (July 1894), 92–93.

23. Justus O. Woods, "The Present Slavery—the Coming Freedom," *JUL*, September 25, 1884, 795–96; Eric Foner, *Reconstruction: America's Unfinished Revolution* (New York: Harper and Row, 1988), 103; idem, *Nothing but Freedom: Emancipation and Its Legacy* (Baton Rouge: Louisiana State University Press, 1983), 90; Port Royal journalist quoted in Saville, *Work of Reconstruction*, 3; Davis quoted in Herbert G. Gutman et al., *Who Built America: Working People and the Nation's Economy, Politics, Culture, and Society* (New York: Pantheon, 1992), 2:76; Joseph P. Reidy, *From Slavery to Agrarian Capitalism in the Cotton Plantation South: Central Georgia, 1800–1880* (Chapel Hill: University of North Carolina Press, 1992), 148. See also David Montgomery, *Citizen Worker*, 118. "Negro Workers: The A.F. of L. or the I.W.W.?" *Messenger* (July 1919), in *The Black Worker: A Documentary History from Colonial Times to the Present*, ed. Philip S. Foner and Ronald L. Lewis, vol. 5: *The Black Worker from 1900 to 1919* (Philadelphia: Temple University Press, 1980), 523–25. An IWW pamphlet declared: "As chattel slaves we were the property of our masters and, as a piece of valuable property, our masters were considerate of us and careful of our health and welfare. Today, as wage workers, the boss may work us to death at the hardest and most hazardous labor, at the longest hours, at the lowest pay. . . . should you be killed at work, the master merely gets another wage slave on the same terms. . . . The white wage worker is little, if any, better off. He is a slave the same as we are, and like us, he is regarded by the boss only as a means of making profits. . . . Our change from chattel slaves to wage slaves has benefitted no one but the masters of industry. They have used us as wage slaves to beat down the wages of the white wage slaves." *Colored Workers of America Why You Should Join the I.W.W.*, in *Black Worker*, 5:506–8. "Experience demonstrates that there may be a wages of slavery only a little less galling and crushing in its effects than chattel slavery, and that this slavery of wages must go down with the other," declared Frederick Douglass in 1883. Quoted in *The Black Worker*, ed. Foner and Lewis, vol. 3: *The Black Worker during the Era of the Knights of Labor* (Philadelphia: Temple University Press, 1978), 35.

24. "Wage Slaves," *JUL* (August 1883), 539; Mitchell, *Organized Labor*, 415. Condemnation of the metaphor continued into the twentieth century. In 1910 H. J. Nieboer decried "careless and rhetorical writers" who used the term in a "lax" way. *Slavery as an Industrial System* (New York: B. Franklin, 1971), 3. Norman Ware warned against the trivialization of the term in *The Industrial Worker, 1840–1860: The Reaction of American Industrial Society to the Advance of the Industrial Revolution* (Gloucester, Mass.: Peter Smith, 1959), xv.

25. "Wage Slaves." See also Wiebe, *Self-Rule*, 93. Garrison Frazier, an ex-slave and Baptist minister, observing emancipation in South Carolina in 1865, stressed this point to the freedpeople: "Slavery is receiving by irresistible power the work of another man, and not by his consent." Quoted in Saville, *Work of Reconstruction*, 11.

26. Justus O. Woods, "Mutualism," *JUL* (December 1883). Workers often contrasted

slavish with "manly" behavior. Martin Shefter, "Trade Unions and Political Machines: The Organization and Disorganization of the American Working Class in the Late Nineteenth Century," in *Working-Class Formation*, ed. Katznelson and Zolberg, 197–276, esp. 203–4; David Montgomery, *Workers' Control in America: Studies in the History of Work, Technology, and Labor Struggles* (Cambridge: Cambridge University Press, 1979), 13.

27. A Pittsburgh glassblower used this term before the Senate Committee on Relations between Capital and Labor in 1883. Leon Fink, *Workingmen's Democracy: The Knights of Labor and American Politics* (Urbana: University of Illinois Press, 1983), 10.

28. Edwin L. Godkin, "The Labor Crisis," *NAR* 105 (July 1867), 213.

29. Conference of Labor Reformers, *Live to help live, an address from Friends of the Workingman, To the Pulpit, the Platform, and the Press in the United States of America* (Boston, 1872), 4, 7, 8, *PAH*, L22; Wendell Phillips, *The Labor Question* (Boston: Lee and Shepard, 1884), 4–5; Stephens quoted in Norman Ware, *The Labor Movement in the United States, 1860–1895* (Gloucester, Mass.: Peter Smith, 1959), 74.

30. "Wage Slavery and Chattel Slavery," *JUL*, May 25, 1884, 702; "Alphega," letter to the editor, *Railroad Telegrapher* (January 1904), 74–75, quoted in Goldberg, "Beyond Free Labor," 67; Charles Pope, "Confidence in Their Own Class," *Labor Standard*, September 3, 1879, quoted in Irwin Yellowitz, *The Position of the Worker in American Society, 1865–1896* (Englewood Cliffs, N.J.: Prentice-Hall, 1969), 102. According to Pope, "wages never, in any country, permanently remain above the amount which may be necessary to provide the laborers with those things without which, from long use, they consider it impossible to exist."

31. *Report of the Bureau of Statistics of Labor of Massachusetts* (Boston, 1870), 158–64, 197, 314–16.

32. Ira Steward, "The Power of Wealth," 8, in PEEH; The most complete examination of Steward's life and ideas appears in David Montgomery, *Beyond Equality*, 249–60. For a full bibliography, see Lawrence Glickman, "Ira Steward," in *American National Biography*, ed. John A. Garraty (New York: Oxford University Press, forthcoming).

33. Arthur Morgan, *Edward Bellamy* (New York: Columbia University Press, 1944), 225.

34. "Wants," *JUL*, August 25, 1886, 2145–55. Similarly, B. W. Williams, a minister from Texas, declared that wages should be based on social needs. Yet he immediately noted that "compensation is, and should be, according to the quality of service rendered." "Wage Workers' Pay: Thoughtful Sermon by a Texas Clergyman," *Knights of Labor*, March 26, 1887, 12.

35. George E. McNeill, *The Eight Hour Primer: The Fact, Theory, and the Argument*, AFL Eight-Hour Series, no. 1 (Washington, D.C.: AFL, 1889).

36. Steinfeld, *Invention of Free Labor*, 187; Roediger, *Wages of Whiteness*, 66; Shklar, *American Citizenship*, 80.

37. Mitchell, *Organized Labor*, 415.

38. James Ellison, "Leaders Wanted," *Tobacco Worker* (March 1902), 7, quoted in Goldberg, "Beyond Free Labor," 158; Mitchell, *Organized Labor*, 415, 416.

39. John Allen Motte, "Labor Unions," *Machinists Monthly Journal* (November 1901), 820–21, quoted in Goldberg, "Beyond Free Labor," 162. See also "A Form of Slavery," *Weekly Bulletin of the Clothing Trades*, February 22, 1907, 3.

40. John Mitchell, "The Workingman's Conception of Industrial Liberty," *AF* (May 1910), 405–10. "To work from fear of want is slavery under a lash more severe than the cruelest drivers' whip," declared Paul L. Vogt, "Savings of Workingmen," *AF* (July 1910), 209–13.

41. George Gunton, "Moral Reasons for a Shorter Working Day," *GIB*, March 25, 1899, 582–83.

42. "Power of Unions," *Stone Cutters Journal* (July 1914), 9, quoted in Goldberg, "Beyond Free Labor," 162.

43. John B. Kelly, "Thoughts of a Working Man," *JUL*, September 25, 1886, 2172.

44. *Richmond Dispatch*, October 5, 1886, in *Black Worker*, ed. Foner and Lewis, 3:106–107.

45. Luke McKenny, "Colored People," *Union Label* (February 1898). Goldberg lists the newspaper as the *Artisan* and dates it in 1899. "Beyond Free Labor," 296.

46. A Lynn, Massachusetts, labor newspaper, quoted in Foner, "Idea of Free Labor," xix; Terence Powderly, *Thirty Years of Labor, 1859–1889* (Columbus, Ohio: Excelsior, 1890), 511.

47. Kazin, *Populist Persuasion*, 60. Saville describes a "battle for regular wages" in the postbellum South. *Work of Reconstruction*, 114.

48. William H. Harris, *The Harder We Run: Black Workers since the Civil War* (New York: Oxford University Press, 1982), 17; "Power of Union," *Union Leader*, July 22, 1905, 18, quoted in Goldberg, "Beyond Free Labor," 160; Mitchell, *Organized Labor*, x. See also "Labor and Independence," *AF* (July 1896), 90–91. Du Bois claimed that workers of all races "paid a wage below the level of decent living" were to some extent enslaved. "The Black Worker" in *W. E. B. Du Bois: A Reader*, ed. David Levering Lewis (New York: Henry Holt, 1995), 606.

49. Ira Steward, "Slavery" and "Freedom and Wealth" in PEEH. For Steward, an inability to consume constituted the essence of slavery: "If laborers ought to consume as little as possible of what they produce, tyrants and slaveholders have always been right. And Thomas Jefferson and William Lloyd Garrison wrong!" "The Power of Wealth," 5.

50. Ira Steward, "A Second Declaration of Independence," July 4, 1879, in *We, the Other People: Alternative Declarations of Independence by Labor Groups, Farmers, Woman's Rights Advocates, Socialists, and Blacks, 1829–1975*, ed. Philip S. Foner (Urbana: University of Illinois Press, 1976), 117.

51. Ibid.; Steward, "Economy and Extravagance," 21, in PEEH.

52. Mullen quoted in Peter J. Rachleff, *Black Labor in the South: Richmond, Virginia, 1865–1890* (Philadelphia: Temple University Press, 1984), 139.

53. Mitchell, "Workingman's Conception of Industrial Liberty," 405–6; Steward, "Freedom and Wealth."

2. Idle Men and Fallen Women

1. Ira Steward, "The Power of Wealth," 1, in PEEH. The Conference of Labor Reformers similarly declared: "Oftentimes the wage laborer, borne down by his comparative poverty, becomes willing to sell his vote, that with the price he may obtain some slight additional comfort or pleasure." *Live to help live, an address from Friends of the Workingman, To the Pulpit, the Platform and the Press in the United States of America* (Boston, 1872), 11, *PAH*, L22.

2. Margaret Dreier Robins, "Editorial," *Life and Labor* 1 (March 1911), 67. On the relation of "community self-governance" to "economic self-determination," see Robert Wiebe, *Self-Rule: A Cultural History of American Democracy* (Chicago: University of Chicago Press, 1995), 13, 39.

3. Ira Steward, "On Distribution of Wealth," 8, in PEEH; idem, "Poverty," in Massachusetts Bureau of Statistics of Labor. *Fourth Annual Report* (Boston: Wright and Pot-

ter, 1873), 416; Marx quoted in Carol Pateman, *The Sexual Contract* (Stanford: Stanford University Press, 1988), 201. As Pateman notes, "The figure of the prostitute can . . . symbolize everything that is wrong with wage labor."

4. On the distinction between metaphor and narrative, see Donald N. McCloskey, *If You're So Smart: The Narrative of Economic Expertise* (Chicago: University of Chicago Press, 1990), 10; J. Hillis Miller, "Narrative," in *Critical Terms for Literary Study*, ed. Frank Lentricchia and Thomas McLaughlin (Chicago: University of Chicago Press, 1990), 66–79; Roger Fowler, ed., *A Dictionary of Modern Critical Terms*, rev. ed. (London: Routledge, 1987), 156.

5. Jeanne Boydston, *Home and Work: Housework, Wages, and the Ideology of Labor in the Early Republic* (New York: Oxford University Press, 1990); Michael Kazin, *The Populist Persuasion: An American History* (New York: Basic Books, 1995), 14.

6. Mary H. Blewett, "Manhood and the Market: The Politics of Gender and Class among the Textile Workers of Fall River, Massachusetts, 1870–1880," in *Work Engendered: Toward a New History of American Labor*, ed. Ava Baron (Ithaca: Cornell University Press, 1991), 92–113.

7. John Galsworthy, "A Statue to Fortitude," *Life and Labor* 1 (February 1911). Samuel Gompers endorsed a subsistence living wage for women without the "anchorage" of a male breadwinner. "A Model Employer," *AF* (October 1896), 161–62. See also Joanne J. Meyerowitz, *Women Adrift: Independent Wage Earners in Chicago, 1880–1930* (Chicago: University of Chicago Press, 1988).

8. Clara Ruge, "Many Ways for Women to Earn a Living," *New York Call*, August 22, 1908.

9. David R. Roediger, *The Wages of Whiteness: Race and the Making of the American Working Class* (London: Verso, 1991), 45.

10. Caroline Dall, *The College, the Market, and the Court: Women's Relation to Education, Labor, and Law* (Boston: Lee and Shepard, 1867), 143.

11. For an overview of the voluminous literature on the "white slave" traffic, see Frederick Grittner, *White Slavery: Myth, Ideology, and American Law* (London: Garland, 1990). Giving shockingly high estimates for the number of prostitutes was a standard element in the critique of modern urban culture: "Women as Bread-Winners," *JUL*, September 27, 1888; Christine Stansell, *City of Woman: Sex and Class in New York, 1789–1860* (Urbana: University of Illinois Press, 1987), 12; Mark Thomas Connelly, *The Response to Prostitution in the Progressive Era* (Chapel Hill: University of North Carolina Press, 1980), 20–23. Another way to condemn moral decay was to hint at prostitution without ever explicitly mentioning it. Describing women who earned low wages, the Social Gospeler Washington Gladden stated, "It is not by charity alone that this starving wage is supplemented. There is a darker side to this picture on which I need not dwell." His audience knew exactly what this "darker side" meant and likely agreed with Gladden that it was structurally connected to the new economy. "A Living Wage," *Kingdom*, August 4, 1898, 812.

Historians of prostitution, notably Christine Stansell, have argued that prostitution was not necessarily tragic for working-class women. I do not challenge this view, which, in interpreting prostitution through a lens other than Victorian sentimentality, has improved our understanding of the lives of the working poor. Instead, in this chapter I examine the significance of rhetoric about prostitution in which such terms as "tragic" appeared with great regularity.

12. As Ruth Rosen notes, commercialization "was seen as encouraging prostitution of all kinds." *The Lost Sisterhood: Prostitution in America, 1900–1918* (Baltimore: Johns Hopkins University Press, 1982), 41. See also Pamela Susan Haag, "Commerce in

Souls: Vice, Virtue, and Women's Wage Work in Baltimore, 1900–1915," in *American Vistas, 1877 to the Present*, ed. Leonard Dinnerstein and Kenneth T. Jackson, 7th ed. (New York: Oxford University Press, 1995), 148–64.

13. Quoted in "Wages and Sin," *Literary Digest*, March 22, 1913, 621–24.

14. Quoted in Thomas J. Kerr IV, "The New York Factory Investigating Commission and the Minimum Wage Movement," *LH* 12 (Summer 1971), 379.

15. "The major factor inducing young women to sell their bodies was the low wages for female labor," writes Timothy J. Gilfoyle. *City of Eros: New York City, Prostitution, and the Commercialization of Sex, 1790–1920* (New York: Norton, 1992), 59–60.

16. Perhaps the fear of prostitution did not rest on its unlikeliness alone, for George Chauncey notes that male prostitution was widespread in New York City. *Gay New York: Gender, Urban Culture, and the Making of the Gay Male World, 1890–1940* (New York: Basic Books, 1994).

17. Wally Seccombe calls this a "willingness to exercise their market prerogatives." *Weathering the Storm: Working-Class Families from the Industrial Revolution to the Fertility Decline* (London: Verso, 1993), 6.

18. "Home, with what the family consumes, is the real point to nearly all the world's work," wrote Steward. All work "ought to be secondary to the original fact of home and family." "Economy and Extravagance," 3, in PEEH.

19. Frederick Engels, *The Condition of the Working Classes in England* (1845), quoted in Eli Zaretsky, *Capitalism, the Family, and Personal Life* (San Francisco: Harper Colophon, 1976), 55; *JSP* quoted in Susan Levine, *Labor's True Woman: Carpet Weavers, Industrialization, and Labor Reform in the Gilded Age* (Philadelphia: Temple University Press, 1984), 141; Edward O'Donnell, "Women as Bread Winners — the Error of the Age," *AF* (October 1897), 186–87.

20. Workingmen's Party of Illinois, "Declaration of Independence," July 4, 1876, in *We, the Other People: Alternative Declarations of Independence by Labor Groups, Farmers, Woman's Rights Advocates, Socialists, and Blacks, 1829–1975*, ed. Philip S. Foner (Urbana: University of Illinois Press, 1976), 102; Rev. B. W. Williams, "Wage Workers' Pay: Thoughtful Sermon by a Texas Clergyman," *Knights of Labor*, March 26, 1887, 12; Gompers quoted in Susan Lehrer, *Origins of Protective Labor Legislation for Women, 1905–1925* (Albany: State University of New York Press, 1987), 142. According to a letter writer to a New York labor newspaper, in "this land of liberty a desperate wage worker may be driven to suicide by helplessly looking upon a starving wife and child." "Crypto Cynic," "The Breadwinners Will Win," *JSP*, March 30, 1884, 2.

21. Martin A. Foran, *American Wages for American Workers* (May 1888), *PAH*, T1169.

22. David Montgomery, *Workers' Control in America: Studies in the History of Work, Technology, and Labor Struggles* (Cambridge: Cambridge University Press, 1979), 13; Nancy A. Hewitt, "'The Voice of Virile Labor': Labor Militancy, Community Solidarity, and Gender Identity among Tampa's Latin Workers, 1880–1921," in *Work Engendered*, ed. Baron, 142–67; Joshua B. Freeman, "Hardhats: Construction Workers, Manliness, and the 1970 Pro-War Demonstrations," *JSH* 24 (Summer 1993), 725–44.

23. Nick Salvatore, *Eugene V. Debs: Citizen and Socialist* (Urbana: University of Illinois Press, 1982), 23. Salvatore writes that manhood "demanded that he secure a living wage." See also Michael Kimmel, *Manhood in America: A Cultural History* (New York: Free Press, 1996), 81–116; Gail Bederman, *Manliness and Civilization: A Cultural History of Gender and Race in the United States, 1880–1917* (Chicago: University of Chicago Press, 1995); E. Anthony Rotundo, *American Manhood: Transformations in Masculinity from the Revolution to the Modern Era* (New York: Basic Books, 1993).

24. Steward, "Extravagance," 2 in PEEH. For astute analyses of the late nineteenth-

century middle-class cult of the physical, see John Higham, "The Reorientation of American Culture in the 1890s," in *Writing American History: Essays in Modern Scholarship* (Bloomington: Indiana University Press, 1970), 73–102; Jackson Lears, *No Place of Grace: Antimodernism and the Transformation of American Culture, 1880–1920* (New York: Pantheon, 1981); Chauncey, *Gay New York*, 112–15.

25. B.D., "Vivid Picture of the Cincinnati Conference," *JSP*, March 13, 1887, 2.

26. Alan Trachtenberg, *The Incorporation of America: Culture and Society in the Gilded Age* (New York: Hill and Wang, 1982), 77. In 1886 Henry George, the United Labor Party candidate for mayor of New York, made this connection explicit. "If a man has others dependent on him . . . then, if he voluntarily chooses poverty, it is a crime—ay, I think the men who have no one to support are shirking their duty." According to George, this social responsibility applied equally to unmarried men since "a woman comes into the world for every man; and for every man who lives a single life, caring only for himself, is some woman who is deprived of her natural supporter." "The Crime of Poverty," *JSP*, September 26, 1886, 1.

27. J. Pickering Putnam, *The Outlook for the Artisan and His Art* (Chicago: Charles H. Kerr, 1899), 15–17. On the historical construction of these gender roles, see Boydston, *Home and Work*; Alan Dawley, *Struggles for Justice: Social Responsibility and the Liberal State* (Cambridge: Harvard University Press, 1991), 21; Kazin, *Populist Persuasion*, 58–59.

28. "Workingwoman's Association Meeting at the *Revolution* Office," *Revolution*, October 1, 1868, 10.

29. In 1865 Ira Steward hoped for the day when "men whose wives and children are laboring in the mills will become ashamed of competing in such a manner, with those whose families do not, and allow them to remain at home, and unite with their fellow workmen in demanding pay enough to support them in their proper sphere." Quoted in Ardis Cameron, *Radicals of the Worst Sort: Laboring Women in Lawrence, Massachusetts, 1860–1912* (Urbana: University of Illinois Press, 1993), 40.

30. Boydston, *Home and Work*, 142–63.

31. *JUL*, March 15, 1887.

32. Lyman Abbott, "The Wages System," *Forum* (July 1890), 528; Florence C. Thorne, "The Trend Toward Equality," *AF* (February 1917), 120–21. Too often, as labor reformer Margaret Dreier Robins wrote, the middle classes wrongly harbored a "belief that the girl is a potential wife and mother only. The fact that she is a bread winner also is forgotten or ignored." "Industrial Education," *Life and Labor* (August 1913), 230.

33. Ida M. Van Etten, *The Condition of Women Workers under the Present Industrial System* (New York: Concord Co-Operative, 1891), 3; Eva McDonald Valesh, "Wage Working Women," *AF* (December 1906), 966. Another way of attempting to preserve gender roles was to criticize the wage system for subverting them. Praising the working-class housewife, even as anxiety increased that she was fast becoming an endangered species, Gompers declared that "the wife or mother, attending to the duties of the home, makes the greatest contribution to the support of the family. . . . in recent years . . . the wife of the wage earner, where the husband has been a fair breadwinner for the family, has taken up beautiful needlework, embroidery, and the cultivation of her better, but heretofore latent, talents." "Should the Wife Help to Support the Family?" *AF* (January 1906), 36.

34. Engels quoted in Pateman, *Sexual Contract*, 133. See also Eileen Boris, "'A Man's Dwelling Is His Castle': Tenement House Cigarmaking and the Judicial Imperative," in *Work Engendered*, ed. Baron, 114–41, esp. 116–17.

35. "Hard Words of a Nobody," *JSP*, March 9, 1885, 2.

36. "Women," *JSP*, May 3, 1885, 1; Dr. Raymond V. Phelan, *Living Wages and the Ballot* (New York: National Woman Suffrage Publishing, 1913); "Hosiers Fear Low Tariff," *NYT*, May 9, 1913, 2; "The Cheapest Commodity on the Market," *Masses* (December 1911), 5; Ira Steward, "The Power of the Cheaper over the Dearer," in *A Documentary History of American Industrial Society*, ed. John R. Commons et al., vol. 9: *Labor Movement, 1860–1880, Part 1*, (New York: Russell and Russell, 1958), 306–29; "A Working Woman," "A Woman to Her Sisters," *JSP*, June 27, 1886.

37. Gompers, "Should the Wife Help?" "A.C.," "Women and Men," *JUL*, January 22, 1887, 2258; Van Etten, *Condition of Women Workers*, 3.

38. Gompers, "Should the Wife Help?"

39. *JUL* (September 1882), 299; Wendell Phillips, *The Labor Question* (Boston: Lee and Shepard, 1884), 31.

40. Alice L. Woodbridge, "Women's Labor," *AF* (June 1894), 66–67.

41. This was the answer to the economist L. T. Hobhouse's question: "If we determine a man's wage on the basis of family needs how are we to determine the minimum wage of a woman?" "The Right to a Living Wage," in *The Industrial Unrest and the Living Wage*, ed. William Temple (London: Collegium, 1913), 72. See also Alice Kessler-Harris, *A Woman's Wage: Historical Meanings and Social Consequences* (Lexington: University Press of Kentucky, 1990).

42. "Women's Right to a Living Wage," *Independent*, January 4, 1915, 6. Another journal noted: "The terrible social evil is largely caused by insufficient pay and constant temptation of weak, ignorant, bewildered girls, whose lives are dull, cheerless, and hopeless, by vicious men who offer them please and change and 'comfort.'" "'Minimum Wage' Movement," *Chautauquan* 66 (April 1912), 148–50.

43. Song quoted in Grittner, *White Slavery*, 118.

44. Similarly, a congressional report on women workers described tempted women as unsatisfied consumers and thus potential prostitutes: "They are feverish and uncomfortable; they want something, but they don't know what it is. They crave, with an intensity we can hardly realize, something to make them forget their discomfort, to divert their minds from the weariness of their lives. That is why they flock to these cheap amusement places." Quoted in Felix Frankfurter, "The Social Evil in Chicago," in *Fourth Report of the Factory Investigating Committee* (New York: J. B. Lyon, 1915), 123, 124.

45. *JSP*, November 23, 1883, 1; Roy Porter, "Consumption: Disease of the Consumer Society?" in *Consumption and the World of Goods*, ed. John Brewer and Porter (London: Routledge, 1993), 58–81.

46. Otis Kendall Stuart, "The Wages of Women," *Knights of Labor*, February 26, 1887, 7. "Obviously, if young women can be kept from selling their souls only as they may be able to satisfy their wants through the sale of their labor, then the amount they must receive for their labor must vary as their wants vary." Frank Barkely Copley, "For and against the Minimum Wage," *NYT*, April 13, 1913, VII, 8.

47. Jay A. Ess, "The Condition of Woman and Her Relation to the Cause of Labor," *JUL*, February 21, 1889; "A Union Man's Wife," "To the Wives of Union Men," *Life and Labor* (September 1911). See also John Swinton, *Striking for Life: Labor's Side of the Labor Question* (New York: American Manufacturing and Publishing, 1894), 63.

48. Davis quoted in Dawley, *Struggles for Justice*, 37; "Woman's Work, Rights and Progress," *AF* (August 1913), 624–25.

49. J. P. Kohler, "The Enemy of Labor," *JSP*, January 23, 1887, 2.

50. W. Whitworth, "The Impending Revolution: Women Underworking the Men, Whom They Turn into Tramps," *JSP*, November 9, 1884.

51. O'Donnell, "Women as Bread Winners."

52. Robins, "Editorial."

53. G. Edward Janney, *The White Slave Traffic in America* (New York: National Vigilance Committee, 1911), 93. "Women's Wages and Morality," *AF* (June 1913), 465–68.

54. Hutchinson quoted in Vivien Hart, *Bound by Our Constitution: Women, Workers, and the Minimum Wage* (Princeton: Princeton University Press, 1994), 63; Paying such a minimum, the Brooklyn Central Labor Union claimed, was the "moral duty" of the state. "Why New York State Should Establish a Minimum Wage for Women and Minors" (1915), in *Selected Articles on Minimum Wage*, ed. Mary K. Reely (New York: H. W. Wilson, 1917), 31–42. As one labor reform journal noted: "perhaps one-fourth of all the working girls do not receive a living wage, are forced to live upon ill-nourishing food, in uncongenial quarters, to clothe themselves from money skimped from their lunch allotment and to deprive themselves of sufficient recreation." "The Wage Question and the Working Girl," *WULLJ* (June 1916), 8–9.

55. Alice Henry, "The Vice Problem from Various Angles," *Life and Labor* (May 1913), 142; Abrahams quoted in Henry Rogers Seager, "The Theory of the Minimum Wage," *American Labor Legislation Review* 3 (February 1913), 105. In promoting the living wage, William Howard wrote: "The value of human labor is not to be determined by the enslaving law of supply and demand but the natural law of life, by the cost of living to him or her who furnishes the labor." In his discussion of the nuts and bolts of the living wage, however, he dropped the feminine pronoun. "To accomplish this it is necessary to establish a unit of labor, based on the cost of living to him who furnishes the least skilled manual labor." "Labor and Life," *JSP*, November 7, 1886, 2. Both friends and foes of the minimum wage agreed that insuring a "living wage" for men would make the minimum wage for women less necessary. The solution, one expert told the New York Factory Investigating Commission in 1912, was "to give a decent living wage to the woman's husband." In this schema, male living wages would make women's wage labor unnecessary. Lehrer, *Origins of Protective Legislation*, 89, 142.

Part II Introduction

1. Gompers quoted in Henry Raymond Mussey, "Eight-Hour Theory in the American Federation of Labor," in *Economic Essays: Contributed in Honor of John Bates Clark*, ed. Jacob H. Hollander (New York: Macmillan, 1927), 235; Samuel Gompers, "A Minimum Living Wage," *AF* (April 1898), 29; "Gompers is Much Excited," *Kansas City Times*, April 10, 1898, *SGP* 4:467.

2. Testimony of George McNeill, *C and L*, 120. In 1871 Charles Cowley, counsel to the petitioners for a ten-hour law, declared: "If before coming here to exhibit their shallowness, these witnesses had devoted a few days to the faithful study of Adam Smith, McCulloch, Ricardo, Mill, or some other writer of authority on political economy," they would have abandoned their "crude notions." *The Ten-Hours Law: Argument Delivered before the Joint Special Committee of the Massachusetts Legislature upon the Hours of Labor, March 22, 1871* (Lowell: Stone and Huse, 1871), 4. William Sylvis regularly quoted "Thomas Malthus, Nassau Senior, Henry Carey, and especially John Stuart Mill." David Montgomery, "William H. Sylvis and the Search for Working-Class Citizenship," in *Labor Leaders in America*, ed. Melvyn Dubofsky and Warren Van Tine (Urbana: University of Illinois Press, 1987), 4.

3. Terence Powderly, Gompers's rival in almost every other way, similarly condemned "the stilted ignorance of Political Economy, as usually taught in the schools." *LM*, 408. The anarchist Dyer D. Lum wrote, "The day has passed when it can be as-

serted as an economic truism that the laws governing production and distribution are invariable natural laws." *Philosophy of Trade Unions*, AFL Pamphlet no. 10 (New York: AFL, July 1, 1892), 12. An important newspaper of the Farmers' Alliance was called the *National Economist*. See Robert C. McMath Jr., *American Populism: A Social History* (New York: Hill and Wang, 1993), 150.

4. See, for example, T. Wharton Collins, *The Right to Labor and Live* (187?), 1, 3, *PAH*, L20; Lemuel Danryid, *History and Philosophy of the Eight-Hour Movement*, AFL Eight-Hour Series, no. 3 (Washington, D.C.: AFL, 1899), 8; Carroll Davidson Wright, *The Relation of Political Economy to the Labor Question* (Boston: Franklin Press, 1882); Ira Steward, "The Power of the Cheaper over the Dearer," 13, in PEEH; John H. Chadwick, *The Living Wage: A Sermon* (Boston: Geo. H. Ellis, 1902), 17; Julie Saville, *The Work of Reconstruction: From Slave to Wage Laborer in South Carolina, 1860–1870* (Cambridge: Cambridge University Press, 1994), 49. Edward Bellamy used the term in his popular novel of 1888, *Looking Backward* (New York: Penguin, 1982), 88.

E. P. Thompson made famous another phrase, "moral economy," to indicate this opposition to political economy, but Thompson's moral economists were far more hostile to the market than were the advocates of social economy. See "The Moral Economy of the English Crowd in the Eighteenth Century" and "The Moral Economy Reviewed," in *Customs in Common: Studies in Traditional Popular Culture* (New York: New Press, 1993), 185–351.

5. See also George Gunton, *Principles of Social Economics* (New York: G. P. Putnam's, 1891). He later changed the title of the journal to *Gunton's Magazine*. Jack Blicksilver, "George Gunton: Pioneer Spokesman for a Labor–Big Business Entente," *Business History Review* 31 (Spring 1957), 1–22; Daniel Horowitz, *The Morality of Spending: Attitudes toward the Consumer Society in America, 1875–1940* (Baltimore: Johns Hopkins University Press, 1985), 30–49.

6. Henry Demarest Lloyd, *The Safety of the Future Lies in Organized Labor* (Washington, D.C.: AFL, 1893), 3–4; Wright, *Relation of Political Economy*, 11, 24. The "living wage," noted E. C. Fortey, "can only be obtained if there are brought to bear on economic questions those ethical principles which are so deeply rooted in our nature." "The Living Wage—an English View," *American Catholic Quarterly Review* 37 (October 1912), 736.

7. "A Living Wage," *Outlook*, September 21, 1895, 458.

8. See, for example, Henry Demarest Lloyd, "Revolution: The Evolution of Socialism," in Chester McArthur Destler, *American Radicalism, 1865–1901: Essays and Documents* (New York: Octagon, 1963), 213–21.

9. Dorothy Ross, *The Origins of American Social Science* (Cambridge: Cambridge University Press, 1991), 42–48, 116. Commons, Ely, and others were criticized for supporting the labor movement. See Leon Fink, "'Intellectuals' versus 'Workers': Academic Requirements and the Creation of Labor History," in *In Search of the Working Class: Essays in American Labor History and Political Culture* (Urbana: University of Illinois Press, 1994), 201–35.

10. Ross, *Origins of American Social Science*, 79–80; Wright, *Relation of Political Economy*, 5–6, 17, 33, 43.

11. Place quoted in Richard Ashcraft, "Liberal Political Theory and Working-Class Radicalism in Nineteenth-Century England," *Political Theory* 21 (May 1993), 254. Journeyman's committee quoted in Sean Wilentz, "Against Exceptionalism: Class Consciousness and the American Labor Movement, 1790–1920," *ILWCH* 26 (Fall 1984), 11.

12. *Annual Report of the Boston Eight-Hour League* (Boston: Boston Eight-Hour League, 1872), 6; Henry George, *The Science of Political Economy*, quoted in "Henry

George's Last Book," *New York Herald*, March 12, 1898, 13; William Cunningham, "A Living Wage," *Contemporary Review* 65 (January 1894), 16–28. Michael Kazin notes that "long, learned arguments like George's against reigning economic orthodoxy were surprisingly popular." *The Populist Persuasion: An American History* (New York: Basic Books, 1995), 32.

13. Bradford Dubois, "What Causes Hard Times?" *JSP*, September 27, 1885, 2. Forty years later, the labor reformer W. Jett Lauck called for the "abandonment of the ruthless economic law of supply and demand." *Political and Industrial Democracy, 1776–1926* (New York and London: Funk and Wagnalls, 1926), 97. George Gunton, *The Economic and Social Importance of the Eight-Hour Movement*, AFL Eight-Hour Series, no. 2, (Washington, D.C.: AFL, 1889), 22. See also J. A. Pollock, "Supply and Demand," *Railroad Trainman* (January 1915), 51–53.

14. Gompers, "Minimum Living Wage," 29. A review of a book by Henry George made a similar point. "Political economy . . . is . . . apt to prove wearisome to the general reader." "Henry George's Last Book."

15. Robert Blatchford, *The Living Wage and the Law of Supply and Demand: A Letter to the Colliers* (London: Clarion, 1895), 12.

16. Wilentz, "Against Exceptionalism," 11.

17. Gompers, "What Does Labor Want? An Address before the International Labor Congress in Chicago," August 28, 1893, *SGP* 3:393; Gunton, *Economic and Social Importance*, 22; Wright, "Relation of Political Economy"; Adam Smith, *An Inquiry into the Nature and Causes of the Wealth of Nations*, book 4, chap. 8 (Oxford: Clarendon Press, 1880), 244; Danryid, *History and Philosophy*, 9; Richard Ely, *Introduction to Political Economy* (New York: Chautauqua Press, 1889), 149; William D. P. Bliss, ed., *Encyclopedia of Social Reform* (New York: Funk and Wagnalls, 1897), 338–39. For scholarly reassessments of Adam Smith consistent with this view, see Istvan Hont and Michael Ignatieff, "Needs and Justice in the *Wealth of Nations*: An Introductory Essay," in *Wealth and Virtue: The Shaping of Political Economy in the Scottish Enlightenment*, ed. Hont and Ignatieff (Cambridge: Cambridge University Press, 1983), 1–44; Mitchell Dean, *The Constitution of Poverty: Toward a Genealogy of Liberal Governance* (London: Routledge, 1991), 122–36; James Kloppenberg, "The Virtues of Liberalism: Christianity, Republicanism, and Ethics in Early American Political Discourse," *JAH* 74 (June 1987), 9–33; Christopher Lasch, *The True and Only Heaven: Progress and Its Critics* (New York: Norton, 1991), 52–55.

3. Defining the Living Wage

1. Roy L. McCardell, *The Wage Slaves of New York* (New York: G. W. Dillingham, 1899), 111. While it was being serialized, the story generated massive public interest; over 7,000 readers sent letters to the *Evening World*.

2. Both the St. Louis and Omaha Populist platforms declared: "Wealth belongs to him who creates it. Every dollar taken from industry without an equivalent is robbery." Chester McArthur Destler, *American Radicalism, 1865–1901: Essays and Documents* (New York: Octagon, 1963), 25–27.

3. Rev. B. W. Williams, "Wage Workers' Pay: Thoughtful Sermon by a Texas Clergyman," *Knights of Labor*, March 26, 1887, 12.

4. The Knights of Labor, who used the phrase "full fruits of his toil" in the preamble to their platform, aimed "to secure to the workers the full enjoyment of the wealth they create." *Labor: Its Rights and Wrongs* (Washington, D.C.: Labor Publishing, 1886), 22,

30. The *New York Call*, June 29, 1908, described a "Fundamental Principle that each worker has an undeniable right to enjoy the full benefit of all that he or she produces." But a couple of weeks later (July 14) in a cartoon demonstrating how rarely workers enjoyed this right, text reading "The Fruit of Workingman's Labor" is set inside a lemon, not exactly the "fruit" that most workers had in mind.

5. Whitman quoted as an epigraph for Sean Wilentz's evocation of "the artisan republic," in *Chants Democratic: New York City and the Rise of the American Working Class, 1788–1850* (New York: Oxford University Press, 1984), 21; George E. McNeill, "To Ira Steward," in *Unfrequented Paths: Songs of Nature, Labor, and Men* (Boston: James H. West, 1903), 95–96; Frank Parsons, *The Drift of Our Time* (Chicago: Charles H. Kerr, 1898), 11; David Montgomery, *Beyond Equality: Labor and the Radical Republicans, 1862–1872* (Urbana: University of Illinois Press, 1981), 238–39.

6. McCardell, *Wage Slaves of New York*, 94.

7. Edward Bellamy's best-selling novel of 1888 also used the term. *Looking Backward* (New York: Penguin, 1982), 222.

8. Testimony of Samuel Gompers, *C and L*, 614.

9. Hugh Lloyd Jones, "Should Wages Be Regulated by Market Prices?" *Beehive*, July 18, 1874; Justus O. Woods, "The Present Slavery—the Coming Freedom," *JUL*, September 25, 1884, 795–96; John A. Ryan, "The Laborer's Right to a Living Wage," *Catholic University Bulletin* 8 (April 1902), 159.

10. The phrase is Richard Oestreicher's. "Labor: The Jacksonian Era through Reconstruction," in *Encyclopedia of American Social History*, ed. Mary Kupiec Cayton, Eliot J. Gorn, and Peter W. Williams (New York: Scribner's, 1993), 2 : 1447.

11. George Gunton, "Hours of Labor," *GIB*, March 19, 1898, 241–49. Haywood declaimed, "Instead of the conservative motto 'A fair day's wages for a fair day's work,' we must inscribe on our banners the revolutionary watchword, 'Abolition of the wage system.'" "Preamble of the Industrial Workers of the World, 1908," in *Rebel Voices: An IWW Anthology*, ed. Joyce L. Kornbluh (Ann Arbor: University of Michigan Press, 1964), 8; Rae quoted in Craig Phelan, *Divided Loyalties: The Public and Private Life of Labor Leader John Mitchell* (Albany: State University of New York Press, 1994), 16–17; John Mitchell, *Organized Labor: Its Problems, Purposes, and Ideals and the Present and Future of American Wage Earners* (Philadelphia: American Book and Bible House, 1903), ix, 415, 416.

12. Gunton, "Hours of Labor," 241. Most living wage supporters acknowledged the (at least temporary) hegemony of the wage system. Some labor groups, however, believed that the wage system would some day be, as the platform of the Knights of Labor put it, "superseded." *Labor: Its Rights and Wrongs*, 33. Ira Steward envisioned "the wage system gradually disappearing through higher wages." *LM*, 144. In the 1920s, a British Communist, R. Palme Dutt, composed a polemic against the "flimsy" living wage policy of the Independent Labor Party. He preferred to see the concept used as a weapon "in the daily struggle between the capitalists and the working class," not as a "social ideal." *Socialism and the Living Wage* (London: Communist Party of Great Britain, 1927), 17.

13. Stephens quoted in William E. Forbath, "The Ambiguities of Free Labor: Labor and the Law in the Gilded Age," *Wisconsin Law Review* (1985), 801.

14. Rev. Wm. J. White, "A Living Wage," *Charities and the Commons*, December 15, 1906, 471.

15. *LM*, 161–62.

16. Slavery meant work without "recompense," a freedman named Jourdan Anderson wrote his ex-master in 1865, in a letter demanding back wages. Leon F. Litwack, *Been in the Storm So Long: The Aftermath of Slavery* (New York: Vintage, 1979), 333–

35. Female factory workers for whom wage labor was "a real source of independence," writes David Zonderman, "did not fear a descent into the ranks of wage labor." *Aspirations and Anxieties: New England Workers and the Mechanized Factory System, 1815–1850* (New York: Oxford University Press, 1992), 15, 188.

17. Lawrence T. McDonnell nicely illustrates this point when he contrasts two pressmen employed at the *Charleston Evening News*, a white man who had followed a "downward path from independent farm ownership or a proud artisanal tradition to . . . wage labor," and a slave who had "risen" into that same world of wage labor. "Work, Culture, and Society in the Slave South, 1790–1861," in *Black and White Cultural Interaction in the Antebellum South*, ed. Ted Ownby (Jackson: University Press of Mississippi, 1993), 125–47.

18. Stanton quoted in Gillian Brown, *Domestic Individualism: Imagining Self in Nineteenth-Century America* (Berkeley: University of California Press, 1990), 4; Tera W. Hunter, "Domination and Resistance: The Politics of Wage Household Labor in New South Atlanta," in *"We Specialize in the Wholly Impossible:" A Reader in Black Women's History*, ed. Darlene Clark Hine, Wilma King, and Linda Reed (Brooklyn: Carlson, 1995), 343–57, esp. 343–44 and 351; Sharon Harley, "When Your Work Is Not Who You Are: The Development of a Working-Class Consciousness among Afro-American Women," *"We Specialize,"* 25–28. Both Hunter and Harley argue that African American women workers often framed demands for justice in terms of wages, although both show that these women also believed that independence required some protection from the wage system as well.

19. Eric Foner, "The Idea of Free Labor in Nineteenth-Century America," in *Free Soil, Free Labor, Free Men: The Ideology of the Republican Party before the Civil War* (New York: Oxford University Press, 1995), xxiv.

20. "Samuel Gompers," *JSP*, July 31, 1887. "Those who . . . fight primarily for the abolition of wage labor" without meeting the needs of workers in the present "have not fully grasped the idea of modern socialism," observed Adolph Strasser, Gompers's fellow cigar maker and union ally. *SGP* 1:71. See also H. M. Gitelman, "Adolph Strasser and the Origins of Pure and Simple Unionism," *LH* (Winter 1965), 71–83. John Mitchell of the UMW similarly wrote: "Trade unionism is not irrevocably committed to the wage system, nor is it irrevocably committed to its abolition. It demands the constant improvement of the workingmen, if possible by the maintenance of the present wage system, if not possible, by its abolition." *Organized Labor*, 415.

21. *LM*, 161–62.

22. Henry Demarest Lloyd, *The Safety of the Future Lies in Organized Labor* (Washington, D.C.: AFL, 1893), 3–4.

23. The style of thinking can be considered part of a strain of American social thought which invokes the "language of the market to articulate higher ideals and principles." Richard F. Teichgraeber III, *Sublime Thoughts / Penny Wisdom: Situating Emerson and Thoreau in the American Market* (Baltimore: Johns Hopkins University Press, 1995), 270–71.

24. Testifying before the United States Strike Commission in 1894, for example, Samuel Gompers said a "principle" had recently been developed by striking English miners which called for "a 'life line' below which point wages dare not fall." *SGP* 3:575. The previous year Henry Demarest Lloyd, who also used the phrase "life line," had given credit to English coal miners for developing the "new words of the living wage." *Safety of the Future Lies in Organized Labor*, 3.

The few contemporary scholars who sought the origins of the term confirmed this chronology. James E. Boyle, *The Minimum Wage and Syndicalism* (Cincinnati: Steward and Kidd, 1913), 72; Sidney Webb, *Industrial Democracy* (London: Longmans, Green,

1899), 587; Henry W. Macrosty, "The Recent History of the Living Wage Movement," *Political Science Quarterly* 13 (September 1898), 416. Although he differed slightly on the timing, the economist Edwin Seligman also attributed English origins to the term: "It is only a few years ago, since 1888 or 1890, that we have heard the phrase living wage used in connection with the miners in England." He noted that the living wage demand was evidence that workers "have gone through an evolution" in their thinking about just compensation. "The Living Wage," *GIB*, March 26, 1898, 262.

25. Hugh Lloyd Jones, "Political and Social Reform," *Beehive*, March 7, 1874, and "Should Wages Be Regulated?" Sidney Webb and Beatrice Webb, *The History of Trade Unionism* (London: Longmans, Green, 1920), 340–41.

26. According to a "Striker," "fair wages" were those above a "living figure." "Fair Wages," *NAR* 125 (September 1877), 324. For debates about the term during the Pullman Strike of 1894, see Nick Salvatore, *Eugene V. Debs: Citizen and Socialist* (Urbana: University of Illinois Press, 1982), 122. An 1897 miner's strike, explained to the public by the AFL as a "great struggle for a living wage," also gained national attention. *SGP* 4: 344–51, 355, 358.

27. Steward twice used the phrase "lowest living wages," which he considered to be little better than "slavery," in "Costs of Increased Wealth," 3, and an untitled section of PEEH; Jones, "Should Wages Be Regulated?"; Samuel Gompers, "A Minimum Living Wage," *AF* (April 1898), 29; Henry R. Seager, "The Minimum Wage as Part of a Program for Social Reform," *Annals* 48 (July 1913), 4.

28. Rev. Dr. Washington Gladden, "A Living Wage," *Kingdom*, August 4, 1898, 813–14; Mitchell, *Organized Labor*, x. The British economist J. A. Hobson declared that "vagueness does not make the demand unreasonable." In fact, its variability and ever-increasing nature were precisely what appealed to Hobson and many other advocates: "A living wage is elastic as life itself." *Work and Wealth: A Human Valuation* (New York: Macmillan, 1914), 196. Advocates often defined the living wage in the negative; for Jones, the living wage was "not a miserable pittance to starve on"; for Gompers and Lloyd, it was a "life line not a dead-line"; and for Edwin Seligman, it was "not . . . simply a bare subsistence wage."

29. Christopher Hill, "Pottage for Freeborn Englishmen: Attitudes toward Wage-Labour," in *Change and Continuity in Seventeenth-Century England* (Cambridge: Harvard University Press, 1975), 219–38. On the "radicalism of tradition," see Craig Calhoun, *The Question of Class Struggle: Social Foundations of Popular Radicalism during the Industrial Revolution* (Chicago: University of Chicago Press, 1981); Sean Wilentz, "Against Exceptionalism: Class Consciousness and the American Labor Movement, 1790–1920," *ILWCH* 26 (Fall 1984), 1–24, esp. 3–5; Leon Fink, "Looking Backward: Reflections on Workers' Culture and Certain Conceptual Dilemmas within Labor History," in *Perspectives on American Labor History: The Problems of Synthesis*, ed. J. Carroll Moody and Alice Kessler-Harris (Dekalb: Northern Illinois University Press, 1989), 5–29.

30. Bruce Laurie, *Artisans into Workers: Labor in Nineteenth-Century America* (New York: Noonday, 1989), 44, 57, 101, 216. The term continued to have appeal in the post-bellum era. Peter James McGuire, chief executive officer of the United Brotherhood of Carpenters and Joiners of America, declared in 1883 that "fully 85 per cent. of the population of this country—the wage-workers—have no hope of ever obtaining a competence." *Report of the Senate Committee upon the Relations between Capital and Labor* (Washington, D.C.: Government Printing Office, 1885), 1:318. See also Paul Krause, *The Battle for Homestead, 1880–1892: Politics, Culture, and Steel* (Pittsburgh: University of Pittsburgh Press, 1992).

31. In 1851 the British social reformer and journalist Henry Mayhew distinguished

between "high" and "low," "good" and "bad," and "fair" and "unfair" wages. *The Unknown Mayhew: Selections from the Morning Chronicle, 1849–1850*, ed. E. P. Thompson and Eileen Yeo (New York: Pantheon, 1971), 463–75. The slogan a "fair day's work for a fair day's wage," writes Gregory Claeys, had deep roots in British working-class culture and "epitomized the just price and fair wage tradition." *Machinery, Money, and the Millennium: From Moral Economy to Socialism, 1815–1860* (Princeton: Princeton University Press, 1987), 189. Sidney Webb claimed that the impetus for the British miners who coined the phrase was the demand of the United Silk Throwers for fair wages. Although they did not use the term living wages, they emphasized not productive equivalence but needs in their definition: "The due reward for our labor may be summed up in these words, Shelter, Food, and Raiment both for ourselves, our wives, and our children." *Industrial Democracy*, 587.

32. *San Francisco Truth*, August 23, 1882. For examples of Powderly's critique of the "wage system," see *LM*, 410, 411.

33. A group of New York workers in 1829, for example, demanded a comfortable living in exchange for "reasonable toil." Victoria C. Hattam, *Labor Visions and State Power: The Origins of Business Unionism in the United States* (Princeton: Princeton University Press, 1993), 80. "The Right of Life . . . carries with it the right to the means of a living," declared a group of working-class radicals in 1883, to be achieved by "rendering the 'full equivalent' to the producer." Henry Demarest Lloyd wished for a day "when every man who works will get a living and every man who gets a living shall work." Destler, *American Radicalism*, 92, 221. The Reverend Joseph Cook, a Knights of Labor sympathizer, included needs in his 1886 explication of fair wages but he retained producerist and market-based components: "A fair day's wages for a fair day's work ought to be at least twice what the laborer must pay for his food, and more, according to his skill and the demand for it." *Labor: Its Rights and Wrongs*, 106–7.

34. "A New Political Economy," *Spectator*, August 18, 1906, 233–35. Another review of Ryan's book noted: "Men have by nature a strict right not merely to a bare subsistence but to a decent livelihood. This right is derived not . . . from the common estimate of what constitutes a just price for work, but from the personal dignity of the laborer." White, "Living Wage," 471.

35. T. Wharton Collins, *The Right to Labor and Live* (187?), 1, 3, *PAH*, L20. See also Wally Seccombe, *Weathering the Storm: Working-Class Families from the Industrial Revolution to the Fertility Decline* (London: Verso, 1993), 8–9. As Craig Calhoun writes, "Workers . . . struggling for higher direct wages were no longer defending a moral economy or notions of a just price." *Question of Class Struggle*, 118.

36. Ira Steward, "A Reduction of Hours an Increase of Wages," in *A Documentary History of American Industrial Society*, ed. John R. Commons et al., vol. 9: *Labor Movement, 1860–1880, Part 2* (New York: Russell and Russell, 1958), 284–301. Steward wrote: "Without attempting to settle . . . how much labor is worth . . . I will make the claim that no man's compensation should be so low, that it will not secure for himself and family a comfortable home — education for his children, and of the influence to which he is entitled by his capacity, virtue, and industry" (295–96). Jones noted that the male worker's living wage should be sufficient to supply "the . . . necessities of his family." "Political and Social Reform." The "labor question," as Carroll D. Wright wrote, embraces "the wants of the wage-laborer." *The Relation of Political Economy to the Labor Question* (Boston: Franklin Press, 1882), 6.

37. Gompers, "Minimum Living Wage"; Lloyd, *Safety of the Future*, 3. See also "Bob Ingersoll on Labor," *JUL*, August 22, 1880, 51.

38. Even the Knights of Labor, an organization with a thoroughly producerist outlook, recognized the difficulty. Claiming that it was possible to measure the "fruits of

production" but admitting the exact quantity of these fruits was not immediately self-evident, the Knights of Labor proposed as "the first step" to "secure to the workers the full enjoyment of the wealth they create," the creation of "bureaus of labor statistics" whose functions would be to "ascertain as nearly as possible how much of the wealth of the world is created by labor." This system, it should be noted, would provide only an aggregate measure of wealth produced and therefore could not determine individual labor yields. "Declaration of the Principles of the Knights of Labor," in *LM*, 485–86.

39. Weber continued: "It thus resembles the medieval 'just price' as determined by the test . . . of whether or not at the given price the craftsmen in question could maintain the standard of living appropriate to their social status." *Economy and Society*, trans. and ed. Guenther Roth and Claus Wittich (Berkeley: University of California Press, 1978), 2 : 871–72.

40. Gompers, "Minimum Living Wage," and *Lowell Mail*, February 9, 1898, *SGP* 4 : 432–35.

41. Robert Ingersoll, "The Infidel," *San Francisco Truth*, September 20, 1882.

42. Gompers, *New York World*, August 28, 1893, *SGP* 3 : 387; Mitchell, *Organized Labor*, 113–14; John H. Chadwick, *The Living Wage: A Sermon* (Boston: Geo. H. Ellis, 1902), 29; "Hurrah for Homestead," *National Labor Tribune*, November 12, 1892, *SGP* 3 : 237. In the past, wrote the novelist Frederick U. Adams, "people were unable to purchase with their wages that which their labor created." The novel's frontispiece announces: "The right of a citizen of the U.S. to demand and to obtain work at wages sufficient to support himself and family shall never be abridged." *President John Smith: The Story of a Peaceful Revolution* (Chicago: Charles H. Kerr, 1897), 38–39.

43. Gompers, "Minimum Living Wage," 29; Williams, "Wage Workers' Pay."

44. For the labor reformer and politician Edwin Chamberlin, the answer to the question "What are wages?" lay in the realm not of needs but of desires: "A ticket to the theatre . . . food, clothing, books and picnics." *The Margin of Profits and Eight Hours* (Boston, 1888), 7, *PAH*, L2336. An AFL official, John Frey, defined wages as "the factor which determines what measure of decency, of comfort, and of opportunity the wage-earner will have in this life." "The Ideals in Labor," *AF* (November 1913), 1059–65.

45. "A Living Wage," *Outlook*, September 21, 1895, 428. H. J. Walls, the longtime leader of the iron molders, made a similar claim in 1877 when he declared that wages should be "gauged, not by the value of services done . . . but by the present necessities of the laborer." Quoted in David Montgomery, *Beyond Equality*, 445. Foster quoted in Henry Raymond Mussey, "Eight-Hour Theory in the American Federation of Labor," in *Economic Essays: Contributed in Honor of John Bates Clark*, ed. Jacob H. Hollander (New York: Macmillan, 1927), 235–36.

46. "The Living Wage," *Outlook*, September 8, 1906, 91.

47. Wm. Howard, "Labor and Life," *JSP*, November 7, 1886, 2.

48. Like most users of the term, living wage advocates did not define the "market." Thomas L. Haskell and Richard F. Teichgraeber III conclude that "there is no consensus" about the meaning of the market. Haskell and Teichgraeber, eds., *The Culture of the Market: Historical Essays* (Cambridge: Cambridge University Press, 1993), 3. David Montgomery writes that the term "has many meanings and many more connotations which are often jumbled together in order to impart some desired ideological message or another." *Citizen Worker: The Experience of Workers in the United States with Democracy and the Free Market during the Nineteenth Century* (Cambridge: Cambridge University Press, 1993), 52.

49. Jones, "Should Wages Be Regulated?" William Howard, "A National Unit of Value for Labor," *AF* (July 1894), 92–93; idem, *Free Land! Free Currency! Free Labor! An Address* (Bethlehem: Times Print, 1880), 6.

50. Wilentz, "Against Exceptionalism," 11, 13.

51. Michael Merrill, "Cash Is Good To Eat: Self-Sufficiency and Exchange in the Rural Economy of the United States," *RHR* 4 (Winter 1977), 42–71; James Henretta, "Families and Farms: Mentalité in Pre-Industrial America," *William and Mary Quarterly* 3d ser., 25 (January 1978), 3–32.

52. G. B. De Bernardi, "Forms of Bondage," *Labor Exchange* (April 1897), 8; Howard, "National Unit of Value," 92–93; idem, *Free Land!* 6.

53. Leon Fink, *In Search of the Working Class: Essays in American Labor History and Political Culture* (Urbana: University of Illinois Press, 1994), 21; Anticipating the minimum wage movement, Howard declared: "The State should establish a national unit of labor and thereby enable the industrian, without consulting his employer, to always earn what his life necessities demand." "National Unit of Value," 93. As Eric Hobsbawm has noted, wage levels, far from being determined by the invisible hand, have always been affected by working-class conceptions of fairness: "The wage structure of a developed capitalist economy was not formed in a void. . . . the worker's wage calculation remained for long, and still to some extent remains, largely a customary and not a market calculation." "Custom, Wages and Work-Load in Nineteenth-Century Industry," in *Labouring Men: Studies in the History of Labour* (London: Weidenfeld and Nicolson, 1964), 347.

54. According to Mary Marcy, wages were "the price of labor-power. Labor-power is a commodity just as stoves, coats and flour are commodities." "Beginners' Course in Socialism and the Economics of Karl Marx: Lesson VII. — Wages," *International Socialist Review* 11 (May 1911), 696.

55. George, *Progress and Poverty* (1879; New York: Robert Schalkenbach Foundation, 1979), 353; Gunton, "Hours of Labor," 243.

56. I am indebted here to the insights of the political theorist Sibyl Schwarzenbach. In her analysis of prostitution, she distinguishes between the selling of one's body and alienation, invoking Hegel's *Philosophy of Right.* Thus, Schwarzenbach describes the sale of one's labor as the ability to "distance" without "alienating" oneself. "Contractarians and Feminists Debate Prostitution," *New York University Review of Law and Social Change* 18.1 (1990–91), 103–30, esp. 112–14. See also Fink, *In Search of the Working Class,* 22.

57. "Crypto Cynic," "The Breadwinners Will Win," *JSP,* March 30, 1884, 2; *The Voice of Labor: Plain Talk by Men of Intellect on Labor's Rights, Wrongs, Remedies, and Prospects* (Philadelphia: H. J. Smith, 1891), 164.

58. On Ricardo's distinction between what he called the "natural" and "market" price of labor, see William A. Scott, *The Development of Economics* (New York: Century, 1933), 117–19. Marx quoted in Maurice Dobb, *Wages* (New York: Harcourt, Brace, 1928), 106. Karl Marx, "What Are Wages?" in *Wage Labour and Capital* (London: Lawrence and Wishart, 1933), 17–27. This was the basis of Marx's argument with his fellow socialist Ferdinand Lassalle, whose "iron law" predicted that wages could never rise above a bare minimum. Philip S. Foner, *History of the Labor Movement in the United States,* vol. 2: *From the Founding of the AF of L to the Emergence of American Imperialism* (New York: International, 1980), 32–33; Laurie, *Artisans into Workers,* 179–80.

59. John A. Ryan, "What Wage Is a Living Wage?" *Catholic World* 75 (April 1902), 2–16; Henry Ward, *The Living Wage: A Religious Necessity* (Philadelphia: American Baptist Publication, 1916); White, "Living Wage," 471.

60. "Labor and Politics," *Nation,* June 13, 1872, 386–87.

61. Gompers, *C and L,* 614; William Cunningham, "A Living Wage," *Contemporary Review* 65 (January 1894), 18–19. Foster quoted in Mussey, "Eight Hour Theory," 235–

36; White, "Living Wage," 471–72. See also Howard, *Free Land!* 6; and Carroll Wright, "The Sort of Talk Needed," *GIB*, March 5, 1898, 222.

62. Gompers, "Letter to the Officers and Members of the New York Stereotypers Association" (February 1888), *SGP* 2:91–92. Williams, "Wage Workers' Pay." A labor newspaper declared that "workers should receive fair liberal wages," which it defined as "enough to support himself and family in a decent manner." "Wages," *San Francisco Truth*, February 18, 1882.

63. Ward, *Living Wage*, 10, 13. See also idem, *The Church and the Social Question: The Declaration of the General Conference of 1916* (Boston: Methodist Federation of Social Service, 1916), 10–12. "Everything necessary to the life of a normal man must be included in the living wage," declared the shoeworkers' journal in 1905. Quoted in Martha May, "The Historical Problem of the Family Wage: The Ford Motor Company and the Five Dollar Day," *Feminist Studies* 8 (Summer 1982), 402.

64. Letter from Bradford Dubois, "What Causes Hard Times?" *JSP*, September 27, 1885, 2; "They Are Looking Further Now," *WULLJ* (December 1906), 11.

65. Mitchell quoted in Alice Kessler-Harris, *A Woman's Wage: Historical Meanings and Social Consequences* (Lexington: University Press of Kentucky, 1990), 9; George Gunton, "American Standard of Living," *Gunton's Magazine* (February 1897), 103–9; John B. Lennon, "Ethics of the Labor Movement," *AF* (September 1913), 731.

66. Mitchell, *Organized Labor*, ix, x. See also Chadwick, *Living Wage*, 19, 24; Testimony of George E. McNeill, *C and L*, 120; and see McNeill, *The Eight Hour Primer: The Fact, Theory, and the Argument*, AFL Eight-Hour Series, no. 1 (Washington, D.C.: AFL, 1889); Gompers, "Minimum Living Wage." "In the United States," Leon Fink has astutely noted, "disillusionment with the older nobility-of-toil ethic was equally evident in Wobbly Big Bill Haywood's admonition, 'the less work the better' and in Samuel Gompers' advice that 'the way out of the wage system is through higher wages.'" "Looking Backward," 15. The line of continuity reached even deeper into history; Gompers was (as was his regular practice) knowingly quoting "that foremost of economic and social thinkers, Ira Steward." Quoted in John Erwin Hollitz, "The Challenge of Abundance: Reactions to the Development of a Consumer Economy, 1890–1920" (PhD. diss., University of Wisconsin, Madison, 1981), 69. Gompers called Steward "the ablest thinker on the economic question," and wrote that "he and Marx . . . are the greatest minds on [economic] matters." *SGP* 1:317–18, 2:426. His demand for "more, more" is quoted in John Kirkby Jr., *The Wages of Tolerance and the Cost of Indifference*, NAM, no. 32 (November 22, 1912). In an address before the National Urban League conference in October 1923, Elwood Street, in language similar to that of white trade unionists, proposed an ever-increasing living wage, which "will always remain a pursuit and never an attainment." "How Minimum Standards of Life May Be Attained," *Opportunity* 2 (January 1924), 14.

67. Despite his advocacy of a "basic living wage," T. H. Marshall feared that need-based wage advocacy could reinforce a "hierarchical wage structure." "Citizenship and Social Class," in *Class, Citizenship, and Social Development* (Garden City, N.Y.: Doubleday, 1964), 113.

4. Inventing the American Standard of Living

1. David Montgomery, *Beyond Equality: Labor and the Radical Republicans, 1862–1872* (Urbana: University of Illinois Press, 1981), 254. Proponents often defined one in terms of the other, as in John Mitchell's comment that "the living wage means the American Standard of Living." *Organized Labor: Its Problems, Purposes, and Ideals and*

the Present and Future of American Wage Earners (Philadelphia: American Book and Bible House, 1903), x. See also Royal Meeker, "What Is the American Standard of Living?" *Monthly Labor Review* (July 1919), 1–13. Peter R. Shergold treats the standard of living as a measurement of wealth in *Working-Class Life: The "American Standard" in Comparative Perspective, 1899–1913* (Pittsburgh: University of Pittsburgh Press, 1982). For philosophical approaches, see Geoffrey Hawthorn, ed., *The Standard of Living* (Cambridge: Cambridge University Press, 1987).

2. Ira Steward wrote, "Low wages . . . mean poverty. And . . . poverty for the masses, returns them back again to . . . chattel slavery." "Poverty," in Massachusetts Bureau of Statistics of Labor, *Fourth Annual Report* (Boston: Wright and Potter, 1873), 411–39. A 1935 AFL pamphlet, decrying threats to the American standard, called the danger of low wages as "great to American workers as the institution of slavery." *The Union Label Comes to America: Talk # 2* (1935), *PAH*, L339.

3. George Gunton, "Moral Reasons for a Shorter Working Day," *GIB*, March 25, 1899, 571. George McNeill celebrated the benefits of "putting money into circulation." *C and L*, 120.

4. W. E. Hart, "High Wages as a Criterion of Civilization," *Social Economist* (May 1891), 176.

5. Steward, "Consumption and Hours of Labor," 2, in PEEH.

6. Steward, "The Political Economy of Eight Hours," 6, 28, ibid.

7. Steward, "Economy and Extravagance," 6, ibid.

8. Ibid. "The laboring classes are taught that 'economy is wealth' and that it would be 'extravagant' to increase their expenditures and luxuries," wrote Steward. "If every body had always economized as much as possible in consuming wealth, there could have been no progress. And all mankind would have remained savages." "Consumption and the Hours of Labor."

9. He concluded that the worker who "distributes his surplus money" could "radiate employment to other workers. . . . Shorten the hours of labor and thereby increase wages, thus enabling all workers to earn and spend liberally." "Economy as a Virtue and Otherwise," *JSP*, September 11, 1886.

10. A. S. Leitch, "Wage Slavery as Viewed by a Wage Slave, III," ibid., May 29, 1887, 2.

11. "Col. Ingersoll on Labor," ibid., March 13, 1887, 1.

12. George E. McNeill, *The Eight Hour Primer: The Fact, Theory, and the Argument*, AFL Eight-Hour Series, no. 1 (Washington, D.C.: AFL, 1889), 11; Knight of Labor quoted in Richard J. Oestreicher, *Solidarity and Fragmentation: Working People and Class Consciousness in Detroit, 1875–1900* (Urbana: University of Illinois Press, 1986), 145; Gunton quoted in William D. P. Bliss, ed., *Encyclopedia of Social Reform* (New York: Funk and Wagnalls, 1897), 1368–80; Edwin Chamberlin, *The Margin of Profits and Eight Hours* (Boston, 1888), *PAH*, L2336. "If labor submits to a low standard of living, low wages will prevail," warned the labor leaders who composed, *The Voice of Labor: Plain Talk by Men of Intellect on Labor's Rights, Wrongs, Remedies, and Prospects* (Philadelphia: H. J. Smith, 1891), 167. The economist Edwin Seligman noted: "If workmen have once been accustomed to a certain high standard of life, they will do almost anything, subject themselves to almost any privation rather than be compelled to accept a wage which will no longer enable them to live according to the standard. They will consider it a degradation against which they will fight to the uttermost." "The Living Wage," *GIB*, March 26, 1898, 259–60.

13. Rev. B. W. Williams, "Wage Workers' Pay: Thoughtful Sermon by a Texas Clergyman," *Knights of Labor*, March 26, 1887, 12; John Mitchell, quoted in Alice Kessler-Harris, *A Woman's Wage: Historical Meanings and Social Consequences* (Lexington: University Press of Kentucky, 1990), 9.

14. See, for example, George Gunton, "American Standard of Living," *Gunton's Magazine* (February 1897), 103–9.

15. Mitchell, *Organized Labor*, 115. Gunton quoted in Bliss, ed., *Encyclopedia of Social Reform*, 1368–80. See also Chamberlin, *Margin of Profits*, 7; Terence Powderly, "The Plea for Eight Hours," *NAR* 150 (April 1890), 465–66.

16. *Voice of Labor*, 163; *The Living Wage*, exhibit no. 37 before the U.S. Railroad Labor Board, (1921), U. S. Department of Labor Library.

17. *Voice of Labor*, 163. "The movement of wages or the purchasing power of a day's work, is the true index of a nation's progress," wrote George Gunton. "Are Wages Really Falling?" *Gunton's Magazine* 15 (August 1898), 81. See also from *Gunton's Magazine*: "Economic Effect of High Wages," 26 (May 1904), 402–11; "High Wages and Cheap Production," 12 (March 1897), 175–79; "Social Influence of High Wages," 13 (December 1897), 417–26; "The Economy of High Wages," 6 (April 1894), 193–99. On "virtue" in the antebellum labor movement, see Sean Wilentz, *Chants Democratic: New York City and the Rise of an American Working Class, 1788–1850* (New York: Oxford University Press, 1984), 92–93. J. G. A. Pocock, "Virtue and Commerce in the Eighteenth Century," *Journal of Interdisciplinary History* 3 (Summer 1972), 119–34.

18. Gunton, "Moral Reasons," 570. McNeill ascribed the progression of civilization to "increased wants . . . from homespun clothes; to cheaply manufactured cottons; to bread; to wine and bread both; to beef and beer; to household furnishings." *C and L*, 120. Ira Steward, "Unemployment," 32, in PEEH. "It is not reasonable to compare the American Standard of Living with the British, the German, the Russian or the Chinese Standards," wrote John Mitchell. *Organized Labor*, 114–15. Gunton argued that "a large number of commodities that are habitually used by American workman are entirely beyond the reach of the French and Belgian laborer." "Some Valuable Wage Statistics," *Gunton's Magazine* (January 1899), 11–19.

19. Frank Foster quoted in Henry Raymond Mussey, "Eight-Hour Theory in the American Federation of Labor," in *Economic Essays: Contributed in Honor of John Bates Clark*, ed. Jacob H. Hollander (New York: Macmillan, 1927), 236; *Voice of Labor*, 163–64.

20. James Duncan quoted in *Labor Terminology*, bulletin no. 25 (Cambridge, Mass.: Bureau of Business Research, 1921), 51; Theresa S. McMahon, *Social and Economic Standards of Living* (Boston: D. C. Heath, 1925). Years earlier, Terence Powderly had expressed a similar blend of solidarity and differentiation. "It is in the interest of all laborers that the price paid for labor should be a good price; whether the labor be skilled or unskilled, of the plow, the loom, the forge, or the shop. The price should be all that the work is worth, due consideration being given to the different cost of living" of the different types of workers. *Richmond Dispatch*, October 12, 1886, *The Black Worker: A Documentary History from Colonial Times to the Present*, ed. Philip S. Foner and Ronald L. Lewis (Philadelphia: Temple University Press, 1978), 3 : 106–7. Wrote George Gunton, "No other theory is able to account satisfactorily for the wide variations in wages paid to laborers in different countries, or in different groups in the same country, or to city, as compared to country laborers, or to men as compared with women." "American Standard of Living," 103–9.

21. McNeill, *Eight Hour Primer*, 10; Gunton quoted in Bliss, ed., *Encyclopedia of Social Reform*, 1231; George Gunton, "Hours of Labor," *GIB*, March 19, 1898, 243. Gunton explored these ideas in *Wealth and Progress: A Critical Examination of the Labor Problem* (New York: D. Appleton, 1887), 88–96.

22. Henry White, "Immigration Restriction as a Necessity," *AF* (June 1897), 67–69. According to Theodore Roosevelt, certain immigrants represented "a standard of living so depressed that they can undersell our men in the labor market and drag them to a lower level." Quoted in Elmer Clarence Sandmeyer, *The Anti-Chinese Movement in*

California, Foreword and Bibliography by Roger Daniels (Urbana: University of Illinois Press, 1991), 107.

23. Samuel Gompers and Herman Gustadt, *Meat vs. Rice: American Manhood against Asiatic Coolieism. Which Shall Survive?* (San Francisco: Asiatic Exclusion League, 1906); Newspaper quoted in Sandmeyer, *Anti-Chinese Movement*, 106. Another newspaper article similarly observed: "In every employment they have entered the Chinese have mastered their work." Nonetheless, it condemned the Chinese because "they live cheaply and can afford to undersell us." "The Terrible Chinee," *NYT*, March 12, 1882, 13. In 1877 the Democratic Party of California called "Chinese coolies" "impregnable to all the influences of Anglo-Saxon life" and thus "voluntary slaves." Gwendolyn Mink, *Old Labor and New Immigrants in American Political Development: Union, Party, and State, 1875–1920* (Ithaca: Cornell University Press, 1986), 102.

24. H. C. Kinne and J. Hoffmeyer, "The Chinese Question," *JUL*, January 25, 1886, 117–18; Gompers quoted in Mink, *Old Labor and New Immigrants*, 97; "The Chinese Must Go! No More Mongolization of Our Country," *JSP*, September 27, 1885.

25. "Chinese Labor," *JUL*, August 15, 1880, 39.

26. Armstrong quoted in Miles S. Richards, "Thomas A. Armstrong: A Forgotten Advocate of Labor," *Western Pennsylvania Historical Magazine* 67 (October 1984), 354; "Chinese Labor," 39; *Boycotter*, February 13, 1886.

27. Steward, "The Political Economy of Eight Hours," in PEEH.

28. Gunton, "Hours of Labor," 243; W. W. Stone, "The Chinese Labor Problem," in *LM*, 432–42; Kinne and Hoffmeyer, "Chinese Question."

29. Debs quoted in Nick Salvatore, *Eugene V. Debs, Citizen and Socialist* (Urbana: University of Illinois Press, 1982), 104; Democratic platform and Foran quoted in Mink, *Old Labor and New Immigrants*, 107, 109.

30. Although generally viewed as the paradigmatic overconsumers, critics sometimes portrayed African Americans in much the same way as they did others with low standards. Wrote Jerome Dowd, "The meager wants of the negro hold their own wages down and also the wages of the white." "Cheap Labor in the South," *Gunton's Magazine* (February 1900), 115.

31. Samuel Gompers, "East St. Louis Riots—Their Causes," *AF* (August 1917), 621–26. White workers also accused black workers of lowering wage standards. This charge was frequently tied to the claim that they were, in Gompers's words, "improvident," a charge never leveled against the Chinese. See, Mark Karson and Ronald Radosh, "The American Federation of Labor and the Negro Worker, 1894–1949," in *The Negro and the American Labor Movement*, ed. Julius Jacobson (Garden City, N.Y.: Anchor, 1968), 159; Philip S. Foner, *History of the Labor Movement in the United States*, vol. 2: *From the Founding of the AF of L to the Emergence of American Imperialism* (New York: International, 1980), 355–61.

32. Chamberlin, "Margin of Profits," 7.

33. Henry R. Seager, "The Minimum Wage as Part of a Program for Social Reform," *Annals* 48 (July 1913), 4.

Part III   Introduction

1. M. E. J. Kelley, "The Union Label," *NAR* 151 (July 1897), 36. Producerism was "a moral conviction," writes Michael Kazin, "that only those who created wealth in tangible, material ways . . . could be trusted to guard the nation's piety and liberties." *The Populist Persuasion: An American History* (New York: Basic Books, 1995), 13. On the

wasteful connotations of the word *consumer*, see Raymond Williams, *Keywords: A Vo-cabulary of Culture and Society* (New York: Oxford University Press, 1985), 78–79.

2. *LM*, 463. Careful not to privilege one aspect of identity over the other, Ira Steward wrote that "every laborer sustains the relation of producer and consumer to the world's wealth." "Economy," 1, in PEEH. See also from *JUL*: "The Rate of Wages," (February 1884); "Eight Hours," February 25, 1885, 644; "Wants," August 10, 1886, 2154–55; "Industrial Ideals, Ch. VI," September 10, 1886, 2157–59. An editorial in the garment workers' newspaper demanded an increase in "the consuming power of the mass, so that an equation between consumption and production can more readily be main-tained." "Unionism against Master and Servant Idea," *Weekly Bulletin of the Clothing Trades*, March 25, 1904.

3. George Gunton, *Wealth and Progress: A Critical Examination of the Labor Problem* (New York: D. Appleton, 1887), 6, 28. On the parallel middle-class recognition that "con-sumers were the only political majority in an industrial society," see David Thelen, "Patterns of Consumer Consciousness in the Progressive Movement: Robert LaFollette, the Antitrust Persuasion, and Labor Legislation," in *The Quest for Social Justice*, ed. Ralph M. Aderman (Madison: University of Wisconsin Press, 1983), 19–47. Clarke Ir-vine, a Missouri worker, wrote that "the best wages and the most regular employment are in those occupations whose products are so cheap and necessary that the con-sumption is almost infinite." "Wages Depend on Demand," *JUL*, August 25, 1885, 1065. The labor leader Theodore Schaffer argued that "inasmuch as the workingman is him-self the consumer he can not purchase unless he has that with which to purchase." *C and L*, 397. Workers claimed that their underconsumption hurt the economy, "since under the wage system, the people can only buy back a portion of their product, the profit-making class must depend on itself alone for the consumption of the remainder." "Declaration of Independence" by the Socialist Labor Party, July 4, 1895, in *We, the Other People: Alternative Declarations of Independence by Labor Groups, Farmers, Wom-an's Rights Advocates, Socialists, and Blacks, 1829–1975*, ed. Philip S. Foner (Urbana: University of Illinois Press, 1976), 145.

4. "What This Label Means: An Organized Demand," *Milwaukee Trades Union League, End of the Century Labor Day Souvenir* (1900), State Historical Society of Wis-consin, Madison.

5. Frank Stricker and Lizabeth Cohen have argued that, even in the affluent 1920s, the cornucopia of consumer goods was not fully available to working-class consumers. Stricker, "Affluence for Whom?—Another Look at Prosperity and the Working Classes in the 1920s," *LH* (Winter 1983), 5–33; Cohen, *Making a New Deal: Industrial Workers in Chicago, 1919–1939* (Cambridge: Cambridge University Press, 1990). In this sense, Gary Cross is correct to argue that "consumerism was a middle-class phenomenon early in the century." This statement, however, does not hold true as a matter of polit-ical ideology. *Time and Money: The Making of Consumer Culture* (London: Routledge, 1993), 135.

6. W. J. Rorabaugh, *The Craft Apprentice: From Franklin to the Machine Age in America* (New York: Oxford University Press, 1986), 88; William H. Sylvis, "A Plea for Rest," in *The Life, Speeches, Labors, and Essays of William H. Sylvis*, ed. James C. Sylvis (Philadelphia: Claxton, Remsen, and Haffelfinger, 1872), 423; Alan Trachten-berg, *The Incorporation of America: Culture and Society in the Gilded Age* (New York: Hill and Wang, 1982), 77. A condemnation of "conspicuous consumption" was a staple of working-class rhetoric. Sean Wilentz quotes a toast of New York artisans: "Less respect to the consuming speculator who wallows in luxury, than to the productive mechanic, who struggles with indigence." Wilentz, "Against Exceptionalism: Class Consciousness

and the American Labor Movement, 1790–1920," *ILWCH* 26 (Fall 1984), 8. The Jacksonian editor William Leggett contrasted "producers of the middling and lower classes" with "the consumers, the rich, the proud, the privileged." Quoted in Kazin, *Populist Persuasion*, 19. Thorstein Veblen introduced the phrase "conspicuous consumption" in his classic 1899 work, *The Theory of the Leisure Class* (New York: Mentor, 1953), 60–80.

7. "Democracy and the Label," *WULLJ* (May 1918), 12; Gus Burquist, "Union Label Is the Bulwark of the United States," *WULLJ* (March 1917); Cross, *Time and Money*, 129; Gompers, "What Does Labor Want? An Address before the International Labor Congress in Chicago," August 28, 1893, *SGP*, 3:393.

8. *The Alarm*, December 12, 1885; Fielden quoted in Paul Avrich, *The Haymarket Tragedy* (Princeton: Princeton University Press, 1984), 182. See also David Montgomery, *The Fall of the House of Labor: The Workplace, the State, and American Labor Activism, 1865–1925* (Cambridge: Cambridge University Press, 1987), 195; Philip S. Foner, *History of the Labor Movement in the United States*, vol. 2: *From the Founding of the AF of L to the Emergence of American Imperialism* (New York: International, 1980), 102, 182. Trachtenberg, *Incorporation of America*, 95. See also Mary H. Blewett, *Men, Women, and Work: Class, Gender, and Protest in the New England Shoe Industry, 1780–1910* (Urbana: University of Illinois Press, 1988), 290.

9. Thomas L. Haskell, "Capitalism and the Origins of Humanitarian Sensibility," *American Historical Review* 90, part I (April 1985), 342; part II (June 1985), 560. J. A. Hobson noted this transformation of working-class identity. "Modern industrial evolution shows a man becoming narrower and more specialized on his producing side, wider and more various on his consuming side. As worker, he is confined to the constant repetition of some section of a process in the production of a single class of article. As consumer, he is in direct contact with thousands of different sorts of workers in all parts of the world, and by his various consumption applies a direct stimulus which vibrates through the whole industrial system. As producer he is the one, as consumer the many." *Work and Wealth: A Human Valuation* (London: Macmillan, 1914), 110.

10. Samuel Gompers, "The Shorter Workday—Its Philosophy," *AF* (March 1915), 166. For an overview of the shorter hours movement, see David R. Roediger and Philip S. Foner, *Our Own Time: A History of American Labor and the Working Day* (London: Verso, 1989). Roy Rosenzweig examines the struggle for control of leisure time but does not address the eight-hour movement in *Eight Hours for What We Will: Workers and Leisure in an Industrial City, 1870–1920* (Cambridge: Cambridge University Press, 1983). Benjamin K. Hunnicutt places the movement in the context of consumer culture, but he interprets it as opposing "the formation of the modern consumer culture and an economy separated from ethical principles." I agree only with the second part of this statement: most eight-hour activists wished to develop an ethical consumer society. "Monsignor John A. Ryan and the Shorter Hours of Labor: A Forgotten Vision of Genuine Progress," *Catholic Historical Review* 69 (July 1983), 386.

11. E. Lewis Evans, "The Union Label," *AF* (September 1897), 143. Contemporaries placed the union label in the context of an emerging consumer culture, relating it to "the change which has come over economic thought" in which the "stress is no longer on production or exchange but upon consumption." Kelley, "Union Label," 33–34. See also "100 Years with the Union Label," *AF* (April 1981), 1–4.

5. Merchants of Time

1. *LM*, 470; E. P. Thompson, "Time, Work-Discipline, and Industrial Capitalism," in *Customs in Common: Studies in Traditional Popular Culture* (New York: New Press, 1993),

352–403; Herbert G. Gutman, *Work, Culture, and Society in Industrializing America: Essays in American Working-Class and Social History* (New York: Pantheon, 1976); Bruce Laurie, "'Nothing on Compulsion': Life Styles of Philadelphia Artisans, 1820–1850," *LH* 15 (1974), 337–66; Mary H. Blewett, "We Are Freeborn American Women: The Persistent Politics of Native-Born New England Women as Nineteenth-Century Industrial Workers," in *Labor in Massachusetts: Selected Essays*, ed. Kenneth Fones-Wolf and Martin Kaufman (Westfield: Institute for Massachusetts Studies, 1990), 124–37; idem, *Men, Women, and Work: Class, Gender, and Protest in the New England Shoe Industry, 1780–1910* (Urbana: University of Illinois Press, 1988), 68–96; David A. Zonderman, *Aspirations and Anxieties: New England Workers and the Mechanized Factory System, 1815–1850* (New York: Oxford University Press, 1992). See also Michael O'Malley, *Keeping Watch: A History of American Time* (New York: Viking, 1990).

2. Marx quoted in *Knights of Labor*, August 27, 1886; Marx quoted in Michael Waltzer, *Spheres of Justice: A Defense of Pluralism and Equality* (New York: Basic Books, 1983), 187. George McNeill wrote, "The eight-hour movement seeks to [give the worker] the advantages now possessed by the capitalist." *LM*, 475.

3. George Gunton, *The Economic and Social Importance of the Eight-Hour Movement*, AFL Eight-Hour Series, no. 2 (Washington, D.C.: AFL, 1889); McNeill, *LM*, 463; Gompers, "Testimony before the Education and Labor Committee of the U.S. Senate" (August 1883), *SGP* 1:317.

4. In a classic statement of this ideology, a "reliable working man" told the Massachusetts Bureau of Statistics of Labor in 1872 that workers needed time for "public duties" and "refined pleasures." David Montgomery, *Beyond Equality: Labor and the Radical Republicans, 1862–1872* (Urbana: University of Illinois Press, 1981), 237–38.

5. Henry Raymond Mussey, "Eight-Hour Theory in the American Federation of Labor," in *Economic Essays: Contributed in Honor of John Bates Clark*, ed. Jacob H. Hollander (New York: Macmillan, 1927), 236–37; Horatio Winslow, "Eight Hours and Revolution," *Masses* (November 1911), 5–6; "The Necessities of the Hour," *Cigar Makers' Official Journal* (November 1876), 2. "Can we enjoy life if our wages are so low that we constantly fluctuate from semi-starvation to abject wants?" it asked. Albert Parsons, the anarchist, served as recording secretary of the Chicago Eight-Hour League in the late 1870s. Parsons believed "the eight-hour day was the starting point from which the labor question as a whole might be resolved." Not all anarchists agreed. Paul Avrich, *The Haymarket Tragedy* (Princeton: Princeton University Press, 1984), 41–42.

6. McNeill, *C and L*, 120; Edwin Chamberlin, *The Margin of Profits and Eight Hours* (Boston, 1888), *PAH*, L2336.

7. "Blessings of Eight Hours," *Weekly Bulletin of the Clothing Trades*, February 22, 1907. See also Philip S. Foner, "Songs of the Eight-Hour Movement," *LH* 13 (Fall 1972), 571–88.

8. Montgomery, *Beyond Equality*, 250; George E. McNeill, "To Ira Steward," in *Unfrequented Paths: Songs of Nature, Labor, and Men* (Boston: James H. West, 1903), 95–96.

9. To this end, Steward lobbied the Massachusetts legislature and worked with the Massachusetts Bureau of Statistics of Labor to promote shorter hour legislation. In 1874 Massachusetts passed the first ten-hour law for women and children.

10. Ira Steward, *Meaning of the Eight Hour Movement* (Boston: the author, 1868), 6–8.

11. Ira Steward, "A Reduction of Hours an Increase of Wages," in *A Documentary History of American Industrial Society*, ed. John R. Commons et al., vol. 9: *Labor Movement, 1860–1880, Part 1* (New York: Russell and Russell, 1958), 285.

12. Ibid., 290, 289.

13. Montgomery, *Beyond Equality*, 256.

14. Walter S. Logan, *An Argument for an Eight-Hour Law* (New York: Knickerbocker Press, 1894), 13; Steward, "Reduction of Hours an Increase of Wages," 285; Samuel Gompers, "The Shorter Workday—Its Philosophy," *AF* (March 1915), 167. See also idem, *The Eight-Hour Workday: Its Inauguration, Enforcement, and Influences* (Washington, D.C.: AFL, 1915), 6; Hyman Kuritz, "Ira Steward and the Eight Hour Day," *Science and Society* 20 (Spring 1956), 120; Steward, "The Power of the Cheaper over the Dearer," 32 in PEEH.

15. Lemuel Danryid, *History and Philosophy of the Eight-Hour Movement*, AFL Eight-Hour Series, no. 3 (Washington, D.C.: AFL, 1899).

16. "The Eight Hour Question," *JSP*, January 31, 1886; Danryid, *History and Philosophy*, 9; George McNeill, *The Eight Hour Primer: The Fact, Theory, and the Argument*, AFL Eight-Hour Series, no. 1 (Washington, D.C.: AFL, 1889). See also Gompers, "The Shorter Workday—Its Philosophy," *AF* (May 1903), 366.

17. Gompers, "Shorter Workday" (1915); "Shorter Workday," (1903), 165–66; Gompers, *Eight-Hour Workday*, 6.

18. Lowell quoted in John G. Sproat, *The Best Men: Liberal Reformers in the Gilded Age* (Chicago: University of Chicago Press, 1968), 211.

19. Steward quoted in Mussey, "Eight-Hour Theory and the American Federation of Labor," 233; "Reduction of Hours an Increase of Wages," 294–95; McNeill quoted in David Montgomery, "Labor and the Republic in Industrial America: 1860–1920," *Mouvement Social* 111 (April–June 1980), 205.

20. "Stone Cutter," "One Trade with Eight Hours," *JSP*, March 2, 1884.

21. Terence Powderly, "The Plea for Eight Hours," *NAR* 150 (April 1890), 464–69.

22. *LM*, 47.

23. Val Fitzpatrick, "Eight-Hour Work-Day," *Railroad Trainman* (January 1916), 3–5. George McNeill stressed that shorter hours would place "the lever of civilization under the humblest man," thus "making him a better man in this world and the world to come." *LM*, 475. "If we want laborers to be moral," George Gunton wrote, "we must first put them where there is an incentive to be clean and wholesome. Morality will not grow in unwholesome and unattractive homes." "Feasibility of an Eight Hour Work Day," *AF* (July 1894), 92.

6. Producers as Consumers

1. Edgar A. Perkins, "The Union Label," *Union Label Advocate*, Duluth, Minn. (December 1897); John Mitchell, *Organized Labor: Its Problems, Purposes, and Ideals and the Present and Future of American Wage Earners* (Philadelphia: American Book and Bible House, 1903), 298.

2. John Graham Brooks, "The Trade Union Label," in *The Making of America*, ed. Robert M. LaFollette, vol. 7: *Labor* (Chicago: Making of America, 1906), 181. Businessmen, Ira Steward wrote, "remember that Foreigners work cheaper than Natives; but forget that Natives buy more of their goods than Foreigners." *Meaning of the Eight Hour Movement* (Boston: the author, 1868). Union labelists never failed to point out that, unlike most other trade union activities, the label was "a distinctly American product," rather than a European import. M. E. J. Kelley, "The Union Label," *NAR* 151 (July 1897), 26–36; Louis J. Humpf, "Best Essay on the Label: Union Label Represents Americanism," *WULLJ* (July 1921).

3. Wm. Wolz, "From the Pacific Coast," *Cigar Makers' Official Journal*, October 10,

1878, 1–2; P. H. Shevlin, "Second Prize Essay," *The Union Label: Its History, and Aims, Prize Essays* (Washington, D.C.: AFL, 1907), 10. Edward J. Spedden, *The Trade Union Label* (Baltimore: Johns Hopkins University Press, 1910), 16. Kelley, "Union Label," 27. Proponents linked the label to the "fight for a living wage": Fred G. Hopp, "The Union Label Is the Flag of Honest Toil, Good Working Conditions, and a Living Wage," *WULLJ* (June 1917); "Can't Live on $840 a Year," *WULLJ* (August 1916); Frances A. Williamson, "Woman's Union Label League," *AF* (July 1906), 171. See also the Chicago *Union Label Bulletin*, January 14, 1900, and November 12, 1902.

4. Mitchell, *Organized Labor*, 293.

5. Walter Macarthur, "First Prize Essay — Union Label Prize Essays," *AF* (July 1904), 574; Kelley, "Union Label," 33–34.

6. "What This Label Means: An Organized Demand," *Milwaukee Trades Union League, End of the Century Labor Day Souvenir* (1900), State Historical Society of Wisconsin, Madison; Letter from G. Bowler, *Weekly Bulletin of the Clothing Trades*, February 1, 1907.

7. Herbert Morley, "The Union Label," *Life and Labor* (July 1911), 203; Charles L. Blaine, "Loyal Dollars and the Union Label," *Life and Labor* (May 1920), 137; "Support Union Labels," *Shoe Workers' Journal* 17 (December 1916), 8–9.

8. *Union Label Advocate* (March 1920).

9. Earl R. Hoage, "Employ Union Labor with Your Own Money," *WULLJ* (October 1916); C. L. Blaine, "Purchase Union Label Goods," *WULLJ* (April 1916), 3–4; *Union Label Advocate* (March 1918), 2; Morley, "Union Label."

10. "Support Union Labels," 8; "The Effect of Labor-Saving Machinery," *Knights of Labor*, September 11, 1886; George Gunton, "Hours of Labor," *GIB*, March 19, 1898, 243; John L. Lewis, *The Miner's Fight for American Standards* (Indianapolis: Bell, 1925), 43. Union label advocates emphasized the aggregate purchasing power of working-class American families. Union members "number nearly 3,000,000 people and this great army of toilers earn each year nearly $2,000,000,000. . . . If this great sum was converted into the proper channels, that is spent for labeled goods, . . . how much easier our lives would be." Anna B. Field, "Work for the Label," *WULLJ* (September 1916), 7. "Low wages are a curse to a community and do not benefit the employer who is eternally scheming to secure them. Good wages mean greater power of consumption. . . . When employers scheme to cut down wages they are sharpening the knife that will in the end cut their own throats." Bro. Chas. H. Litchman, "Starvation Wages," *JUL* (June 1883), 492. See also "Beyond Contradiction: Rich Men Profit by Labor Unions and High Wages," *Weekly Bulletin of the Clothing Trades*, October 29, 1902, 2.

11. "Support Union Labels," 8.

12. John Graham Brooks, "The Trade-Union Label," *Bulletin of the Department of Labor* 15 (March 1898), 207; Mitchell, *Organized Labor*, 298; Ida M. Van Etten, *The Condition of Women Workers under the Present Industrial System* (New York: Concord Co-Operative, 1891), 10.

13. Robert Hunter, "Unionism and Union Labels," *Shoe Workers' Journal* 17 (April 1916), 3–4.

14. Ibid., 4; Morley, "Union Label."

15. David Montgomery, *Workers' Control in America: Studies in the History of Work, Technology, and Labor Struggles* (Cambridge: Cambridge University Press, 1979), 18–27; Matthew Woll, "The Trade Union Label," *WULLJ* (July 1916), 4.

16. Testimony of Samuel Gompers, *C and L*, 628; Peter J. Brady, "Constructive Work on the Union Label," *Union Label Advocate* (May 1918), 1–2; Spedden, *Trade Union Label*, 64, 73.

17. "Trade Unionists of Philadelphia," *Vindicator and Union Label Advertiser*, undated Superior, Wisconsin, newspaper in Collection of material regarding union labels dated from late 1800s to mid-1900s, State Historical Society of Wisconsin Library, Madison. See, for example, "Be Consistent—Buy Union Label Goods with Union Earned Money," *WULLJ* (March 1916). A Hamilton, Ohio, labor organization asked workers to "be consistent . . . and purchase nothing but union-made goods." "A Short Label Sermon," *Butler County Press*, December 11, 1903, 3. A Chicago organization asked: "How can a union man consistently object to the capitalist for refusing to employ union labor, while at the same time he refuses to employ union labor himself? The wage earner spending his wages is an employer of labor in the largest sense of the word; and should so spend his wages to promote in other crafts conditions he desires as his own. This he can do by demanding goods bearing the union label." "Unionists Should Employ Union Labor," *Union Label Bulletin*, November 12, 1902.

18. In *Organized Labor*, Mitchell treated them together in a chapter titled, "The Label and the Boycott." Organized labor began to use both tactics at about the same time. See Michael Gordon, "The Labor Boycott in New York City, 1880–1886," *LH* 16 (1975), 184–229; David Scobey, "Boycotting the Politics Factory: Labor Radicalism and the New York City Mayoral Campaign of 1886," *RHR* 28–30 (1984), 280–325. Boycotts, David Montgomery writes, marked an attempt to "impose a mutualistic morality on the marketplace." *Citizen Worker: The Experience of Workers in the United States with Democracy and the Free Market during the Nineteenth Century* (Cambridge: Cambridge University Press, 1993), 147.

19. Mitchell, *Organized Labor*, 292; Macarthur, "First Prize Essay," 573; E. Lewis Evans, "The Union Label," *AF* (September 1897), 143. See also Blaine, "Loyal Dollars," 137.

20. On middle-class consumer organizations, see David Thelen, "Patterns of Consumer Consciousness in the Progressive Movement: Robert LaFollette, the Antitrust Persuasion, and Labor Legislation," in *The Quest for Social Justice*, ed. Ralph M. Aderman (Madison: University of Wisconsin Press, 1983), 19–47; Florence Kelley, "The Consumer and the Near Future," *Survey*, April 5, 1919, 5–7; idem, *Twenty Five Years of the Consumers League Movement*, National Consumers' League Women in Industry Series, no. 10, reprinted from the *Survey*, November 7, 1915.

21. Mitchell, *Organized Labor*, 293. On middle-class support for organized labor, see Michael Cassity, *Defending a Way of Life: An American Community in the Nineteenth Century* (Albany: State University of New York Press, 1989).

22. Williamson, "Woman's Union Label League," 171. In 1910 garment workers' organizer Pauline Newman left behind male union venues to direct union label activity toward the public at large, especially socially minded women. Gus Tyler, *Look for the Union Label: A History of the International Ladies Garment Workers' Union* (Armonk, N.Y.: Sharpe, 1995), 290–93.

23. Dana Frank points out that the reality of sex roles in working-class life was often "far less neat" than in the norm assumed by union label activists. "Gender, Consumer Organizing, and the Seattle Labor Movement, 1919–1929," in *Work Engendered: Toward a New History of American Labor*, ed. Ava Baron (Ithaca: Cornell University Press, 1991), 273–95.

24. "If the wives, mothers, and daughters of all union men would . . . use their influence the cause would take more rapid strides than ever before in its history. We do not mean that they shall take the stump or do anything unwomanly. They have in their hands a weapon that is more effective." "Attention, Wives and Daughters of Union Men!"

Tri-City Labor Voice, May 9, 1903. Similarly, a Columbus, Ohio, newspaper noted: "The wife and mother who is alive to her own and her family's interests should keep in mind the fact that if her husband or sons are union men, she should buy only union-made goods when there are to be had. To buy other goods is to give employment not to her husband and sons, but to those who are not so near or so dear to her. Just think of a wife who will buy goods made by a man who just a year before took her husband's job." "Women and the Union Label," *Labor World*, April 6, 1907, 3; Field, "Work for the Label."

25. Gus Burquist, "Union Label Is the Bulwark of the United States," *WULLJ* (March 1917).

26. Macarthur, "First Prize Essay," 573; Williamson, "Woman's Union Label League," 171; "Female Labor and the Unions," *WULLJ* (October 1917), 4.

27. Yet Kelley noted that many still resisted this role. "There are few or no union labels on women's ready-made clothing or other articles used exclusively by women, or made only by them. . . . Neither men nor women have yet come to a realization of the economic importance of women either in production or consumption." "Union Label," 30.

28. Shevlin, "Second Prize Essay," 14.

29. It described the league as "a movement calculated to encourage the support of trade union labels among women, and especially among women who are not wage earners. The house-wife is not usually considered a wage earner, but she has a great deal to do with the spending of the earnings of the husband, and if she spends the husband's money for non-union products, she is discharging some union workman, putting a non-union workman in his place, and eventually tending toward the discharge of her own husband. . . . It is just as bad for a man's wife to spend his money for non-union products as it is for him to do it himself." "Support Union Labels," 8–9.

30. "To the Ladies," *Union Label Advocate*, Duluth, Minnesota (October 1898); "Labor Must Patronize the Union Label," *WULLJ* (August 1921), 6; Laurel Koster, "Women Put Biggest Bar on Union Labor," *WULLJ* (September 1916), 7; Dana Frank, *Purchasing Power: Consumer Organizing, Gender, and the Seattle Labor Movement, 1919–1929* (Cambridge: Cambridge University Press, 1994), 218–20. As a union label pamphlet noted with alarm: "The wives and house-keepers of good union men were buying unlabeled goods, and crooked dealers were laughing . . . that through the attraction of a 'markdown' or the 'bargain counter' they were sending dishonest wares right into the homes, and even into the very mouths of the men who boasted and talked loudest about the 'boycott.'" Collection of Material regarding Union Labels, State Historical Society of Wisconsin, Madison.

31. Brooks, "Trade-Union Label," 206; Mitchell, *Organized Labor*, 298; Rev. Wm. J. White, "A Living Wage," *Charities and the Commons*, December 15, 1906, 471–72; Kelley, "Union Label," 33.

32. White, "Living Wage," 471–72; Macarthur, "First Prize Essay," 573. On the impersonality of consumption in the market economy, see E. P. Thompson, "The Moral Economy of the English Crowd in the Eighteenth Century," in *Customs in Common: Studies in Traditional Popular Culture* (New York: New Press, 1993), 256.

33. Gunton, "Rights and Wrongs of Trade Unions," *GIB*, January 7, 1899, 343; idem, "Consumers' Leagues and the Sweatshop," *GIB*, March 4, 1899, 503.

34. Gunton, "Consumers' Leagues and the Sweatshop," 518; idem, "Rights and Wrongs of Trade Unions," 335.

35. Gunton, "Rights and Wrongs of Trade Unions," 336–37.

36. Starr Hoyt Nichols, "Another View of the Union Label," *NAR* 165 (October 1897),

432, 436, 439–40, 442. Nichols also objected that the label limited consumers "in their choice of goods, since many excellent goods are not offered because they lack the union label." Another kind of middle-class critique of the label emerged from the organized business community. See, for example, *The Union Label a Detriment to Business: Statement by the L. S. Starrett Company regarding Their Discontinuance of the Use of the Union Label*, NAM, no. 23 (1911).

37. Maud Nathan, "Notes and Comments: The Consumers' Label," *NAR* 166 (February 1898), 251, 253, 250, 254.

38. Spedden, *Trade Union Label*; James E. Boyle, "The Union Label," *American Journal of Sociology* 9 (September 1903), 171. Despite these criticisms, M. E. J. Kelley noted that union labels were popular in many trade union communities. "The demand for articles bearing the union label originated with members of trade unions acting in their capacity as consumers, and so far very few outside the working class have taken any interest in the union label." "Union Label," 29.

39. Benjamin Hunnicutt writes: "Historians have yet to come to grips with the fact that the work week was reduced gradually but steadily for a century before the Depression and has remained stable since then. Nor have they explained why the cause of shorter hours was a crucial liberal reform from the 1830s to the 1930s, but since then it has dropped from view." "Monsignor John A. Ryan and the Shorter Hours of Labor: A Forgotten Vision of Genuine Progress," *Catholic Historical Review* 69 (July 1983), 385–86. See also idem, *Work without End: Abandoning Shorter Hours for the Right to Work* (Philadelphia: Temple University Press, 1988); Gary Cross, *Time and Money: The Making of Consumer Culture* (London: Routledge, 1993).

Part IV Introduction

1. Sidney Webb, *Industrial Democracy* (London: Longmans, Green, 1899), 588. In the United States, middle-class interest in the living wage was linked in the nineteenth century to patterns of labor conflict and in the twentieth to debate about minimum wage laws, which intensified after passage of the first state minimum wage law in 1912. World War I set off a new wave of interest, especially after the National War Labor Board adopted a policy of a "living wage for all workers" in 1918. *Family Budgets of American Wage Earners: A Critical Analysis*, Research Report no. 41 (New York: National Industrial Conference Board, September 1921). The biggest outpouring came in the early 1920s. A widely debated text was James J. Davis, "A Living and Saving Wage" (1922), Department of Labor, Chief Clerk's Files, 167/832, National Archives, Washington, D.C. The *Times* article ("Mr. Gompers' Slogan," November 13, 1907, 8) noted: "The doctrine of a living wage is highly ethical and admitted theoretically by nearly all."

2. Edwin V. O'Hara, *A Living Wage by Legislation: The Oregon Experience* (Salem: Oregon State Printing Department, 1916), iv; Davis, "A Living and Saving Wage."

3. A. N. Holcombe saw "a new stage, which marks a distinct advance over the old." "Minimum Wage Boards," *Survey*, April 1, 1911, 32–33.

4. James C. Young, "What Is a Worker's Living Wage? New Issue of Capital and Labor," *NYT*, November 19, 1922, VIII, 3. As early as 1903, the minister John H. Chadwick, an advocate of an expansive living wage, criticized such narrow interpretations. *The Living Wage: A Sermon* (Boston: Geo. H. Ellis, 1902), 17.

5. See, for example, Dorothy Douglas, "Ira Steward on Consumption and Unemployment," *Journal of Political Economy* 40 (August 1932), 532–43.

7. Subsistence or Consumption?

1. Samuel Crowther, "Who Wants a Living Wage?" *Collier's*, December 30, 1922, 8, and January 6, 1923, 8, 25. James C. Young, "What Is a Worker's Living Wage? New Issue of Capital and Labor," *NYT*, November 19, 1922, VIII, 3; James J. Davis, "A Living and Saving Wage" (1922), Department of Labor, Chief Clerk's Files, 167/832, National Archives, Washington, D.C.; idem, "A Saving Wage," *NYT*, March 19, 1922, 8.

2. *Adkins et al., Constituting the Minimum Wage Board of the District of Columbia, v. Children's Hospital of the District of Columbia*, 261 U.S. 525. The case was argued on March 14, 1923, and decided on April 9, 1923. For analyses of the decision, see Alice Kessler-Harris, *A Woman's Wage: Historical Meanings and Social Consequences* (Lexington: University Press of Kentucky, 1990), 33–56; Vivien Hart, *Bound by Our Constitution: Women, Workers, and the Minimum Wage* (Princeton: Princeton University Press, 1994), 122–29.

3. Crowther, "Who Wants" (1922), 8. One month earlier, a Catholic priest claimed that "our industrial resources . . . are sufficient to provide more than a living wage for a very large proportion of the workers." James F. Cronin, C.S.P., "The Workingman and His Wages," *Catholic World* 116 (November 1922), 225. Aaron I. Abell, "The Reception of Leo XIII's Labor Encyclical in America, 1891–1919," *Review of Politics* 7 (October 1945), 464–95.

4. Francis A. Walker, *The Wages Question: A Treatise on Wages and the Wages Class* (New York: Henry Holt, 1876); Evans quoted in Hart, *Bound by Our Constitution*, 68.

5. Pope Leo XIII, *Rerum Novarum*, quoted in John A. Ryan, *A Living Wage: Its Ethical and Economic Aspects* (New York: Grosset and Dunlap, 1906), 33; Father Cuthbert, "The Ethical Basis of Wages," *Catholic World* (July 1922), 453–67. See also the Reverend John D. Callahan, *The Catholic Attitude toward a Familial Minimum Wage* (Washington, D.C.: Catholic University of America, 1936). The Church Association for the Advancement of the Interests of Labor, an organization of Protestant reformers, called for the living wage in 1887. Henrietta A. Keyser, "A Living Wage," in Joint Commission of Social Service of the Protestant Episcopal Church, *Social Service at the General Convention of 1913* (New York: Church Missions House, 1913), 76–78. See also Edwin B. Robinson, "The Church and the Wage-Earner," in *The Christian Ministry and the Social Order*, ed. Charles S. MacFarland (New Haven: Yale University Press, 1909), 149.

6. Information about the history of minimum wage legislation has been gleaned from the following sources: Elizabeth Brandeis, "Minimum Wage Legislation," in John R. Commons, Don D. Lescohier, and Brandeis, *History of Labor in the United States* (New York: Macmillan, 1935), 3:501–39; Irene Osgood Andrews, "Minimum Wage Legislation," app. III, in *Third Report of the Factory Investigating Commission* (Albany: J. B. Lyon, 1914); Rudolf Broda, "Minimum Wage Legislation in the United States," *International Labour Review* (January 1928), 24–50; Alice S. Cheyney, "The Course of Minimum Wage Legislation in the United States," *International Labour Review* (July 1938), 26–43; "Minimum Wage Laws of the United States," *International Labour Review* (May–June 1921), 205–17; Kessler-Harris, *Woman's Wage*; Susan Lehrer, *Origins of Protective Labor Legislation for Women, 1905–1925* (Albany: State University of New York Press, 1987); Hart, *Bound by Our Constitution*; Robyn Muncy, *Creating a Female Dominion in American Reform, 1890–1935* (New York: Oxford University Press, 1991).

7. As early as 1900, "living wages" appeared on the platform of the Social Democratic Party. In 1936 the Communist Party called for "Jobs and a Living Wage for All."

Theodore Roosevelt, "The Minimum Wage," *Outlook*, September 28, 1912, 159–60; James E. Boyle, *The Minimum Wage and Syndicalism* (Cincinnati: Stewart and Kidd, 1913), 10; *The Living Wage*, Exhibit no. 37 before the United States Railroad Labor Board (1921), U.S. Department of Labor, 113–15; *National Party Platforms*, rev. ed., comp. Donald Bruce Johnson (Urbana: University of Illinois Press, 1978), vol. 1.

8. W. Jett Lauck, *The New Industrial Revolution and Wages* (New York: Funk and Wagnalls, 1929), 118–19.

9. Jonathan Grossman, "Fair Labor Standards Act of 1938: Maximum Struggle for a Minimum Wage," *Monthly Labor Review* (June 1978), 22–30; George E. Poulsen, *A Living Wage for the Forgotten Man: The Quest for Fair Labor Standards, 1933–1941* (Selinsgrove: Susquehanna University Press, 1996).

10. William Giles, "Social Discontent and the Labor Troubles," *American Journal of Sociology* 9 (September 1903), 173; Michael O'Kane, "Wages and the Principles of Justice," *American Catholic Quarterly Review* 24 (April 1899), 175; White quoted in Lauck, *New Industrial Revolution and Wages*, 104.

11. Samuel Gompers, "A Minimum Living Wage," *AF* (April 1898), 25–30; idem, "A Minimum, Not a Uniform Rate of Wages," *AF* (January 1902), 20. See the Introduction for Gompers's 1898 definition.

12. It defined the minimum as "a living wage for all who devote their time and energy to industrial occupations." "A Platform of Industrial Minimums," *AF* (September 1912), 721–22.

13. E. R. A. Seligman, "A Living Wage," *GIB*, March 26, 1898, 257; Boyle, *Minimum Wage and Syndicalism*, 71–72; idem, "The Legal Minimum Wage," *Forum* (May 1913), 576–84. In 1910 a trade unionist apologized for defining a living wage as a subsistence wage in an earlier article: "My use of the term a 'living wage' was unfortunate as suggesting a minimum wage barely sufficient to sustain life." He called instead for raising "the scale of wages as high as possible." "Mr. Shaw's Scheme of Capitalizing Labor," *AF* (July 1910), 687.

14. Henry W. Macrosty, "The Recent History of the Living Wage Movement," *Political Science Quarterly* (September 1898), 440; E. E. Clark quoted in "The Question of the Minimum Wage," *Outlook* 73 (March 1903), 722. See also Seligman, "Living Wage," 257.

15. William Cunningham, "A Living Wage," *Contemporary Review* 65 (January 1894), 18; Although minimum wage legislation "seems the most expeditious way to insure a more just wage for workers," Gompers warned that "it is but a step—and a logical step—from legal fixation of wages to compulsory service at those wages." "Judicial Dissent Points Out Danger," *AF* (June 1914), 468–72; "A Trade Unionist" and "The Minimum Wage-Board and the Union," *Unpopular Review* 4 (December 1915), 387–411.

16. Boyle, *Minimum Wage and Syndicalism*, 73; B. C. Forbes, *The Highest Possible Wage and How to Attain It* (New York: B. C. Forbes, 1923), 7; Crowther, "Who Wants" (1922), 8; bureau quoted in *Living Wage*, 39.

17. *Living Wage*, 39; Learned Hand, "The Hope of the Living Wage," *New Republic*, November 20, 1915, 66–68; "The Worker's Right to a 'Living Wage,'" *Literary Digest*, November 11, 1922, 8. Middle-class proponents claimed that the question of how women could live on low wages was "very difficult to determine" since "the answer depends not only upon what standard is assumed but also upon the way in which the wages, whatever they are, are used." "Minimum Wage Laws for Women," *Nation*, April 10, 1913, 350–51.

18. See the comments of Balch, a Boston attorney, George Anderson, and a commission member, Edward F. McSweeney, who contrasted the "Christian view of the living wage," which was "based on the unit of the family," with the "legal minimum wage . . .

based on the pagan unit of the individual," in Henry Rogers Seager, "The Theory of the Minimum Wage," *American Labor Legislation Review* 3 (February 1913), 92–155.

19. Cunningham, "Living Wage," 18–19; Henry R. Seager, "The Minimum Wage as Part of a Program for Social Reform," *Annals* 48 (July 1913), 4. William Smart argued that the living wage should provide not merely a subsistence income "but a minimum determined by a customary level of comfort, based on . . . national wealth." *Studies in Economics* (London: Macmillan, 1895), 45. The Philadelphia Bureau of Municipal Research concurred with this need-based definition. *Living Wage*, 37.

20. Benjamin Kline Hunnicutt, "Monsignor John A. Ryan and the Shorter Hours of Labor: A Forgotten Vision of Genuine Progress," *Catholic Historical Review* 69 (July 1983), 384–402. It was this opposition to unleashed consumption that put Gompers at odds with religious leaders. It seemed to him that ministers were often "on the side of the wealth possessors as against that of the working men whenever there is a contest for a living wage. . . .Is it any wonder under such circumstances that the Church and labor unions have drifted apart?" *SGP* 3:500–501.

21. Ryan, *Living Wage*, 72–73; idem, "The Problem of Complete Wage Justice," *Catholic World* (August 1916), 623; "The Worker's Right to a 'Living Wage,'" 9; Ryan, "The Underpaid Laborers of America; Their Number and Prospects," *Catholic World* (May 1905), 156; E. C. Fortey, "The Living Wage—an English View," *American Catholic Quarterly Review* 37 (October 1912), 731.

22. "Statement of the New York Retail Dry Goods Association" (1915), in *Selected Articles on Minimum Wage*, ed. Mary K. Reely (New York: H. W. Wilson, 1917), 163.

23. Rome G. Brown, *The Minimum Wage, with Particular Reference to the Legislative Minimum Wage under the Minnesota Statute of 1913* (Minneapolis: Review, 1914), 4–5. Brown used the masculine pronoun even though the Minnesota law applied only to women.

24. Joseph Lee, "What the Minimum Wage Means to Workers—a Criticism," *Survey*, November 8, 1913, 157; *Washington Evening Star* quoted in "Worker's Right to a 'Living Wage,'" 9; *Adkins v. Children's Hospital*, 538, 557–58.

25. Brown, *Minimum Wage*, 17, 9; "Statement of the Dry Goods Association," 163.

26. Letters of Rebekah G. Henshaw and Florence Kelley, "The Minimum Wage," *Survey*, March 27, 1915, 638–39; Crowther, "Who Wants a Living Wage," *Collier's*, January 6, 1923, 8. Some did acknowledge the difficulty of measuring individual production. Samuel Crowther admitted, "What makes it hard for the ordinary worker to see that his wages come out of production is that he either produces some tiny fraction of the finished product that has no relation in his mind with the eventual product, or he works upon an article at a comparatively low wage and sees it ordered retail at a high price." Crowther, "Who Wants" (1922), 26.

27. "Worker's Right to a 'Living Wage,'" 7; "A New Political Economy," *Spectator*, August 18, 1906, 233–35; Harleigh Hartman, *Should the State Interfere in the Determination of Wage Rates?* (New York: National Industrial Conference Board, 1920), 28. Another critic challenged "the doctrine that every man has a natural right to a living wage." "The Living Wage," *Outlook*, September 8, 1906, 91.

28. "There is an irrevocable law of nature that . . . if one man is paid more than he earns, another must receive less than his production entitles him to," wrote John Kirkby Jr., in *The Disadvantages of Labor Unionism*, NAM, no. 2 (November 7, 1909), 24.

29. "The Living Wage Discussed: Edward Atkinson, Samuel Gompers, and Professor Seligman before the Nineteenth Century Club," *New York Daily Tribune*, March 11, 1898. "Neither the employer nor the workingman can make the rate of wages," Atkinson concluded, invoking the power of the market in a manner not unfamiliar to proponents

of labor's consumerist turn. "That is fixed by the community of consumers who buy the goods." Young, "What Is a Workers' Living Wage?" For a similar critique of English workers' living wage demands, see F. C. Chappell, "The 'Living Wage' Fallacy," *Annalist*, September 17, 1923, 365, 379. "The Earned Wage," *NYT*, December 3, 1922, II, 6; "A Privileged Wage," *NYT*, September 22, 1922, 8; Victor Morowetz, "The Living Wage Question," *NYT*, December 3, 1922, IX, 8. In the same issue M. L. Dunham questioned why industrial workers should be the sole beneficiaries of living wages based on needs. "The Farmer's Wage."

30. *Bunting v. Oregon* quoted in Lehrer, *Origins of Protective Legislation*, 70; Crowther, "Who Wants" (1922), 8. See also William E. Forbath, "The Ambiguities of Free Labor: Labor and the Law in the Gilded Age," *Wisconsin Law Review* (1985), 767–817; Kessler-Harris, *Woman's Wage*, 47. The opinion in the earliest Court decision to invoke the term "living wage" quoted Cardinal Manning: "A workingman is a free man . . . to sell as he wills, wherever and for whatsoever time he will and at whatsoever price he can." *Hopkins et al. v. Oxley Stave Co.*, No. 789, Circuit Court of Appeals, Eighth Circuit, 83 F. 912 (November 8, 1897), 938.

31. Brown quoted in Lehrer, *Origins of Protective Legislation*, 67; NAM, no. 33 (May 20, 1913), 21; Crowther, "Who Wants" (1922), 26; Railroad Labor Board quoted in "Worker's Right to a 'Living Wage,'" 7.

32. Giles, "Social Discontent," 174–75; "Worker's Right to a 'Living Wage,'" 7.

33. Crowther, "Who Wants" (1922), 26; J. Laurence Laughlin, "Wages and Producing Power," *Atlantic Monthly* (October 1913), 444–53. And in the September issue, see John Bates Clark, "The Minimum Wage," 290.

34. Crowther, "Who Wants" (1922), 8; Seligman, "Living Wage," 257.

35. "The Saving Wage," *Nation*, June 14, 1922, 710.

36. *Adkins v. Children's Hospital*, 556, 558–59.

8. The Living Wage Incorporated

1. David MacGregor Means, "Municipal Progress and the Living Wage," *Forum* (September 1895), 12.

2. Steve Fraser and Gary Gerstle define the New Deal order as "an ideological character, a moral perspective, and a set of political relationships . . . that decidedly shaped American political life for forty years." Fraser and Gerstle, eds., *The Rise and Fall of the New Deal Order, 1930–1980* (Princeton: Princeton University Press, 1989), xi. See also David Plotke, *Building a Democratic Political Order: Reshaping American Liberalism in the 1930s and 1940s* (Cambridge: Cambridge University Press, 1996), 1, 162–89.

3. Roosevelt quoted in Michael J. Sandel, *Democracy's Discontent: America in Search of a Public Philosophy* (Cambridge: Harvard University Press, 1996), 260. On the consumerist transformation of the later New Deal, see Alan Brinkley, "The New Deal and the Idea of the State," in *Rise and Fall*, ed. Fraser and Gerstle, 85–121; idem, *The End of Reform: New Deal Liberalism in Recession and War* (New York: Knopf, 1995), 65–85.

4. Schlesinger quoted in Robert Collins, "Growth Liberalism in the Sixties," in *The Sixties: From Memory to History*, ed. David Farber (Chapel Hill: University of North Carolina Press, 1994), 26. On the rejection of quantitative economic issues in favor of qualitative concerns in the 1950s, see Irwin Unger, *The Best of Intentions: The Triumph and Failure of the Great Society under Kennedy, Johnson, and Nixon* (New York: Doubleday, 1996), 17–18. See also David M. Potter, *People of Plenty: Economic Abundance and the*

American Character (Chicago: University of Chicago Press, 1954); David Riesman, *Abundance for What? And Other Essays* (Garden City, N.Y.: Doubleday, 1964).

5. Economists and planners in the 1920s stressed consumption as "the key to a healthy economy." Alan Dawley, *Struggles for Justice: Social Responsibility and the Liberal State* (Cambridge: Harvard University Press, 1991), 305. See also "Labor Needs a Living Wage," *NYT*, June 24, 1920, 14; "The Living Wage," *NYT*, November 14, 1920, II, 2; W. R. Ingalls, "Paying the Living Wage," *NYT*, December 24, 1922, VIII, 8.

6. Lizabeth Cohen, *Making a New Deal: Industrial Workers in Chicago, 1919–1939* (Cambridge: Cambridge University Press, 1990).

7. In his 1928 presidential address to the Taylor Society, Morris Cooke called on his peers to recognize the crucial role for labor in the development of a mass consumption society. Steve Fraser, "The 'Labor Question,'" in *Rise and Fall*, ed. Fraser and Gerstle, 61. Ruth Milkman notes that support for "high wages had become the key to control over labor" in the 1920s. *Gender at Work: The Dynamics of Job Segregation by Sex during World War II* (Urbana: University of Illinois Press, 1987), 23.

8. James J. Davis, "The Living and Saving Wage," 1, Department of Labor, Chief Clerk's Files, 167/832, National Archives, Washington, D.C.; "The Saving Wage," *Nation*, June 14, 1922, 710.

9. Davis, "Living and Saving Wage," 2, 3, 4; *C and L*, 133, 490–91; National Industrial Conference Board, Acc. 1057, ser. I, box 2, transcript 8, Monthly Meeting, October 23, 1930, Hagley Library Archives, Wilmington, Del.

10. J. H. Richardson, *A Study on the Minimum Wage* (London: George Allen and Unwin, 1927), 19; Michael O'Kane, "Wages and the Principles of Justice," *American Catholic Quarterly Review* 24 (April 1899), 182, 180; "The Wage Question," *American Catholic Quarterly Review* 11 (April 1886), 325; Aaron I. Abell, "The Reception of Leo XIII's Labor Encyclical in America, 1891–1919," *Review of Politics* 7 (October 1945), 466. Henry R. Seager conceded that there were some employees whose "work is not worth a living return to their employers." "The Minimum Wage as Part of a Program for Social Reform," *Annals* 48 (July 1913), 4.

11. James E. Boyle, *The Minimum Wage and Syndicalism* (Cincinnati: Stewart and Kidd, 1913), 14. See also Robert Bruere, "Can We Eliminate Labor Unrest?" *Annals* 81 (January 1919), 95. Filene quoted in "The Minimum Wage—What Next? Seven Governors and a Score of Citizens Discuss the Decision and the Way to Further Progress," *Survey*, May 15, 1923, 219–20; J. A. Norton, "The Living Wage—What Is It?" *Industrial Management* (September 1919), 211–12; Anthracite Coal Commission quoted in *The Living Wage*, 51, exhibit 37 before the United States Railroad Labor Board (1921), U.S. Department of Labor Library, Washington, D.C.

12. J. A. Hobson, "Influence of a Legal Minimum Wage upon Employment," in *Selected Articles on Minimum Wage*, ed. Mary K. Reely (Minneapolis: H. W. Wilson, 1913), 19; "Good and Evil in the Fuller Dinner-Pail," *Literary Digest*, April 21, 1923, 17.

13. Seager quoted in "Warns against Hurried Passage," *NYT*, April 13, 1913, VII, 8; Brooks, "The Minimum Wage and Its Consequences," *Living Age* (April 1912), 370–72. William Allen White, reflecting the influence of the working-class proposals, wrote that "wages must be set in reference to the cost of living. Labor otherwise becomes a commodity, and . . . we shall get our labor down to a point where certain standards of citizenship are also forgotten." Quoted in W. Jett Lauck, *The New Industrial Revolution and Wages* (New York: Funk and Wagnalls, 1929), 104.

14. James F. Cronin, C.S.P., "The Workingman and His Wages," *Catholic World* 116 (November 1922), 224; Father Cuthbert, "The Ethical Basis of Wages," *Catholic World* (July 1922), 454. As late as 1913 Gilbert Slater remarked that the wage system was of

"comparatively recent" origins and that it was still uncommon in most of the world. "Trade Unionism and the Living Wage," in *The Industrial Unrest and the Living Wage*, ed. William Temple (London: Collegium, 1913), 107.

15. Alice Henry, "The Living Wage," *Life and Labor* (July 1913); Walter Lippmann, "Campaign against Sweating," *New Republic*, March 27, 1915, in *Selected Articles on Minimum Wage*, ed. Mary K. Reely (New York: H. W. Wilson Company, 1917), 42–55. "A bare subsistence wage is not enough and would mean the stagnation of our civilization," noted William Kenyon in 1922. "It may be said that a living wage is a wage which . . . will insure the lowest paid worker an income sufficient to maintain himself and family at a level of health and modest comfort and with a reasonable degree of security." Quoted in Lauck, *New Industrial Revolution*, 101–2.

16. Elizabeth Brandeis, "Minimum Wage Legislation," in John R. Commons, Don D. Lescohier, and Brandeis, *History of Labor in the United States* (New York: Macmillan, 1935), 3:513; Gompers, *AF* (May 1923), 400–401; "An Appeal from the Supreme Court," *New Republic*, April 25, 1923, 228–29. Elsewhere Gompers noted: "The law of the U.S. declares that 'the labor of a human being is not a commodity or article of commerce.' . . . The five justices trampled it underfoot, together with the great army of women wage earners in our country." "Minimum Wage—What Next," 221–22.

17. Letter to Florence Kelley, June 14, 1923, Records of the National Consumer's League, box B21, folder: Correspondence, Ryan, John A., DD, 1923–1933, Library of Congress, Washington, D.C. "How much of the good things of life must be within the laborer's reach in order that he may have a decent livelihood?" asked Ryan in 1902, making it seem an open-ended question rather than one settled by market forces. "What Wage Is a Living Wage?" *Catholic World* 75 (April 1902), 3. See also Ryan, "Rome Brown and the Minimum Wage," *Survey*, March 13, 1915, 660–61.

18. Ryan, "What Wage," 2.

19. In 1912 the Massachusetts Minimum Wage Board condemned the fact that the "wage value of . . . the labor of women is not fixed by any other economic law than that of supply and demand." "Report of Commission on Minimum Wage Board, Massachusetts" (January 1912), in *Selected Articles on Minimum Wage*, ed. Reely (1913), 14. Ryan wrote, "Whatever may be the measure of justice in wages, it certainly is not the mere operation of unrestricted competition, and the so-called law of supply and demand." "'Earning' the Minimum Wage," *Survey*, November 6, 1915, 150.

20. An Australian judge quoted by Samuel Crowther, "Who Wants a Living Wage?" *Collier's*, December 30, 1922, 26. On the Australian living wage law, see Henry Demarest Lloyd, "A Living Wage by Law," *Independent*, September 27, 1900, 2330–32.

21. J. W. Sullivan, "Business Methods in Marketing One's Labor," *AF* (April 1911), 287; "Report of Commission on Minimum Wage Board," 16; Edwin V. O'Hara, *A Living Wage by Legislation: The Oregon Experience* (Salem: Oregon State Printing Department, 1916), xix; Cuthbert, "Ethical Basis of Wages," 454–55.

22. Lippmann, "Campaign against Sweating," 44.

23. In 1915 Nearing denounced the "American Wage" as "anti-social" because it was "fixed wholly independent of social relations." Quoted in Susan Lehrer, *Origins of Protective Labor Legislation for Women, 1905–1925* (Albany: State University of New York Press, 1987), 91. In 1916 he condemned the view that the worker receives wages "in proportion to his product." In truth, he wrote, wages "are never fixed on that basis." *A Scott Nearing Reader: The Good Life in Bad Times*, ed. Steve Sherman (Metuchen, N.J.: Scarecrow Press, 1989), 66–67; Nearing, "What Are Men Worth?" *Railroad Trainmen* (October 1916), 872–73.

24. "The Minimum Wage Problem," *Independent*, March 14, 1912, 584–85; O'Hara, *Living Wage by Legislation*, xiv; "Freedom of Contract a Fiction," *AF* (November 1911),

913. In 1912 Theodore Roosevelt declared, "Under the present industrial conditions, to leave wages in all cases to free competition must sometimes mean that under the pressure of the competition the freedom to starve outright or else to starve slowly by accepting a wage insufficient to sustain life as it should be sustained." "The Minimum Wage," *Outlook*, September 28, 1912, 159–60.

25. The "fair share" for workers central to moral capitalism was typically defined in consumerist terms. Cohen, *Making a New Deal*, 209, 286. See also "Reuther Challenges Our 'Fear of Abundance,'" *NYT Magazine*, September 16, 1945, quoted in Nelson Lichtenstein, *The Most Dangerous Man in Detroit: Walter Reuther and the Fate of American Labor* (New York: Basic Books, 1995), 220. For examples of organized labor's postwar living wage campaigns, see *UE Fights for a Better America: Picture History of UE Members in Their Struggle for a Living Wage, Job Security, and the Preservation of Their Union* (New York: United Electrical, Radio, and Machine Workers of America, 1946); Joseph Gaer, *Let Our People Live: A Plea for a Living Wage* (New York: CIO Political Action Committee, 1945). On the "tense and temporary bargain" of the post–World War II years in which union members gained "steady work at a family wage," see Jackson Lears, *Fables of Abundance: A Cultural History of Advertising in America* (New York: Basic Books, 1994), 236.

26. Lichtenstein, *Most Dangerous Man*, 221. In discussing the 1920s, Kazin writes: "'Consumer' was no longer the pejorative label it had been at the beginning of the industrial revolution." He continues, "The ordinary producer and his family were beginning to shade into a related identity — the eager, self-aware consumer." *The Populist Persuasion: An American History* (New York: Basic Books, 1995), 76, 143, 145. Fraser, "The 'Labor Question,'" 57.

27. Alan Brinkley declares: "The belief that consumption was the engine driving the economy, and hence a positive social good, was largely new to the industrial world," and he names the Progressive economist Simon Patten "the first important spokesman for such ideas in the United States." *End of Reform*, 67, 71.

28. "It is extremely difficult to know just where workers' orientation to moral capitalism came from," writes Cohen. She speculates that "long-standing expectations about America, particularly workers' own desire to acquire property," played a role, as did the largely failed example of 1920s-style welfare capitalism. But the living wage ideology also marked an important antecedent. *Making a New Deal*, 315.

29. There are important exceptions to this generalization. Most notable is Cohen, *Making a New Deal*. Jean-Christophe Agnew has noted that "the pervasive promise of American consumerism inspired the labour militance of the 1930s and after." "Coming Up for Air: Consumer Culture in Historical Perspective," in *Consumption and the World of Goods*, ed. John Brewer and Roy Porter (London: Routledge, 1993), 31.

30. Arguing for the new consumerist interest of Keynesians, Michael Sandel quotes John Maynard Keynes's comment that "consumption . . . is the sole end and object of economic activity" but does not note that Keynes was paraphrasing Adam Smith. *Democracy's Discontent*, 250, 267.

31. Roosevelt quoted in Persia Campbell, *Consumer Representation in the New Deal* (New York: Columbia University Press, 1940), 17.

Coda: Interpreting the Living Wage and Consumption

1. In his speech, Douglas declares that Lincoln evokes sympathy for "black slave labor," but "he never . . . makes reference to the condition of labor here in the North [where] 'free' citizens must toil at shattering looms in soulless factories and never see

the sun. . . . What kind of liberty is this?" Robert Emmet Sherwood, *Abe Lincoln in Illinois: A Play in Twelve Scenes* (New York: Scribner's, 1939), 133.

2. The living wage is a paradigmatic "keyword" as defined by Nancy Fraser and Linda Gordon, a "taken-for-granted commonsense belief that escapes critical scrutiny." "A Genealogy of Dependency: Tracing a Keyword of the U.S. Welfare State," *Signs* 19 (Winter 1994), 310. On the obfuscating qualities of "tradition," see Eric J. Hobsbawm and Terence Ranger, eds., *The Invention of Tradition* (Cambridge: Cambridge University Press, 1983).

3. On the living wage in America, see Alice Kessler-Harris, *A Woman's Wage: Historical Meanings and Social Consequences* (Lexington: University Press of Kentucky, 1990); Martha May, "Bread before Roses: American Workingmen, Labor Unions, and the Family Wage," in *Women, Work, and Protest: A Century of U.S. Women's Labor History*, ed. Ruth Milkman (Boston: Routledge and Kegan Paul, 1985), 1–21; idem, "The Historical Problem of the Family Wage: The Ford Motor Company and the Five Dollar Day," *Feminist Studies* 8 (Summer 1982), 399–424; Maurine Wiener Greenwald, "Working-Class Feminism and the Family Wage Ideal: The Seattle Debate on Married Women's Right to Work, 1914–1920," *JAH* 76 (June 1989), 118–49; Ron Rothbart, "'Homes Are What Any Strike Is About': Immigrant Labor and the Family Wage," *JSH* 23 (Winter 1989), 267–84; Mary H. Blewett, *Men, Women, and Work: Class, Gender, and Protest in the New England Shoe Industry, 1780–1910* (Urbana: University of Illinois Press, 1988); Stephanie Coontz, *The Social Origins of Private Life: A History of American Families, 1600–1900* (London: Verso, 1988); Nancy Fraser, "After the Family Wage: Gender Equity and the Welfare State," *Political Theory* 22 (November 1994), 591–618; Vivien Hart, *Bound by Our Constitution: Women, Workers, and the Minimum Wage* (Princeton: Princeton University Press, 1994).

The British scholarship on the living wage has been theoretically and historiographically influential, beginning with the Webbs, who traced the origins of the term far more carefully than any contemporary historian. See Sidney Webb, *Industrial Democracy* (London: Longmans, Green, 1899); Sidney Webb and Beatrice Webb, *The History of Trade Unionism* (London: Longmans, Green, 1920); Hilary Land, "The Family Wage," *Feminist Review* 6 (1980), 55–78; idem, "The Mantle of Manhood," *New Statesman*, December 18, 1981, 16–18; Sonya Rose, "'Gender at Work': Sex, Class, and Industrial Capitalism," *History Workshop* 21 (Spring 1986), 113–31; idem, *Limited Livelihoods: Gender and Class in Nineteenth-Century England* (Berkeley: University of California Press, 1992); Jane Humphries, "The Working Class Family, Women's Liberation, and Class Struggle: The Case of Nineteenth Century British History," *Review of Radical Political Economics* 9 (Fall 1977), 25–41; idem, "Class Struggle and the Persistence of the Working-Class Family," *Cambridge Journal of Economics* 1 (September 1977), 241–58; Wally Seccombe, "Patriarchy Stabilized: The Construction of the Male Breadwinner Norm in Nineteenth-Century Britain," *Social History* 2 (January 1986), 53–76; idem, *Weathering the Storm: Working-Class Families from the Industrial Revolution to the Fertility Decline* (London: Verso, 1993); Michelle Barrett and Mary McIntosh, "The 'Family Wage': Some Problems for Socialists and Feminists," *Capital and Class* 11 (Summer 1980), 51–72; Harold Benenson, "The 'Family Wage' and Working Women's Consciousness in Britain, 1880–1914," *Politics and Society* 19 (March 1991), 71–100.

4. Some historians use the term "family wage" to connote the ideal of male breadwinner, and others use it in precisely the opposite meaning to refer to the wages earned by an entire family. "Given the propensity for confusion," Wally Seccombe elects "to steer clear of the term altogether." *Weathering the Storm*, 234 n. 138. While Seccombe is correct to note the historiographical confusion, the historical record, at least in the

United States, is clear: workers and, until the Progressive Era, reformers could be counted on to use the term "living wage."

5. William Smart, *Studies in Economics* (London: Macmillan, 1895), 29; John A. Ryan, "What Wage Is a Living Wage?" *Catholic World* 75 (April 1902), 5. For recent calls for a return to the "family wage," see William Tucker, "A Return to the 'Family Wage,'" *Weekly Standard*, May 13, 1996, 27–31; Allan C. Carlson, "What Happened to the 'Family Wage'?" *Public Interest* 83 (Spring 1986), 3–17; Bryce Christensen et al., *The Family Wage: Work, Gender, and Children in the Modern Economy* (Rockford, Ill.: Rockford Institute, 1988), vii.

6. The family wage took on special importance for twentieth-century welfare reformers. Christensen et al., *Family Wage*, vii; Fraser, "After the Family Wage," 591.

7. "Testimony of Gompers before the U. S. Strike Commission" (August 25, 1894), *SGP* 3:575; "Living Wages for Labor," *NYT*, March 11, 1898, 2; John A. Ryan, *A Living Wage: Its Ethical and Economic Aspects* (New York: Grosset and Dunlap, 1906); James J. Davis, "A Living and Saving Wage" (1922), Department of Labor, Chief Clerk's Files, 167/832, National Archives, Washington, D.C.

In England the same was true. In 1914 J. A. Hobson wrote: "A minimum or living wage is the usual name for this demand" that "remuneration shall be regulated on the basis of human needs of a family living in a civilized country." *Work and Wealth: A Human Valuation* (New York: Macmillan, 1914), 190, 196.

8. By the end of World War II the living wage was indeed a long-standing ideal with a seventy-five-year history. Ruth Milkman, *Gender at Work: The Dynamics of Job Segregation by Sex during World War II* (Urbana: University of Illinois Press, 1987), 40, 107, 125.

9. In a pioneering article on the subject, for example, Martha May argued that the "family wage ideology emerged in the first half of the nineteenth century." "Bread before Roses," 3. In this article, May also claims that E. L. Godkin used the term living wage in 1872. In fact, Godkin did not use the term, although he did speak of "a comfortable subsistence." "Labor and Politics," *Nation*, June 13, 1872, 386–87. May quotes a paraphrase of Godkin which appeared in Sidney Fine, *Laissez Faire and the General-Welfare State: A Study of Conflict in American Thought, 1865–1901* (Ann Arbor: University of Michigan Press, 1964), 60. Linda Gordon suggests that the term "living wage" "evolved" from the "family wage"—the opposite of the historical trajectory traced in this book. *Pitied but Not Entitled: Single Mothers and the History of Welfare, 1890–1935* (New York: Free Press, 1994), 53, 290–91.

10. L. T. Hobhouse remarked in 1913, while the term was relatively new, that the "notion of the living wage is not in any sense a novel conception." "The Right to a Living Wage," in *The Industrial Unrest and the Living Wage*, ed. William Temple (London: Collegium, 1913), 64–65. See also Mary H. Blewett, "Manhood and the Market: The Politics of Gender and Class among the Textile Workers of Fall River, Massachusetts, 1870–1880," in *Work Engendered: Toward a New History of American Labor*, ed. Ava Baron (Ithaca: Cornell University Press, 1991), 92–113, esp. 92. David Zonderman notes that some employers in the antebellum period paid wages for the entire family at a factory to the male head of household. Zonderman calls this a "family-wage policy." *Aspirations and Anxieties: New England Workers and the Mechanized Factory System, 1815–1850* (New York: Oxford University Press, 1992), 178.

11. See Jeanne Boydston's pioneering analysis of the historical construction of the male breadwinner, *Home and Work: Housework, Wages, and the Ideology of Labor in the Early Republic* (New York: Oxford University Press, 1990), 153–63. Indeed, what Wally Seccombe calls the "male-breadwinner ideal" would be a better label for what most his-

torians now call the "family wage." Seccombe argues that the norm of the male bread-winner came in the late nineteenth century "to be articulated by male trade unionists in a new form . . . the notion of a 'living wage' for men." *Weathering the Storm,* 111. In another useful approach, Ardis Cameron treats the family wage as an ideology and metaphor which "reflected and constructed working-class identity and consciousness." *Radicals of the Worst Sort: Laboring Women in Lawrence, Massachusetts, 1860–1912* (Urbana: University of Illinois Press, 1993), 40–41, 65–66.

12. Sean Wilentz, "Against Exceptionalism: Class Consciousness and the American Labor Movement, 1790–1920," *ILWCH* 26 (Fall 1984), 1–24, esp. 10; Michael Fogarty, *The Just Wage* (Westport, Conn.: Greenwood, 1961).

13. Eric Foner, "The Idea of Free Labor in Nineteenth-Century America," in *Free Soil, Free Labor, Free Men: The Ideology of the Republican Party before the Civil War* (New York: Oxford University Press, 1995), xiii.

14. Amy Bridges, "Becoming American: The Working Classes in the United States before the Civil War," in *Working-Class Formation: Nineteenth-Century Patterns in Western Europe and the United States,* ed. Ira Katznelson and Aristide R. Zolberg (Princeton: Princeton University Press, 1986), 157; David Brody, "The Old Labor History and the New: In Search of an American Working Class," *LH* 20 (Winter 1979), 111–26; Bruce Laurie, *Artisans into Workers: Labor in Nineteenth-Century America* (New York: Noonday, 1989), 3–14. On the intellectual milieu in which the Commons school developed, see Dorothy Ross, *The Origins of American Social Science* (Cambridge: Cambridge University Press, 1991), 202–4; Leon Fink, "'Intellectuals' versus 'Workers': Academic Requirements and the Creation of Labor History," in *In Search of the Working Class: Essays in American Labor History and Political Culture* (Urbana: University of Illinois Press, 1994), 201–35.

15. The phrase appears in John R. Commons, Don D. Lescohier, and Elizabeth Brandeis, *History of Labor in the United States* (New York: Macmillan, 1935), 1 : 19; Selig Perlman, *A Theory of the Labor Movement* (New York: Augustus M. Kelley, 1928). On Perlman's use and eventual abandonment of the term, see Fink, "'Intellectuals' versus 'Workers,'" 216, 230 n. 61.

16. John Bodnar, "Immigration, Kinship, and the Rise of Working-Class Realism in Industrial America," *JSH* 14 (September 1980), 45–46. Though not himself a new labor historian, Christopher Lasch sums up this scholarship well when he calls the acceptance of wage labor "an indication of the narrowing of political debate in the twentieth century." *The True and Only Heaven: Progress and Its Critics* (New York: Norton, 1991), 206–8.

17. The new labor history, Richard Oestreicher notes, has interpreted "diverse phenomena not previously thought of in class terms" as part of a "republican critique of American capitalism." "Urban Working-Class Political Behavior and Theories of American Electoral Politics, 1870–1940," *JAH* 74 (March 1988), 1260.

18. Wilentz defines "essentialism" as "a model of modern history which supposes that the existence of capitalist wage relations should produce, in a direct way, particular forms of working-class political thinking and behavior, undertaken by a clearly delineated, self-conscious proletariat in opposition to other classes." He defines "exceptionalism" as the assumption "that a powerful working-class socialist movement . . . is the *sine qua non* of true class consciousness." "Against Exceptionalism," 2, 3.

19. Ibid., 6. David Montgomery similarly criticizes the exceptionalist model because it "diverts attention from the ways in which workers in the United States battled the wage system of labor." Montgomery, "Editor's Remarks," *ILWCH* 26 (Fall 1984), v; Laurie, *Artisans into Workers,* 9.

20. David Montgomery is correct to note that the Catholic family wage doctrine differs from the Marxist goal of "the abolition of wages through the distribution of goods and services according to needs." But most living wage advocates promoted a consumerist view of wages, which shared an affinity with Marxian notions of need-based justice. "Response to Harold Benenson, 'Victorian Sexual Ideology and Marx's Theory of the Working Class,'" *ILWCH* 25 (Spring 1984), 27.

21. Merrill, "History by the Neck," *Nation*, June 22, 1992, 862–64. See also Seccombe, *Weathering the Storm*, 6.

22. Historians have rightly noted labor's opposition to both wage labor and nonproducers in the antebellum era. See Foner, "Idea of Free Labor," xiii.

23. Werner Sombart, *Why Is There No Socialism in the United States?* trans. Patricia M. Hocking and C. T. Husbands (White Plains, N.Y.: International Arts and Sciences Press, 1976), 105–6.

24. Walter Benn Michaels, *The Gold Standard and the Logic of Naturalism* (Berkeley: University of California Press, 1987), 14 n. 16. On the "tendency in both academic and intellectual circles to denigrate . . . consumption," see Colin Campbell, "Consuming Goods and the Good of Consuming," *Critical Review* 8 (Fall 1994), 503–20.

25. See, for example, John Brewer and Roy Porter, eds., *Consumption and the World of Goods* (London: Routledge, 1993).

26. In 1985 Michael Denning asked, "What is the relation of the culture of American workers to this culture of abundance?" Since then, many historians have begun to answer this question. "Class and Culture: Reflections on the Work of Warren Susman," *RHR* 36 (1986), 110.

27. Daniel Horowitz, *The Morality of Spending: Attitudes toward the Consumer Society in America, 1875–1940* (Baltimore: Johns Hopkins University Press, 1985), 30.

28. Kathy Peiss, *Cheap Amusements: Working Women and Leisure in Turn-of-the-Century New York* (Philadelphia: Temple University Press, 1986); Susan Porter Benson, *Counter Cultures: Saleswomen, Managers, and Customers in American Department Stores, 1890–1940* (Urbana: University of Illinois Press, 1986); Roy Rosenzweig, *Eight Hours for What We Will: Workers and Leisure in an Industrial City, 1870–1920* (Cambridge: Cambridge University Press, 1983); Lizabeth Cohen, *Making a New Deal: Industrial Workers in Chicago, 1919–1939* (Cambridge: Cambridge University Press, 1990); Francis G. Couvares, *The Remaking of Pittsburgh: Class and Culture in an Industrializing City, 1877–1919* (Pittsburgh: University of Pittsburgh Press, 1984); George J. Sanchez, *Becoming Mexican American: Ethnicity, Culture, and Identity in Chicano Los Angeles, 1900–1945* (New York: Oxford University Press, 1993).

29. Horowitz, *Morality of Spending*, 168. For an influential early formulation of this position, see Gareth Stedman Jones, "Class Expression versus Social Control? A Critique of Recent Trends in the Social History of 'Leisure,'" *History Workshop* 4 (Autumn 1977), 163–70.

30. Richard Wightman Fox and T. J. Jackson Lears, Introduction to *The Culture of Consumption: Critical Essays in American History, 1880–1980* ed. Fox and Lears (New York: Pantheon, 1983), xi. Lisa Tiersten argues that historians have viewed "consumer culture as [an] outgrowth of middle-class culture," and suggests that "we need to look more closely at the role of consumer culture in social stratification and class formation." "Redefining Consumer Culture: Recent Literature on Consumption and the Bourgeoisie in Western Europe," *RHR* 57 (Fall 1993), 119, 139.

Index